Six Women and th

Marguerite-Yerta Méléra and

Gabrielle Yerta

Alpha Editions

This edition published in 2023

ISBN : 9789357955201

Design and Setting By
Alpha Editions
www.alphaedis.com
Email - info@alphaedis.com

Contents

PREFACE

This little book gives a very graphic and interesting account by an eye-witness—who knows how to write!—of life in the occupied provinces of France under the daily pressure of the German invasion. There are many repulsive and odious incidents recorded here of the German occupation, but, mercifully, few "atrocities," such as those which make of the French Governmental Reports, or that of the Bryce Commission, tales of horror and infamy that time will never wash out. These pages relate to the neighbourhood of Laon, and the worst brutalities committed by German soldiers in France seem to have happened farther south, along the line of the German retreat during the battle of the Marne, and in the border villages of Lorraine. But the picture drawn of the Germans in possession of a French country district, robbing and bullying its inhabitants, and delighting in all the petty tyrannies of their military régime, is one that writes in large-hand the lesson of this war. "There must be no next time!" If Europe cannot protect itself in future against such conduct on the part of a European nation, civilisation is doomed.

And that this little book under-states the case rather than over-states it, can be proved by a mass of contemporary evidence. I pass for instance from Madame Yerta's graphic account of the endless "requisitions," "perquisitions," "inquisitions," to which the inhabitants of Morny in the Laonnois were subject in 1915, to a paragraph in this week's *Morning Post* (Tuesday, September 18), where a letter found upon a German soldier, and written to a comrade in Flanders from this very district, gleefully says: "We take from the French population all their lead, tin, copper, cork, oil, candlesticks, kitchen pots, or anything at all like that, which is sent off to Germany. I had a good haul the other day with one of my comrades. In one walled-up room we found fifteen copper musical instruments, a new bicycle, 150 pairs of sheets, some towels, and six candlesticks of beaten copper. You can imagine the kind of noise the old hag made who owned them. I just laughed. The Commandant was very pleased."

No doubt the Commandant was of the same race as the Von Bernhausens or the Bubenpechs, whom Madame Yerta pillories in these lively and sarcastic pages. It would be too much indeed to expect that any Frenchwoman who had passed through fifteen months of such a life should write with complete impartiality of her temporary masters. She would be less than human were it possible. Yet in the sketches of the two German officers "Barbu" and "Crafleux," billeted on the "six women," there is no more than a laughing malice, and an evident intention to be fair to men who had no evident intention to be cruel. But of the bullying

Commandant, Lieutenant von Bernhausen, and of the officer, Lieutenant Bubenpech, who succeeded him as the absolute master of the French village which is the scene of the book, Madame Yerta gives us portraits in which every touch bites. The drunken, sensual manners of such men, combined with German conceit and German arrogance, make up a type of character only too real, only too common, to which throughout the districts where the Germans have passed, French experience bears inexorable and damning witness.

It is clear, however, that these six brave women—Madame Valaine, her four daughters and her daughter-in-law, the writer of the book—were well able to take care of themselves. The tale of their courage, their gaiety, their resource under the endless difficulties and petty oppressions of their lot, lights up the miserable scene, kindling in the reader the same longing for retribution and justice on a barbarian race, as burnt in their French hearts.

Madame Yerta describes for us how neighbours helped each other, how they met in the farm kitchens, behind their closed doors and windows, to pass on such news as they could get, to pray for France, and scoff at the invader; how they ingeniously hid their most treasured possessions, how they went hungry and cold because the Germans had robbed them of food, clothing and blankets—(they are doing it afresh at this very moment in occupied France and Belgium!)—and how village and town alike would have starved but for the Spanish-American Relief Commission.

The result is a typically French book, both in its lightness of touch and in the passionate feeling that breaks through its pages. The old Latin civilisation makes the background of it—with its deeply rooted traditions, its gifts of laughter and of scorn, its sense of manners and measure, its humanity, its indomitable spirit. When the writer at last, after fifteen months of bondage, sees once more the fields of "la douce France," she puts simply and sharply into words the thoughts and sufferings of thousands—thousands of ill-treated, innocent and oppressed folk—to whom, as we pray, the course of this just war will before long bring comfort and release.

Her book deserves a wide audience, and will, I hope, find it.

MARY A. WARD.

September 1917.

PART I

"It is no longer the pillar of fire. It is the pillar of cloud, it is the dark shadow of invasion that approaches."

CHAPTER I

As you know only too well, in the year 1914 war set Europe on fire. That is to say, you the men made war, and we the women had but to comply. Let us be honest and true: whereas you, heart of my heart, now gone to fight for your country, wished for this contest with the enthusiasm, spirit, and rage of youth, I wished for it too, but with terror, anguish, and remorse. Such is the difference.

The Place? The Île de France, the part of my country blessed among all, sweeter to my eyes than the most loudly sung; and in the Île de France, Morny, a village of the Laonnois, situated on a level plain. At ten miles' distance, to the west of Morny, Laon is perched on a steep low hill. To the north, fields and meadows stretch out as far as the eye can reach, and towards the south, the forest of St. Gobain makes a long dark blot on the landscape; beyond, a blue line of mountains closes the horizon like a wall. This peaceful scene, with its green meadows, fertile fields, rich forests, villages nestling among orchards, with its good-humoured tenants wrapt up in a love of their country, sums up the treasures of the Île de France. But it is also "the seasoning of the French pie, this rotten ferment whose canker-like nature, frivolity, inconstancy, and folly, have spread into the noblest parts of France." You were not aware of this? No more was I, but I learned it from Hummel's *Geography*, published in 1876 for "German families," and it is a conviction that Teutonic babies imbibe with their mothers' milk.

The *dramatis personae*? Six women, I have said. My mother-in-law, her four daughters, and I. Let me introduce them. Mme. Valaine, my mother-in-law, charms by her gentle dignity and by her handsome face, still young under waving grey hair. As to her daughters, when they all were little girls in pinafores, an old woman once cried out at the sight of their childish beauty, "One is prettier than another." To which my husband—at that time a teasing schoolboy—retorted, "One is naughtier than another." We do not believe this last assertion. I will only maintain that their beauty has grown with them.

Geneviève, the eldest, is my favourite sister, another me; and for a long while we have not been able to do without one another. A supple shape, a lovely expressive face fringed with golden hair, clear eyes between black eyelashes, added to a fine intellect and well-poised faculties, make of her a privileged being. Her steadfast character always deals straightforwardly, whereas mine, just as tenacious, does not disdain manœuvring.

Her sisters are tall and graceful. Yvonne has large black eyes, a tiny mouth, and splendid golden locks. She is the musician of the family; thinks nothing better in the world than the harmony of sweet sounds, and lives only for her art. Antoinette bears proudly an imperial beauty and a bachelor's degree, which she has recently carried off. As to Colette, the pet child of the family, by turns charming and execrable, she counts seventeen summers, and rejoices our eyes with the sweetest face ever seen, a rose-bud complexion, and cornflower eyes.

Two representatives of the opposite sex intrude upon this company of women. My husband first. He is the tallest, the handsomest of the sons of men. "When I see him, I think I behold a young god," said one of our friends a few years ago; and I shall not cheapen these terms of praise by any description of him. If I confide to you that he is growing bald on his temples, be sure you don't go and tell him so; the loss is due to sojourns in Saigon and Panama; for this half of myself is a true globe-trotter, and has seen the whole world—without me alas! He is a man of great learning, and is deeply skilled in philology and theology. Such as he is, I adore him, and think it better to own it honestly, for fear my partiality might remain unperceived. The other specimen of the sterner sex, with whom I have to deal here, is a small Parisian boy, nine years old, owner of the most flippant tongue. By a stroke of carelessness he was sent to us for a fortnight, and like many another has now to stay as a prisoner on account of the Invasion.

Out of common politeness I have not yet mentioned my own person. The task of describing it is hateful. Of this self fortunately there is not much—fifty kilos at the utmost. In other words, I am slender. I have a pink and white complexion and very long auburn hair, a small insignificant nose, a large mouth, and serious eyes. I am generally called "Grandmother," in memory of a time when we acted *Little Red Riding Hood.* My husband always calls me Mr. Monkey, your Poisonous Ladyship, or Mrs. Kid, vexatious names, truly, for a woman. We live in Paris the greater part of the year, but it is with pleasure that the whole family meets every summer in our country-house at Morny, to spend its holidays.

When, about the 20th of July 1914, Geneviève, Yvonne and I arrived in the dear old place, my husband and Colette had been enjoying it for a fortnight; my mother-in-law and Antoinette were expected shortly. We had taken with us little Pierre Prat, whose mother, a good friend of ours, could not leave Paris for the present, and the health of the interesting boy required the country. We had hardly exchanged the usual kisses, and renewed our knowledge of the place, we were hardly seated at the dinner-table, when Colette cried out: "Oh, grandmother, how lovely! Fancy, there will be a war. The day it is declared I shall dress like a boy and become a soldier!"

"Of course, you will cut your beautiful locks, besmear your cheeks, and there you are. But tell me in earnest, Posy, do you think there will be a war?"

I suppose my husband has a name of his own, but no one knows it. For the whole family he is "Brother," and I call him "Posy."

Now Mr. Posy thought war unavoidable, and began to expound the reasons that strengthened his opinion.

A little tired of the journey, happy to be again in the country, I listened to the deep sounds of the dear voice I had not heard for the last fortnight, but gave little heed to the meaning of his words. Besides, I was so sure there would be no war at all! We began to lead a blissful life; we enjoyed walks in the large garden, and praised the sun and the green. What delightful holidays we would have! The mere thought of it led to lyrism. O Nature! O Idyll! O blessed rest!

At first nothing happened to trouble our peace. It will be remembered that the newspapers were rather encouraging. Optimism prevailed; my husband alone talked of an impending conflict; but he wished it so eagerly that I thought he might be mistaken in his prophecies. "War is talked of every year," I said; "it is but a summer topic."

On the 26th of July there were alarming rumours, confirmed the day after. We then began to talk of war, to talk always about that, to talk of nothing else. Colette herself held no other conversation, and from her crimson lips dropped no other words than mobilisation, armament, concentration.

I shall never forget the night when troops crossed the village. I saw war that night, war, the man-eater, the great killer, war himself. The hour was grave. France was preparing to withstand her enemies, and was sending her armies to protect the frontiers. Troops marched through the village the whole night. First came the foot soldiers, who filed off to the strains of the "Marseillaise" and the "Chant du Départ." Leaning out of my window, in a nightgown, I tried to catch sight of something, and I saw only a black flood, endlessly rolling on. The sight of this dark mass which marched on and sang was striking indeed. The young voices had an accent of resolution and rage, and gave the impression that all hearts throbbed as if by one impulse. The men knew they were marching on to death, and they sang as the volunteers of '92 may have sung. Sometimes there was silence, and nothing was to be heard save the sound of steps as rhythmical as a heavy shower.

As the first battalion passed, my husband laid his book aside, lifted up his head, and declared: "There can be no more doubt of it now." And resuming his Henri Houssaye and his cigarette, he buried himself again in his reading. I was not so easily resigned to the situation. A certitude had seized upon me too. "It is war." I was trembling like a leaf, shaken by the wind, and I could not master my emotion. I was not frightened, I felt easy in my mind, but my body—was it due to primeval memory, to misgivings, or to the terrible thought that has been handed down from wars of yore? I do not know—but my frightened body was trembling convulsively.

When I was not leaning out of the window, I thought, lying by the side of my husband: "War is coming, may God protect us!" I clasped his dear head in despair, I kissed him in an agony, and said over and over again: "War will carry him off." And I thought: "All over France the roads are covered with troops, and thousands of women, close to the man they love, are listening to the steps of the soldiers and the rumbling of the cannon; broken-hearted, they kiss an adored face, and with bitter tears repeat: 'War will carry him off!'"

Cavalry followed infantry; then came gunners, cannon, and powder-carts. The heavy pieces rolled on with the noise of thunder, and shook the house to its foundations. It was about three o'clock in the morning. A cold mist fell as if reluctantly from the cloudy sky. The night was less dark, and the moving forms passed slowly like shadows before my sight, horses, cannon, and gunners wrapt up in their cloaks. Dark in the dark haze, the outlines of men and animals seemed to sketch a new dance of death, in the midst of which the grim monster might have appeared at any moment. I was so deeply impressed by this phantasmagorical marching past that I almost expected to see Death go up behind a gunner or get astride a cannon. I felt intensely that I was seeing war, war and death. War, the terrible tyrant, was marching along, and nothing would impede his progress.

Still more foot soldiers. The men sing no more. Dawn is unfavourable to enthusiasm. You set forth in the evening sanguine of success, seeing at the end of the road Victory, Triumph, and Glory. But when morning comes, dark and cold, your exaltation sinks. Not that you feel less resolute, but behind the brilliant phantoms your fancy had conjured up the night before, you see grimacing slaughter and death and fire.

Day broke bright and clear. In the sun's lively beams all fears melted away. There will be a war? Be it so. The men will go and fight, and we too will do something for France. The following week was a medley of enthusiasms and sadnesses. At last war and revenge were no more mere words; at last Germany would be crushed. Too long our enemy had wronged us; we would wreak a tardy but fearful vengeance for our still unavenged disgrace, for grievous humiliations daily inflicted on us.

enge, O sun, you rise, and your first rays make our hearts sing like the granite of old Egypt. We lived in a fever. War, which approached, cast its shadow before, but it was a bright shadow, the shadow of Glory, of more than human courage, of manifold heroism. It was the pillar of fire which, shielding our hearts from the enemy and the terrors to come, hid them from our eyes. The passing breath of enthusiasm quickened the beating of our hearts. As to myself, I put a good face upon the matter, but all the time I thought with anguish: "It is war. I shall be alone.... War will sever us from all we love, blood and tears will be shed everywhere. May God save France, and have pity upon us!"

On the 2nd of August war was an unquestioned fact: mobilisation was proclaimed. My husband has served in the Navy, and had to go to Cherbourg the next day. We then began preparations for the departure of our sailor, who increased my cares by saying over and over again: "Don't expect me to remain in the Navy, there is nothing to do there. I will be sent to the east of France, and see the white of the Prussians' eyes."

The luggage being ready, we went for a stroll in the village. War was of course the one topic of the day. To qualify them for the toils of Mars, the men had duly sacrificed to Bacchus, and their patriotism was none the less fiery for that. Most women were silent. Many had cried their eyes quite red. One day more, and they would be alone with groups of small children. A very young woman, almost a girl, declared with a toss of her light hair: "Bachelors who have but their own body to care for ought to go and fight, that's right, but fathers of a family!..." Her neighbour next door, Mme. Turgau, nodded assent. She had a baby in her arms, and was pensively listening to her husband who, hot with anger, was speechifying not very far off. In his quality of orator, he discoursed not only upon Germans, but upon spies also. In the morning two Germans had been arrested in Laon, and the day before a man who was going to blow up a bridge had been shot. But look! Two strangers appeared at the corner of the street. All faces grew serious, and Turgau, advancing towards the men, demanded their papers. When they refused to show them, the crowd grew nervous, and Turgau thought himself insulted. Cries and bad names filled the air, until the soldiers, astonished at the uproar, took the culprits away to examine their papers.

The lover of justice came back home greatly pleased with himself. People gathered round him, and declared: "Policemen, gendarmes, all humbug! Fortunately we are here to maintain order." And all together they went to the next inn, and from the adventure drew this moral lesson: No more strangers, France for Frenchmen!

Pleasant and peaceful, the last evening was drawing to its close, the last of many evenings that will never come again. The following morning I went to the station with my husband. There was a large crowd on the platform. The men, high in spirit, seemed delighted to go off to the army. Silent and gloomy, the women stood close to their husbands, and their eyes betrayed a sadness past remedy. Then came the train, full of soldiers of the reserve, singing at the top of their voices. All get into the crowded carriages, a whistle is heard, the train moves forward. A last kiss, a last handshake. The dear face leans out of the window, my eyes raised up towards it, until its features disappear and vanish in the distance. It is all over; he is gone; they are gone. Towards Glory, towards Death! Who knows? I came back home, forlorn and sad. In vain Colette's endearing words and Geneviève's warm affection awaited me; love had deserted the house.

The following days glided by tiresome and empty, but fortunately we soon found an occupation. A regiment of artillery was formed in the neighbourhood. Two batteries were quartered in Morny, and willing needlewomen were required to put the uniforms of the soldiers into good condition. Very well. There are no opportunities for high deeds, let us be content with small ones. We put together needles, scissors, and thread, and thus armed ran to the school where other women were already working. And what work! We were told to shorten trousers, to let jackets out, to sew stripes, and to stitch numbers on collars and sleeves. A noisy and merry activity prevailed in the yard. When off duty, the soldiers gathered about the big nut-tree, whose shadow protected the needle-women from the sun. Harmless jokes were exchanged, and Germany of course had to bear the brunt of them. There was a tailor, a giant with a jolly face, who declared that he would get all he wanted on the other side of the Rhine, and for a ball of thread or a missing button would send you straight to Berlin. These good-natured and simple ways were all the more touching on account of the dangers which lay ahead. And, what we highly appreciated, the soldiers behaved like gentlemen. We spent many hours with them, and never heard a rough or coarse word. For truth's sake, I must say their Captain kept a sharp look-out upon his men. He was about forty-five, had nice eyes and a kindly face. We heard his name, and found out that he was a famous man, whose works we greatly admired. We had common friends too, and it was not long before we became real comrades, and told him how eager we were to be of some use to our country.

"Don't you think we might nurse a few wounded soldiers in our house?" we asked.

The Captain was good enough to like the idea.

"All right," he said, "if your rooms are large enough and airy."

"Come and see yourself."

The Captain came first alone, and the day after with two Surgeon-Majors. They made calculations, and then declared that we might receive thirty soldiers. Two empty houses our neighbours offered out of kindness would contain twenty other beds. Fifty soldiers would compose quite a sufficient ambulance, and to our heart's delight we might devote our strength to the wounded.

"In Laon, they will be only too pleased to send you convalescents," M. Vinchamps told us; "plenty of patients will soon fill the hospitals; and a doctor from the town will come every day to tend your invalids."

This medical visit did not remain the only one M. Vinchamps paid us. About nine o'clock, his day's work over, our new friend came round and knocked at the window. Our talk was chiefly on war, the only topic we took an interest in.

"Men are good for nothing," M. Vinchamps said; "courage is their only gift. That is why I am delighted with the present war. At peace, men are out of their right element."

"Then you must improve the occasion, and make the best of it, for certainly there will be universal peace after the present war, and you men will be for ever out of your element."

No one answered, and our silence called up a picture of dead and wounded stretched upon a plain where a battle had taken place. And again we talked of Belgian courage, of that heroic Liége which had to face such fearful odds, and did not yield to brute strength. We likened the storming party to the turbulent waters which beat furiously against a dyke. But we knew the dyke was strong, and would not give way.

The Germans were not highly appreciated by Captain Vinchamps.

"They are not intelligent," he declared.

"But——"

"They are not. I do not deny their qualities. They are fine imitators, but no creators. They make good use of others' inventions, and derive benefit from discoveries they would be unable to make themselves. Their talents— quite practical—are not what is called intelligence. Cuvier, Pasteur, Lamarck have no rivals on the other side of the Rhine, and their work no equal. Besides, consider that for fifty years our neighbours have thought of but one goal: a victorious war."

"But that is very important just now."

"Never mind. Intelligence will get the better of brute strength and crush it."

The mere thought of victory sent a thrill of rapturous joy through our hearts.

On going out through the yard, lit up by the moon's rays, the Captain listened to the whistle of the trains, and said with a smile:

"Food for powder!"

At full speed the trains rolled on both lines day and night; the food for powder went by without ceasing.

Food for powder!

And yet the expression is not right. For the soul of every man was awake. At the call of war all men were ready to fight and to die; all shouted "victory," in the assurance that it would come to us.

In the village our confidence met some distrust. Mme. Tassin, who acts as housekeeper when we are away, tossed her grey head.

"I was young when I saw *them* for the first time in '70. What shall I do at my age if they come here now?"

Geneviève was filled with horror at the mere suggestion. In the farm near by Mme. Lantois expressed the very same unreasonable fears. "Do you think we shall have them here?" she asked a young lieutenant, who was as bitterly disgusted as we were.

Meanwhile our gunners were ready from head to foot, and their horses from mane to hoof. We heard the last exhortations of the Captain to his men, and the next day we got up at four o'clock in the morning to see them off. It was magnificent. The sun shone in triumph upon the martial train; the flower-covered cannon had a good-humoured air; the horses pawed the ground; and the gunners had not smiles enough to throw to us, nor caps enough wherewith to salute us.

Captain Vinchamps, before he took leave, introduced his horse. It was a "skittish" little mare, he thought, clever and sweet-tempered. Once more we wished him success, and once more hoped that the war would spare him and his men; and all, soldiers, officers, and horses, galloped off, and were soon hidden from our sight amid the poplar trees in the sun and the dust.

The last soldier had departed. The village was empty of men, and the women from sunrise to sunset were working in the fields. We led an uninteresting life. In fact we did not live in Morny, but in Belgium where our soldiers were fighting. Our overburdened minds looked forward passionately to the result of the first conflict. What was going to happen?

CHAPTER II

First came a letter from my husband. He had written it in the first fever of war. The letter was a week late, and he marvelled at the splendid eagerness and union of France. "'Tis the world upside down," he wrote. "In my detachment, out of 1200 seamen, not one was missing or drunk on getting to Cherbourg. As to myself, I am more decided than ever not to go to sea. I will see the Prussians face to face. Yesterday I had a talk with a field officer, and he promised to get me an interesting post. That is a good thing; I now depend only on him."

I thought I saw him rubbing his hands with satisfaction. An interesting post! It means, doesn't it, to run into jeopardy, to seek after perilous missions? Oh, dare-devil! oh, heart of stone! Wrapped up in his joy, he has no thought for the pangs of those whose hearts are hanging upon his life!

Soon after there arrived unexpectedly Mme. Valaine and Antoinette, whose journey had been greatly delayed by the mobilisation. We had got but scanty news from Paris, and listened in amazement to their descriptions of the capital, the fine frenzy of the soldiers leaving for the front, the plunder of German shops, and then in our turn told them the little that we had seen in the country.

When our stories and greetings were finished, it was time to prepare rooms for the travellers.

I will seize upon the occasion to give a short description of our dear old house. Notched like a saw, the gabled front presents a row of shutters, which, like grey eyelids, secure us from indiscreet looks. To the right and the left two large iron gates, always carefully closed, lead one into a paved yard, the other into a narrow road, planted with trees. The side of the house, looking out on the high-walled garden, throws off the reserve in which the front is shrouded; windows and doors are always wide open to the air, the sun, and the creepers, whose branches penetrate even the rooms themselves. Inside, a passage separates the house into two parts, the dining- and the drawing-rooms on one side, and on the other the bedrooms and the kitchen. Geneviève, Colette, and Mme. Valaine have their rooms downstairs. Upstairs the attic has been cut up pleasantly into three. Outside, parallel with the house, a small building opens into the yard, containing a wash-house, a room—the small room—a coach-house, a stable, and the whole is topped by an attic.

The house—this does not allow of discussion—is too small, or the family is too large, and Antoinette, who wanted a room to herself, declared: "I will settle in 'the small room,'" and we could not get it out of her head, although we enlarged,—with some complacency—upon the dangers she might run alone by night.

"The walls are high, the doors strong. I am not afraid, and then there are the dogs."

Indeed, Gracieuse and Percinet, the collies we dote on, live next door, and have sharp sets of teeth which they show to all intruders.

"Grandmamma," said Antoinette the next morning, "last night, about twelve...."

"The proper time for crimes."

"I was startled out of my sleep."

"You were dreaming of the Germans."

"No, no. Some one was in the attic above my room."

"There you are! A spy! Have you run him in?"

"Without joking, Grandmamma. I heard steps quite clearly."

"Do you know that deserters are said to have escaped near Morny?"

In process of time the deserters were proved to be dormice, but we thought the mistake amusing, and ever after called the attic "the deserter's attic." Life went on. Dull, spiritless, insignificant in Morny; immense, tremendous, and tragical beyond there in the North and the East. We longed for the postman the whole day long. He had few letters for us, but he still brought papers. We read them carefully, and we were none the wiser. We ought to have read between the lines, but we could not. I assure you that, during the end of August, we were deaf and blind. Our reason refused to believe the testimony of our senses. We saw thousands and thousands of people whom Belgium and the North had cast away, the Belgian army driven back from Flanders, the staff officers settle in Laon, and we never came to the right conclusion.

In the case of floods—long before they are out—birds fly with hasty wings, beasts hurry away, and even snails climb up the trees. Less clever than the beasts of the field, we were unconscious of the threatening inundation even when the country round us already lay under water, and floating wrecks were visible on all sides.

One morning, at an early hour, we went with our arms full of provisions to the station where seven trains had stopped, crowded with refugees. In an instant the poor people had stripped us of our burden, and by way of thanks answered our anxious questions.

For thirty-six hours they had been travelling, men, women, old people, children, invalids, crowded in the narrow carriages, and yet they were happy to get away, to escape, as they thought, from a nightmare. Furious bombardments, pitiless fights, burning villages—they had witnessed, and told to us all the horrors of war. They had seen corpses in some places so thickly packed that they remained standing, and the sight haunted them, as did the horrible smell of hundreds of dead bodies burning on funeral piles, or floating in long files down rivers of sinister aspect.

For the first time we realised the actual atrocity of war, and with a shrinking of the heart we eagerly questioned the lieutenant who convoyed the train, as to what had happened.

"Madam, I know nothing. I have been told an important battle is imminent. Belgium is in ruins."

"And we shall not go to Germany, and impose upon the aggressors the law of retaliation!"

"Of course we shall. Be patient. They shall rue it dearly. But when?"

The hordes that covered the roads were still more miserable than the travellers we had just seen.

Day after day they trudged grimly along. We saw vehicles of all kinds, carriages, carts, wains drawn by horses, oxen, donkeys, and even dogs, loaded and overloaded with women, children, sick people, huddled together with old clothes, kitchen utensils, articles of food for the people, and straw for the animals. The men relieved the sorry jades by pushing or pulling, and on both sides of the road rolled a flood of ragamuffins. The women, with urchins hanging on to their skirts, bore babies in their arms; boys and girls rode on bicycles; with great toil old and infirm people dragged along heaps of shapeless burdens, tools, saucepans, and the most unexpected objects of every kind.

They went on without rest, and with only one wish, to get farther away, and the very dogs followed, lolling their tongues out, their tails curled between their legs, with a feeling of the universal distress visible in their eyes.

Some faces looked tragical, even desperate, but on most of them was impressed a gloomy resignation.

"The Prussians are coming!" they had heard, and snatching some hastily made parcels, they had fled away with no other purpose than flight.

They were but a distracted herd, flying from a destroying wave; they possessed neither hearth nor home. All that they had was lost, burnt, plundered, and every one of them was but a cypher in the nameless crowd that besought the pity of France.

This human torrent had its dregs. There was no excuse for those who were harsh to the fugitives—and they were plenty—but society was upset, and the worst elements came to the surface. Plunder-fed vagabonds, always to be met in public calamities, profited by the woes of others, filched from the rich, took toll even of the poor, ransacked abandoned houses, and on their way back still managed to commit highway robbery and to steal purses. Thanks to these scoundrels, many honest and pitiful people were involved in the suspicion which wanderers often arouse. Fortunately our people in Morny are trustful enough, and they did their best to assist the helpless and relieve the hungry. Even in the poorest houses the peasants deemed it a point of honour to share their food and lodging with the wanderers. Several nights running, we gave hospitality to unfortunate families, first to Belgians and then to people of the North, small manufacturers of the neighbourhood of Fourmies. All told the same heart-rending stories: the order to evacuate, the house left ten minutes after, the bewildered flight on the road. Many had fled of their own free will, driven by the breath of terror the Prussians spread abroad; but all were way-worn, all talked of sleepless nights, hunger, thirst, and suffering.

"Alas," said a young girl, "there are some still unhappier than we are! Graves have been dug by the wayside; one woman has lost her mother, another her baby."

And under their breath they whispered the nameless deeds, the monstrous crimes committed by the Germans.

Their stories left us half incredulous, and if terror seized upon our soul, it was a far-off, unselfish terror. It did not occur to our minds that the tempest was lowering overhead; we refused to believe that the dyke over there had already given way, and that we ourselves might be overrun by the tumultuous flood of invasion. And then, on Wednesday, August 26, three Belgian officers announced that 12,000 Belgian soldiers, "the remainder of an army forty thousand strong," would march through the village the next day at five.

The excited people gathered in knots on the road long before the appointed time, and having nothing else to do let their tongues run on. Much news was exchanged, some of which seemed insipid, and some thrilling.

The *Journal de Laon*, born with the war, ceased to come out owing "to postal difficulties." This organ surely suffered from a secret blemish: it was not born to live. Indifference.

No trains came from the North. Indeed! And we had been told everything would go on miraculously well, as soon as the mobilisation was over. Astonishment.

The people of the "Terres Rouges"—a remote quarter of Morny—persuaded that the Prussians were approaching, made a great slaughter of their plumpest pigs and poultry, and devoured them hastily. "It is so much gained," they wisely thought. What a droll idea! Hilarity.

But ... and this seemed odd. The ladies of the Red Cross, leaving the wounded in the lurch, scampered away last night. Shame upon them! Surely the strait-laced nurses would never be guilty of indiscretion, and yet they commit strange blunders. Reprobation.

The staff is established in Laon. Ah! Ah! That is worthy of note. It will be interesting to see the town in its new aspect of headquarters. Interest.

And here are the newspapers a neighbour has brought straight from Paris! Change of Ministry. Formation of a Ministry of National Defence. Oh! Oh! This is somewhat curious. They are hiding things from us. Anxiety.

While the village was busy in discussion, time went on, and the Belgian army also. About seven, the boys that stood sentry over the road came on shouting:

"Here they are! Here they are!"

They were coming indeed, white with dust, but still gallant-looking. First came lancers, then gunners, a few foot-soldiers, and again lancers. Here and there a spiked helmet topped a lance's point as a trophy, and the gunners, along with their guns, dragged a canteen carried off from the enemy. For three hours they went at a gallop, and for three hours we shouted our throats sore, and the whole village with us:

"Bravo! Long life to Belgium! Success to the brave!"

The soldiers, still galloping, answered at the top of their voice:

"*Vive* France! Down with Germany! Hurrah for the French women!"

And, rushing forward, we shook all the hands that were stretched towards us. That night I think we shook 12,000 hands as 12,000 men went along. We ran, we were everywhere. Colette was madly imprudent, and I wondered at her not being run over or crushed under the wheels of the cannons. At last, about half-past ten, the village was silent, as we made our way home with hoarse voices and tired arms, thinking only of our beds. There will be time enough for serious politics to-morrow.

The next day we went to Laon, Geneviève and I. If we were uneasy and disquieted, where could we better calm our fears than in Laon? The official reports were vague but rather encouraging, the officers optimistic. The civilians thought there was no room for hesitation, and unhesitatingly ran away. Many were already off. The cowards were frightened, like hares, by the shadow of their ears. Our scorn was greater even than their haste. We reserved our sympathies for the soldiers whose bright uniforms gave a pleasant liveliness to the town. We were less pleased with the checks put upon our movements. Passports had to be produced at every corner of the streets, and then, after two hours waiting among a noisy and ill-smelling crowd, to be signed in a guardroom. This was—if necessary and comprehensible—very tiresome.

All the same we felt uneasy on our way home. We were infringing the regulations, that was as clear as day. "It is strictly forbidden to take any provisions out of the town," the orders said. But there is no use talking of obedience to hungry women, and we had—with what pains—carried off from a greedy grocer rice, sugar, salt, and other precious things, that ran short in the country. Fortunately we saw the Mayor of Morny driving by, and from him we gratefully accepted a lift for the sake of our parcels.

The evening was lovely, the country smiling in the setting sun. The harvest, somewhat delayed for want of men and horses, drew to its close, and beetroot promised a splendid crop. Everything spoke of peace and plenty. The Mayor with a word broke the spell. "From this place," he said, pointing at a hill disgraced by the presence of a factory, "the cannon was audible yesterday."

"It is mere hearsay," he added, daunted by our protestations, and we all came to the conclusion the hearers had but singing in their ears.

Thus at the side of the Mayor we made a sensational entrance into Morny.

At home they had taken in two Belgian soldiers, whose lucky star had led to our door. In great haste the family had prepared a huge omelette, a solid beefsteak, a comfortable salad. Then to pay their share they had talked. Alas, what they said was not encouraging:

"We have been beaten; the Germans are gaining ground." They knew nothing more. The next day we had another Belgian to feed. Our ward, Pierrot, met him in the street in quest of a dinner, and, showing him the way, had brought the soldier into the dining-room. Our new guest told us frightful stories, and talked of defeat and high treason; but, on the other hand, he boasted of such high deeds he had performed himself that we listened wholly unmoved to his wondrous tales.

Defeat! Treason! We had no fear on that score. In spite of a vague alarm, we apprehended no real danger. Some uneasiness stole first over our minds when we got a telegram from Mme. Prat claiming Pierrot back. It was the 30th of August. We ran to the station, and were there told with the greatest serenity:

"There is no train going to Laon to-night."

"To-morrow will do, then; there is no hurry."

We thought no more of the journey, for the majors' dinner took place that very evening. All that wore a uniform were sure to arouse an admiring interest. The soldiers were overwhelmed with love and adulation. A little more, and we would have prostrated ourselves at their feet. It was but right. What sacrifices could we make to match what they gave us: their strength, their life, their youth? And they were France herself; they were ourselves. Every woman who spoiled a trooper said to herself: "My son too is a soldier."

On this Sunday, then, the village was overjoyed to hear that soldiers would be billeted on it.

"A good thing. We shall see some officers, and perhaps hear some news." And we kept our eyes open, ready to snap up the first piece of gold lace that would come on. The said lace happened to be on the sleeve of a surgeon-major, who to our anxious questions gave us an evasive answer, and seized time by the forelock.

"Oh, madam," he said to my mother-in-law, "shall I dare ask you...."

"Dare ask it, sir."

"To lend us your kitchen and your dining-room? We are ten surgeon-majors, and we have nowhere to dine."

"Certainly, my house is at your disposal."

"But say nothing about it! It is not here that our quarters are."

His companion, a giddy-brained youth fresh from the schools, who hitherto had not opened his mouth, cried out:

"We will say that the ladies are relations of ours. Mademoiselle will not refuse to declare I am her cousin."

The haughty Antoinette did not like the joke, and snubbed the joker. Then Esculapius' disciples went away, to return speedily. We exchanged a great many low bows, and, the ceremony performed, left the gentlemen for fear we should disturb them. They seemed to want rest, judging from their worn-out faces. We heard that one of our guests who had just fallen into a doze was the famous Professor X, and we beheld his tired face with some respect. In a clandestine meeting we had decided:

"We shall have supper in the garden."

"We will drink a cup of milk, and eat bread and butter."

We are not of those who believe in the necessity of dining. Of course, out of respect for our stomachs, we give them tolerable cheer, but occasionally we are content with a cup of cocoa and a slice of bread. And that night we had other fish to fry than to feed ourselves. Besides, we were unlucky enough to have no maids at all at that time; the only one we had left had refused to stay any longer in a place likely to be invaded.

Our modest meal over, we ran into the house. In the kitchen, the dinner was getting on well. A savoury smell rose from the saucepans. A giant scullion was helping a cook, who pontified solemnly. This strange cook hid beneath his apron, assumed for the occasion, a uniform covered all over with decorations. Beneath the trade of cook, also assumed for the occasion, he hid that of an engineer in civil life, in military life that of an hospital orderly. He was tall, spare, pale, red-haired, and he looked unalterably calm.

"Where are the Germans?" we asked the engineer-cook. "Will they come here? What ought we to do?"

He feared the Prussians would reach Morny, and in his opinion we had better avoid the meeting.

"Are we to run away, then, and wander about like the Belgians? Or shall we take a ticket to Marseilles, Algiers, or Timbuktu? Is that far enough?"

Our interlocutor stilled our impatience with the slow sounds of his voice. Really now, he had a castle ... in the air?... No, but in Brittany, where his sister would be delighted to receive us.... And the head cook, while draining dry his fried potatoes, gave us the address of his mansion in Brittany. After the advice of the kitchen, we wanted the counsels of the dining-room. A few sleepy-heads had already gone to bed, among others the celebrated physician and the giddy-brained youth, who had grown extremely serious. The remainder of the learned party were chatting together amid the smoke of tobacco and the flowers on the table. Without more ado we went in, and asked the usual questions:

"Where are the Germans? Will they come here? What ought we to do?"

A long conversation ensued. Alas, our guests were as pessimistic as could be. The head major, a small man, thick-set, energetic, and dark, did not hide from us the truth that we should see the Germans, and, still worse, that they would lay siege to Paris. Grief and indignation prevented us from looking at our own situation; we thought but of the country itself.

"Why," Geneviève cried out, "you think the Germans will conquer us! You are expecting another '70?"

"Never! never! The Germans will be beaten. Should they go to Marseilles and Bordeaux, I should still believe in their final defeat, but the moment is a critical one. We have been beaten; it is a certain fact; there is no use being blind to it, and the Germans will go to Paris."

A clear voice rose at the end of the table:

"You talk as if we were lost," Colette said. "We are retreating? It may be a wise measure. Our men are ready for anything. The Germans in Paris!—but you do not know our soldiers!"

"Very good," said the neighbour of Colette, a tall, fair-haired man. "Do try to convince my friends; these ten days I have dinned the same arguments into their ears. But you must excuse our despondency; weariness is the cause of it; these last three weeks we have hardly slept. And what do we see of war? Nothing that is not horrible and disheartening—battle-fields after the fight, the dead, the wounded, the stragglers—nothing that elevates, and idealises men."

So the talk went on, and the dining-room rang with the praises the doctors bestowed on their heroic patients. They spoke chiefly of the terrible weariness of the men.

"They are overcome with sleep," they said, "and to such an extent that they don't wake up, even when we dress their wounds."

A few minutes after, Colette said to her neighbour:

"It is delightful to discuss with you. At least, you always agree with me!"

We all burst out laughing, and at this fit of gaiety the majors went softly out for fear they would wake up the officers and the refugees whom we were sheltering.

CHAPTER III

Sleep was long in coming that night. After much talking we were still at a loss what to think. Were the Germans really at our gates? "I cannot believe it," groaned Geneviève; "it is a collapse; it is the end of all things."

"If we are invaded, what shall we do?"

The next day we renewed the discussion.

"If the Prussians come, we have but to wait for them with a bold face," said Geneviève and Colette. Mme. Valaine hesitated.

"Mother," exclaimed Yvonne and Antoinette, "we cannot stay here. Think of the risks we run."

"What shame," retorted Colette, "to run away like a troop of rabbits! I had never thought you were such cowards!"

The others repeated with one accord:

"And if mother was taken as a hostage? The Germans are capable of anything; they have already committed many atrocities."

Our perplexity was great.

About ten o'clock there dropped from the sky three new surgeons, and, pressing on them a cup of coffee, we renewed our anxious questions. They told us plainly that the Germans were gaining ground, and that we were sure to see them.

"What do you advise us to do?" cried my mother-in-law.

"Madam," Dr. Seseman declared—he was bearded, jovial, and fatherly— "Madam, if you were relations of mine, I should urge your departure."

"Well, the die is cast, we shall go," declared Mme. Valaine.

"Yes," I said, "but the house is not in order."

A few days ago, as I went to Mme. Lantois to buy some eggs, the farmer's wife told me with great satisfaction:

"I feel quieter now, my house is in order."

It was as much as to say that all she set store by had disappeared; the family had hidden, buried, and walled up whatever they had been able to hide, bury, and wall up.

Our guests of yesterday's dinner had told us that the owners of a northern farm had unpaved a yard, dug a huge hole, huddled in pieces of furniture and pictures, and then filled up and repaved it. This farm could await the invaders: it was in order. But our house was not in order—that was obvious enough.

"You have here," said our visitors, "a beautiful Empire clock. It would be a great pity to have it sent to Germany."

"And this lovely console table—and those vases...."

A few minutes after the two officers, with whom we were gravely discussing, asked:

"Where is our friend Laison?"

"In the garden with Colette, digging holes...."

"Is he? then we will too."

And soon after, our visitors, in their shirt-sleeves, seemed to strive who would dig hardest; and we, just as busy, ran in all directions, and brought in objects of every kind.

In order to carry out our plan, we had to look for a favourable place. In front of the house stretches a velvet lawn planted here and there with firs and pretty reeds. We could do nothing there. But beyond there are beds in the gardens, shaped like a lozenge, a crescent, and what not, box-edged and planted with shrubs. That was the right place, and we proved it by digging there six or seven big holes. The largest received the drawing-room clock, carefully wrapped up in oilcloth, with other clocks almost as dearly cherished. On this side, we buried silver, on that, old china, with a great deal of bustle and haste.

"Is the old Rouen jug buried? And my yellow tea-set? I will bury that too; it is too lovely to lose."

The work drew to an end, and, by a masterpiece of cunning, we strewed the newly-dug ground with dry leaves, twigs, and small pebbles.

Dr. Laison went into ecstasies about the garden he had made over the grave of the clocks. He was thinking himself a match for Le Nôtre, when he gave a start. "What is that?" The buried treasures, indignant at their ill-usage, protested against it by the voice of the Empire clock, which began to strike the hour. As we listened to the silvery yet hollow sound which came from the earth, we were reminded of a tale by Edgar Poe. But we had to apply our thoughts to other cares, and hide the linen and clothes. After our guests were gone—loaded with grateful blessings—we hardly spared the time to swallow a hasty dinner, and went to give the finishing touch to our work.

Now there is between the ceiling of my bedroom and the roof a very dark and lofty space that might serve as a very good hiding-place; but the ladder was too short to get to it, so we put it on a table, and I, astride on a beam, concealed in the accommodating shadow the things which my sisters-in-law, posted on the ladder like so many tilers busy with new roofing, handed up to me. We spread out and heaped up, at first linen, then clothes, furs, shawls, carpets, curtains, eider-down coverlets, and a big lion-skin; with many exertions we even hoisted up to the loft a console table. Colette, standing on tiptoe at the other end of the attic, declared:

"It looks quite empty; you can put in more things."

"Thanks! We are quite stiff enough for once. Thank Heaven the Germans don't come every day, or we should not be equal to the job."

Downstairs we took down looking-glasses and pictures, and concealed them as well as we could behind cupboards and bed-curtains. They showed a little, but we hoped the Germans would see nothing of them. We could not bury water-colours or oil-paintings, could we?

At last the house was in order, and we went out for a little stroll. The village was silent, dead, not a cat in the streets; all the doors and windows were closed. It was evident that every one was giving himself wholly up to the very sport we had just enjoyed. All were vying with one another in hiding their treasures, and were racking their brains to find unknown holes and undiscoverable hiding-places. I wish to state here that there is a gap in our public instruction, a want in our literature. Since we are provided with such alarming neighbours, every school-master should devote two hours a week to teach our youth what precautions to take in case of invasion. Moreover, in my leisure hours, I intend to write a book on "The Art of Concealing applied to Invasion." This may open a new field of literature, for they will certainly lose no time in answering the work from the other side of the Rhine with "The Treasure-seeker's Guide, or a Hand-book for the Complete Plunderer." We shall have, therefore, to study the question and improve the art of hiding. In this respect, it is true, an ancient instinct may serve as a guide, an instinct which has had no better chance of expansion than in the corner of France we belong to. This rich country has excited the lust of all conquerors. Before the Christian era the Romans subdued it, and later on the Franks laid hands upon it. Attila, as Colette said but yesterday, may have sent a few patrols down here. Then came the Normans, who levied contributions on us; and the English, who took their ease at the inhabitants' cost during the Hundred Years' War. Later the troops of Philip the Second plundered us, and last century, 1814, 1870—two inauspicious dates—we knew the strangers twice more. Therefore, when the alarm spread, "the enemy are advancing," the order of the day, which we knew by right of inheritance, went round: "let us hide, let us hide!" All kept on hiding, and we hid too.

And our departure? We had decided to go, that was well and good; but how should we go? We could not by railway, and we could not find a horse and a carriage in the village for their weight in gold. Mme. Valaine went in haste to M. Laserbe, who was setting out with three carts drawn by oxen. He promised to take us and our luggage with him, as little luggage as possible.

"Never fear, I will tell you in good time. There is no danger for the present."

These words gave us confidence. We would fly, but whither, in this train of sluggard things? I have mentioned the ridges that lie to the south and the west of Morny. In the country these modest hills are pompously called "the mountains." Now every one was convinced the Germans would shun "the mountains." An army always goes along valleys, does it not? And what would the enemy do in this uneven region, where orchards and pasture grounds alternate with rocks and woods? "It is not the right place to fight in," the people said. And in a hamlet in this happy part of the country lives an old relation of ours, Mme. Laroye. We decided to go to Cousin Laroye; we were sure she would receive us with open arms; there we should see what to do next, and, when once the enemy had passed over both sides of "the mountains," we could get to Switzerland, the South of France, or Brittany as we chose.

Meanwhile, after this busy day, we really wanted rest, and to-night at least we would sleep our fill. But we do not shape our own ends.... At half-past two we were up. Foot soldiers passed in the street. At three we were standing at the window, busy pouring out wine or coffee. Our poor, poor soldiers! So cheerful, so lively, so full of gay spirits but a month ago, in what a state did we see them return!

Bent, way-worn, they marched painfully. Yet they marched; but as soon as they were ordered to stop, they dropped on the ground, and many fell asleep on the spot. Still, when they heard we were giving something to drink, they came tumbling one over another, and gathered around the window. A captain advanced, quieted the disturbance, and ordered the sergeants to distribute the bottles of wine by sections. At the sight of this officer, I suddenly understood the gravity of the hour. Dark-haired, with firm and yet fine features, he bore in his eyes the bitterness of the retreat, the horror of the defeat. A look on his tragic face informed me of the truth better than long speeches. Beaten! We were beaten. France was lost....

O God! is it possible? Has God suffered this? No, no, it is not so; I see now the flames, that protest in the feverish eyes: "We will die, but we will struggle to the end." Yes, dear soldiers, brave heroes, you will struggle against the enemy, happy that you can still take an active part, while we, we can but wring our hands in despair, and support your courage with love and earnest prayers. In this terrible moment, our eager goodwill could do no more than ask: "Do you want a cup of coffee? The water is boiling."

"Madam, with pleasure." Then some one called the officer, and he had to go without his coffee, for which, by the way, many were eager.

The village was awake, and all were desirous to bring food and drink to the soldiers. But the soldiers were so many that a great number certainly got nothing at all.

Day broke, and the men still passed on, always as dusty, always as tired, all regiments, all arms mixed in confusion. We did our best to relieve as many as we could. In the morning the crowd grew thinner; we saw only stragglers and cripples. How many we took in to comfort and nurse I cannot say; they were too many. I remember the clerk of the telegraph pointing to his right hand, of which the fingers had been shot off.

"What shall I do now?" he said. "And the girl I am engaged to, will she marry me?"

"Of course she will, or she would not be French!"

And then came a soldier wounded in the leg, and, in spite of his sufferings, he hobbled on with a stick. In admiration, he indicated Antoinette with a movement of his chin, and declared in his Lorraine brogue:

"That girl there, she has dressed my wound much better than a trained nurse."

A little linesman moved our pity still more, and even now we cannot talk of him without emotion. He was very young, with a childish face; his motionless features expressed an immense stupor, a grievous surprise. What! that war! That was war! This wonderful thing we had so often heard of! It was this retreat, these toils, these sufferings! For three weeks he had not taken off his shoes, and his blistered feet were so swollen that the poor fellow could hardly walk. Geneviève washed his poor feet, and Colette, the over-fastidious Colette, wiped and bound them up with tender care. We got him fresh socks, and the little foot soldier, after a comfortable breakfast, went on his way again. As he left us, he looked around him with amazement depicted on his face, and said:

"The Germans will punish you for that."

In these busy hours we had many opportunities to wonder at the energy and vitality of our race. As soon as the soldiers, spent with fatigue and disheartened, had rested a bit and swallowed something hot, they renewed their vigour and even recovered gaiety enough to tell us their adventures, to laugh at the German shells, which often do not burst, and whose fragments run over the cloth of their uniforms, they assured us, without doing any harm.

"But"—and there they dropped their voices to a whisper—"we have been beaten, because there are traitors among the generals...." This opinion drove us to despair. We did not give credit to it, but what would happen if the men reposed no trust in their chiefs? And what could we answer to the poor fellows? I recalled to Geneviève's memory Captain Vinchamps' saying: "Beaten soldiers always call out treason, and they are not wrong; a traitor is not merely a man who basely and selfishly sells his country; he is a traitor too when he is not equal to his duty."

We did our utmost to hearten our guests of a moment, to cheer them physically and morally; and then one after another they resumed their journey. A touching detail: every lame soldier was attended by a comrade, who took charge of him, carried his knapsack, held him up, and was as careful of him as a mother of her child. About noon, when all had gone away, Yvonne and Colette, who kept a watchful eye upon the street, cried out: "Something is happening towards the pond," and set off running thither. They found that a soldier had suddenly gone mad. Half-naked, up to his waist in water, he shrieked and gesticulated, and four men had a hard struggle to master him.

Trifling as it was, this incident brought the people's excitement to its highest point.

"He is a Prussian," said one. "He is a spy," retorted another. This time the people snatched at their luggage, were off in an instant, and came back an hour after. The level-crossings were not open to civilians for the present, or at least to carriages. Our state of mind was that of a fish caught in a net. Terror spread amain, and won complete power over the public mind. None knew what he dreaded, and all men reasoned themselves out of reason. Our arguments were proved absurd and grotesque by the event. A mist was over us; it was no more the pillar of fire; it was the pillar of cloud. It was no more the shadow of approaching glory; it was the black shadow which impending invasion casts before.

News kept coming.

"The Prussians are at Marle."

"No, they have been driven back."

"Perhaps they won't come down here."

Driven back! Oh, you simpletons! Have you not just seen our army pass? Are you not conscious of the void, which draws on the enemy like a cupping-glass?

In the village, so lively, so busy but a few days ago, is there a single uniform left?

At heart the people felt uneasy; the cars were loaded, the horses harnessed, the drivers on the look-out. Animals and people were but waiting for a signal to rush upon an unknown fate.

The signal came.

It was about six. Tired, I was lying down in the drawing-room, when all of a sudden a gun-shot resounded in the air, and directly after followed sharp firing. At a bound I was up in the attic, at another I flew to the garret window. Like a gargoyle stretched out on the edge of the roof, I scanned the horizon. Northward a light puff of smoke vanished in the upper branches of the poplar trees. Nothing was to be heard; but I beheld the confused flight of all creatures that were out in the fields. A man standing in a car lashed his bewildered horse with all his might; fowls and even pigeons hurried away to poultry-yard and dovecot.

What had happened? I hastened down. The house was empty. I jumped out of the window. At the corner of the street I caught sight of Geneviève. I ran after her as fast as I could; we met at the cross-road, where a crowd had gathered.

"What is the matter?" A patrol.... An English patrol.

We cast a look at the field-grey backs which rode away on big horses. English? it may be!

"But at what did they fire?"

"It was a signal."

"No, they have shot carrier-pigeons."

"You are mistaken, they have arrested a spy."

In fact they had taken away a French soldier, bareheaded, who looked about him with a profoundly ironical air.

"Oh," murmured the crowd, "it was easy to see he was a spy; he seemed to laugh at us."

He was laughing at you! I am sure he was, the poor man! English soldiers! English soldiers! Oh, you blind of one, of two eyes, threefold idiots, how foolish you have been! They were twelve in number, and the village was armed, and the men were there, and Prussians in flesh and bone, as quiet as can be, took the high road to Laon!

We, quiet too, came back home. There now! We had had our warning! Our hearts were still throbbing violently, but all the same we plucked up courage again.

"The English keep watch and ward!"

Each one laughed at his friends' fright. We thought particularly ridiculous the attitude of one of our neighbours, Marthe Tournillart, a tall young woman, ruddy-cheeked and dark-haired, who at the first shot had rushed headlong on her overloaded barrow. Resolutely she laid hold of it, and with her two children hanging on to her skirts, fled away bewildered but energetic, she knew not where; but she fled straight into the hottest of the fight, had one taken place.

Nevertheless the passage of the patrol was looked upon as suspicious. "We put no trust in this lump of flour," the peasants thought, like La Fontaine's mice. "If we hear the guns now, it is the right moment for flight."

Yvonne ran to M. Laserbe. When and how were we to go? The messenger came back struck with dismay. Laserbe refused to take charge of us! The traitor! And he had pledged his word! He alleged he had no places left. Well, what were we to do? Whither could we turn? Could we go on foot? To-night?

Mme. Valaine hesitated. She thought it dangerous in this troubled time to run away by night through woods and fields.

"We will see what to-morrow brings," she said.

"Mother, to-morrow may be too late," retorted Antoinette.

"The first thing to do," said I, "is to have supper. There is a soup on the table which will give you wings."

It was about nine. Hazardous times do not improve punctuality. We sat down to table, and had hardly enjoyed a few mouthfuls of the soup I had boasted of, when hasty steps resounded in the street; we heard a knock at the shutter. We rushed forward.

"The Prussians are coming," whispered one of our neighbours. "They are ten miles away. They have been seen on their way to Morny. French officers have been to the Mayor's, and have pulled down the flag. Every one is going. Good-bye; we won't lose time...."

I am going, you are going, we are going. Go on, oh flock of sheep!

Our own house is greatly alarmed. Mme. Valaine does not know which way to turn. "Make haste, we must go at once. Get our things ready." Thinking Laserbe would take us, we had packed up just what was necessary, and what was necessary meant thirteen bags. We must discard them. Feverishly we unpacked and abandoned the heavy bags; bundles would do. A little linen, one or two light dresses, cloaks, shawls, a basket filled with food, and we were quite ready. Had I not early in the morning buried in the depths of the garden a sealed-up glass jar full of jewels? And with the gold pieces my mother-in-law had brought from Paris, had I not made a band I wore around my waist? We were ready, no doubt of it.

We did not know what to do with the bags we were bound to abandon. We dragged them upstairs to a loft next my bedroom, thrust them into it all topsy-turvy, and hurriedly heaped up big logs at the entrance. Everything was in order; the dogs were on their chains; we had but to go.

Here we are in the street, all doors shut, and off we go. We wait one minute to calm our hearts and to drop a tear.

Dear little house, white walls, virginia creepers, when shall we meet again? And what will you look like? Let us begone! It is time for action, not for regret.

Our neighbours next door, the couple Tillard, were putting the donkey in their cart all ready for flight.

I have read somewhere that people should help one another in misfortune, and so I blurted out: "Oh, M. Tillard, I suppose you are driving to 'the mountains.' We are going too. Would you kindly take one of our parcels with you?" At a loss what to answer, Tillard muttered between his teeth:

"Hum! already loaded.... Don't know which way...."

That is enough. "Thank you.... I understand." Another pause, this time at M. Lonet's, my mother-in-law's brother. Stern-faced, with knotted brows, our uncle refuses to go. Not he! He is fonder of his house, of his gardens, than of anything, and the Germans cannot scare him away. He bends on our caravan a glance of mingled scorn and pity, and, on going out, Geneviève whispered in my ear as a last protest:

"He is not a coward."

If fear could not enter M. Lonet's heart, it reigned in the village. The whole place was deserted, and we were among the last to go. Here and there a flickering light showed that hasty preparations were still being made in a few houses. Terror oozed from the closed shutters, hostile to the expected foe, and from the doors, which presently the dwellers would half open, to sneak away. At the end of the village, in a yard, a lantern moved to and fro, a horse was harnessed, people hurried up and down.

"Lucky rogues," Colette cried out, "who possess a cart!"

That is true. Our bundles already seemed heavy to bear. But, full of courage, we went on, left the high road, crossed Cerny-les-Bucy, dead, empty, mute. Another struggle and we were in the open country. Thus we marched on—a strange little train, six women, attended by a small boy and two dogs—silent, with heavy hearts, and then a voice complained:

"It is so heavy."

Yvonne had taken charge of the dogs, and had perhaps the hardest work, for these animals, as soon as they are out of doors, pull on their chain, until they almost tear out your fingers.

The road was deserted. Nobody in front of us, nobody behind. We were safe from attack. We decided to rest awhile. Halt! We gathered our luggage into the middle of the road, and sat down in a ditch. Speechless, we looked at and listened to the night.

I shall never forget the night of our flight, as I watched it in that meadow. Silvery night studded with stars, lit up by the moon, warm and sweet and so quiet! Fields and meadows, bathed in moonlight, stretched on all sides. Southward a wood showed like a shadow, and from the damp meadows rose a mist, which followed the brook. You might have said that large puffs of cotton wool hung in the air upon invisible threads, above which emerged the tops of pollarded willows. Not a sound was heard. Only far away a carriage rattled, or a dog barked; and close about us the crickets sang their shrill song. A god-like presence filled the world, and the serenity of inanimate things contrasted sharply with the mad fear of men which swept us away. On this same night, uniformly kind to all, whole armies marched, dreaming of death and destruction, while thousands of wayworn fugitives wandered on towards uncertainty, misery, despair.

Boom, boom! Two formidable detonations from the fort of Laniscourt shook the air, and aroused us from the torpor which crept over us. Was it a signal? We did not know. We went on. Go, take up your burden again, hasten, the way is long. We went on, but slowly; we were tired, and baggage always retards the advance of an army. Poor snails that we were! The flood was approaching; it had driven us away; and if in our unreasoning prudence we resembled snails, we had not the good luck to carry a house with us. What shelter should we get? Where should we lay our tired heads? We advanced anyhow, our ears pricked, our eyes on the look-out. An alarm! This shadow on the road, which moves on...! black, apocalyptical, it passed by, and greeted us without astonishment:

"Good-night, ladies; a beautiful night, isn't it?"

We recognised old Lolé, a well-known beggar, bent with age, loaded with a wallet full to the brim. Another shadow, a white one this time, crossed our path a few steps farther on; it was a small dog, which did not stop, but hurried on his way to Morny. The times were hard for dogs too.

"And then, look behind that stack—two, three, five dark forms ... they are people, aren't they?" But, still more afraid than we, they hid themselves, and we passed on triumphantly. Without striking a blow, we crossed the woods, and got to the fields again. On approaching Mons-en-Laonnois we heard eleven strike. The silvery sound of the bell seemed to drop from a very high tower, from the starry sky, perhaps. Here we made a feeble and vain attempt to get a carriage. No one in the streets; the very garret windows were shut up, the doors barricaded. At the end of the village, we halted. We were hungry, for the good reason that we had left on the supper-table the creamy milk and crusty cake, which were to end our frugal meal. But we had taken with us a few savoury chicken *pâtés*, which my prudent mother-in-law had made the day before. We cut slices of bread and butter, and, sitting by the wayside, made an excellent meal. We were gay, but our gaiety was fictitious. We laughed at a light anxiously flickering behind a shutter. It seemed a prey to nameless terror, and, conscious of our own courage, we made merry over it. The poor thing surely believed a German patrol was feasting at the gate!

Two hours after, we got to Vaucelles, then to Royaucourt. We were tired to death, and made up our minds to seek shelter. All the barns were full of refugees, all the yards were encumbered with refugees' horses, all the streets were crowded with refugees' vehicles. We too were refugees now.

"Will there be any room for us," we wondered, "no matter where, so long as we can rest?" We stopped in front of Mlle. Honorine's inn: "Good accommodation for man and beast." It was just what we wanted. We gave a knock at the door.

"Mademoiselle, mademoiselle, open the door, please ... just a small room, only chairs to sit down." But none so deaf as those who won't hear. Nothing would have roused Mlle. Honorine from her sweet slumbers.

At length we made up our minds to rest outside, on the threshold of the unrelenting house. An accommodating bench very kindly welcomed three of us, Geneviève and Antoinette, wrapped up in their cloaks, stretched on the stony ground of the courtyard. As to myself, I chose for a resting-place a flight of steps. Crouching down in a comfortable corner, with Pierrot nestled in my arms, I covered our bodies with my shawl, and summoned sleep in vain. The stone was very hard. Yet I was comfortable, and had no mind to go away. But we soon remembered we were running away, and that it was high time for us to be off again. "Get up! get up! It is half-past two." We rose reluctantly, yawned, cleared our throats, stretched ourselves. Antoinette was so weary and so ill that we had much trouble to move her. At length we were all up. We cursed the household that had behaved so unkindly to the poor wanderers, and, leaving the inhospitable village, we turned to the right. The road wound its way through the woods. The moon had gone down; it was pitch dark; our hearts quivered with fear; our eyes searched into the shades of night; and we strained our ears like the dogs. The poor beasts disapproved of our nightly expedition, and sniffed at tufts of grass with great anxiety.

"This black mass here, lying on the wayside, is it a dead body? No, it is but a log. And there, those white spots, aren't they faces? No, they are birches. Don't you hear a noise of steps? No, it is the breaking of a dead branch." We stopped to take a little breath. We were out of the forest; we had reached the top of the hill. Quite bare, it was not really a plateau, for the ground spread itself out in large waves. We walked along, dragging our luggage up and down the road. Geneviève and I carried the heaviest bag, and tried many experiments to make it lighter. We put it on our shoulders like an urn, on our back like a sack of flour. Like the queen of the turtles, we hung it on a stick, of which each of us took an end. From time to time we stopped a minute to change hands, or to listen to far-away noises. Then a slight quivering broke the stillness. We thought we heard a distant rumbling. Sometimes there were explosions—bridges were being blown up. Day was already breaking. A pallor whitened the sky towards the east. We reached Urcel, prettily placed among orchards on the slope of a hill. Worn out, we sat on the edge of the pavement like so many swallows on the edge of a gutter. We were in high spirits, we exchanged jokes, and all of a sudden:

"Yvonne, Yvonne, laughter will end in crying...."

Indeed, the poor girl, still half-choked with laughter, was now sobbing bitterly. We gathered round her, and tried to comfort her.

"Get up, get up, the inn will be open in a minute, and we shall have a cup of coffee. Come."

At the first glimmering of the dawn, the shop opened a shutter like a fearful eyelid.

We went in. The landlady, in a dressing-gown, with her black hair loose over her shoulders, dragged herself along, and raised her weeping eyes.

"Oh, Heavens! they are coming here, aren't they? What an unhappy, poor creature I am! What will become of me? And my daughter, aged fourteen years? What will become of us?"

The woman's despair amused us, and we tried to comfort her.

"The Prussians will never reach this out-of-the-way place. Perhaps a patrol or two will come, and that is all. All the world is seeking refuge in 'the mountains.' Everybody knows the Prussians won't come here."

On leaving Urcel, we plunged into the misty shadows of a valley. But when we got on the other side it was glorious, dazzling. The sun was just rising, and beneath its first beams the country smiled and glistened. The meadows, bathed in dew, sparkled as though decked with gems; the air was mild, nature thrilled with joy, a lark carolled to the sun. Pierrot, drunk with light and space, danced about like a little faun, and we ourselves, for an insect, for a flower, for a bush covered with bright berries, leapt like goats. Our thoughts were lighter than the soft mists melting in the sun.

War! It is but a myth.

Invasion! an idle tale.

Danger! an illusion.

Weariness, pangs, mental sufferings, all were forgotten. We were young, we were strong; we breathed the fresh air with ecstasy, and the splendour of the hour intensified our love of life. Danger is life. War is victory, and blessed be the hand which bestows on mankind black nights and white mornings, dull cares and consoling joys.

With light hearts we took to our cheerful road. We marched for one hour, and then doubts arose.

"Mother, you have taken the wrong road, I am sure. Chevregny is not so far...."

Yet at a turn of the road we caught sight of Chevregny, nestled in verdure, crouched in a hollow way. We marvelled at the pointed steeple, at the red tiles or blue slates of the roofs. So we prepared to make an entrance into the village worthy of us and it. We sat by the wayside and took small looking-glasses and powder-puffs out of our leather bags. Powder is as necessary to women as to soldiers, isn't it? We did our hair, brushed our dresses, and then went down the village street quite smart. We turned to the right and entered the big farm of Mme. Laroye. Surprise, exclamations! Arms lifted up to the sky, and then clasped around us in a close embrace! Boundless friendship and endless hospitality were promised us.

"But tell us, dear cousin, who are all these people we see gathered in your domain?"

Mme. Laroye had already given hospitality to twenty-one refugees in her barns and cart-sheds, and had received into the bargain certain solid citizens of Laon, persons whom she honoured with her friendship and best rooms. We did not allow them to move from their quarters.

"If mother is provided for, dear cousin, it is all that we want. Don't bother about us; we will sleep in the hay-loft; it will be delightful."

When these matters were settled, we refreshed ourselves. How delightful it was after that painful night to take a bath, to loll in an armchair, to sit at table where fresh bread, golden butter, and transparent jam smiled upon us. We found a charm in the smallest pleasures, and thought:

"Now we are quiet, now we are in safety, we shall suffer nothing at the hands of the abhorred invader; we shall not see the shadow of their helmets on our walls; we shall not hear the tramping of their horses on our pavements; the booming of their cannon will not roll over our hearts!"

But what did we hear?

We stood up, speechless with horror.

The street rang with loud cries, and those cries were:

"The Prussians! The Prussians!"

PART II

Frenchman! I saw thy child
Who cried alone on the road.
I have comforted him. I have reassured thy wife.
Thy field lay fallow, I have tilled it.
When Peace reappears again on earth
May thou reap the fruits of my labour!

Published in German in the *Lillerzeitung*, translated into French, and
reproduced in the *Gazette des Ardennes*.

CHAPTER IV

Placid and heavy on their placid, heavy horses, they slowly advanced along the street. Of giant stature, they came on, revolver in hand, with the self-reliance of brutal strength. Their red-edged caps made their hard-featured faces still harder. It was a sight to strike Nature herself with horror, and, hidden behind the muslin curtains, we sobbed bitterly. The guests, huddled together in the dimly lighted room. Were silently weeping; the women crossed themselves, and watched over their children as if it were old Bogy's steps they heard. The men tugged nervously at their moustaches, and shook their fists in the empty air. Our gestures made the poor people uneasy.

"Heavens!" the women groaned, "don't show your face at the window!"

"Don't open the curtains!"

"Don't draw their attention to the house!"

"How frank they are," an old woman whimpered. "How splendid to be frank like that! As to myself, I could not be so." I suppose she meant courageous, but courage was not in question. We thought of nothing; we felt nothing; we were only looking at the men. We were glaring with all our eyes at a sight that crushed our souls. Grief left a huge void in our hearts. The enemy was there, and it was all up with us! I think we had suffered less if we had seen the Germans arrive in a town. A town is always somewhat of a courtesan. It gives a hearty welcome and hospitality to every one; it is daily a prey to strangers of ill repute. If invasion beats against its walls, if a hostile army crosses its streets—one human flood succeeding so many others—the town scowls at the foe, and then loses all memory of him. But there in a small village, hidden in a fold of the French ground, in a tiny hamlet which a hostile mind never chose for a shelter, the presence of the invaders seems to profane the very grass; and ever after the poor little place will remain an unhallowed spot, which bloodshed and years will not purify again.

After the horsemen had passed, there rolled along cannon and powder-carts, whose rumbling set our teeth on edge.

"Grandmother, look there!" cried out Colette.

On a powder-cart, looking very unhappy, sat the small dog we had met in the meadow.

So the Germans had traversed Morny; they had followed close upon us.

At last there came an end to the procession. The street was empty. No one uttered a word, and we ran away to cry to our hearts' content. House, yard, barns were all crowded with people. I took refuge in the garden. Nature seemed covered with an ashen veil, the very sun was obscured. Had the radiant morning really begotten this sad noon? Like a wounded animal looking for a dark shelter, I fled to the orchard, and crouching down in a corner close to the wall I wept most bitterly, without knowing why. Some one called me; I had to go back to life, or rather a life, unknown, unsuspected, in which all was changed. The Prussians were advancing through France.

On arriving at the house I met only with grief-stricken features and swollen eyes. We had no mind to eat. Only a few refugees, already indifferent, and the dogs did not lose their appetite. But standing at the dining-room windows we saw a sight worth seeing. The Prussians had taken possession of the village, and were looking for what they might lay their hands upon. They seemed to think little Mme. Laineux' shop had been created for their own special use, and they set about plundering it according to rule. They went up, three steps at a time, got among the groceries, made their choice, and came back, their arms filled with bottles and bags. In short, they carried away all that was eatable and drinkable in the house. They went up and down without interruption like two rows of ants busy stripping a sack of flour, one row full, the other empty. The grocer's wife, a small woman, dark and pale with large black eyes, stood by, unable to withstand the plunderers. She locked the door. The first soldier who encountered that obstacle went to the window, broke a square, turned the door-handle, and muttering threats reopened the door.

With a look of despair, Mme. Laineux went and fetched an officer who was eating upstairs.

"Come and see what your men are doing."

The officer came, looked round, and declared:

"C'est la kerre, Matame!"

And he went back to his lunch.

The shop cleared out, the men made farther search into the house, and discovered a small store-room, which they emptied with equal activity. For the pleasure of the thing, they cut stockings to transform them into socks, and spilled ink on petticoats and blouses. The last comers took the trap from the coach-house, the horse out of his stable, put the horse in the trap, and drove off with a light heart.

A bitter disenchantment filled our tired hearts. Nothing would have astonished us. In the afternoon two soldiers entered the farm, but at the sight of the yard crowded with men and dogs, withdrew. Broken down with weariness, we went early to bed. A ladder about twenty feet high led to a square opening through which we climbed into the hay-loft. There every one of us made a hole in the hay and buried herself in it. Now, in theory, hay offers a soft and sweet-smelling couch. The reality is slightly different. You may find comfort in this bed if you are wrapped up in cloaks and shawls to keep out the cold of the night, but the odour of the hay will make you sneeze, you will soon feel stiff in your legs, and hard blades of grass will prick your ankles and your neck.

Despite minor annoyances, my companions were very soon slumbering. For my part I could not sleep. I was feverish and ... my golden waistband played tricks and got into my ribs. The slanting light of the moon gave an added pallor to the faces of the four sleeping girls, whose presence on their bed of hay, beneath the beams of the loft which spiders had covered with their grey lace, was astonishing enough. It seemed as though the four heads had been put there for a whim, and the bodies laid down somewhere else. I fell into a doze. I saw hundreds of Prussians pass before my eyes, laden with goods, and carrying away the very houses. Then there came a multitude of galloping horses, which all vanished from my sight, and I was asleep.

The next day an impudent sunbeam woke us up by caressing our eyelids. In the barn below the refugees were bustling about noisily. The first moment after awaking was cruel; we had, as Stendhal says, "to learn our misery afresh." One after the other, like fowls getting out of the henhouse, we went down our long ladder, and ran off to wash and to hear the latest news.

That day also was a day of tears.

The villagers, frightened to death, had not dared to unlock their doors, and we heard only in the morning that a French convoy had been taken by surprise and captured by the Germans at Neuville, no more than two miles from Chevregny.

Then a scout—a fact completely unconnected with the former—had been killed by the enemy at a cross-way, near Mme. Laroye's house. We went to see the place, where the two white roads cross each other; large reddish spots still marked the ground. Kneeling down, we kissed this blood which cried for revenge, and from our inmost soul we besought Heaven that France should be victorious over her enemy, so that her heart's blood might not be shed in vain.

Some peasants, who had witnessed the scene, gave us an account of it. In great numbers the Germans came down the road. All of a sudden, two French scouts appeared on the outskirts of the wood, saw the enemy, fired at them, and then turned back. One of them was lucky enough to get under cover, but the other, severely wounded, was unhorsed, and fell down. Stretched by the wayside he made an attempt to get up, but his adversaries rushed upon him, and in a confused scuffle beat him to death with the butt-ends of their guns, and rode away at full gallop.

The victim was to be buried that very morning, and as we wished to be present at the funeral, no time could be lost. When we arrived at the churchyard two men were already digging a narrow grave. The body, wrapped in a white sheet, was lying on a stretcher. There was no coffin. Soldiers should lie in the soil for which they have died. The red spot beneath his head grew larger little by little, and the blood that trickled down made a dazzling rill in the white sand. We approached him with a shrinking heart. With pious hands the grave-digger lifted up the sheet to show us the face of the dead man. An aquiline nose and a firm chin were still distinguishable. The rest of the features were clotted with blood and shapeless. Nearly choked with sobs, we could not help wondering from which wound the blood had flowed, when suddenly the truth flashed upon us, at a gesture of the old grave-digger, who pointed at what were, but the day before, the boy's eyes. His eyes! oh, you cowards! villains! They had not only beaten him to death, they had put his eyes out! He was defending himself like a brave soldier. He was alone against twenty, and they had murdered him. There on the white road, in the sunshine, they had committed their crime; the shades of night had fallen upon him before he descended to the tomb.

Oh, vengeance! vengeance! We wept, we cried, and nothing could comfort us. We wept over the gallant soldier of France, who fell so near us; we wept over all the dead and wounded, and above all we wept—oh, narrowness of the human heart!—over the one soldier we loved, whose uncertain fate tortured our hearts. Oh, my Posy, my treasure, my love, my pride, have you not asked for a dangerous mission? Have you received your death-wound, outnumbered in some lonely corner? Have they...? the terrifying thought! ... oh, his eyes! ... his eyes!... It was beyond endurance. Crushed with grief, I fell senseless. When I came to myself the priest had said the usual prayers, and was gone. My companions stood up, shedding silent tears. The two villagers gloomily filled the grave, and the earth fell with a hollow sound on the poor body. One of the men broke off in the middle of his work, and told us of the scout's death. What he said confirmed what we had already heard. "Curse them!" he cried out, and, with a gesture of rage, seized his spade, and began again to fill the grave.

But we had not done with emotion yet.

"Do you know that the Germans took three hundred prisoners yesterday?" some one asked us. "You will see them pass on the road."

The churchyard is terraced to the street, which runs down a steep hill, and thence already we caught sight of a few horsemen, closely followed by soldiers on foot. They were French. At the sight of the enemy, our grief, all of a sudden, turned to wrath and madness. Here they were in our own country, the very same we saw yesterday, no doubt. They were those perhaps who had blinded and killed the scout, and they were taking our brothers to captivity. Oh, for the power to strike, to kill those men! To hurl down upon them some of those big stones, half loosened by time! We shuddered at the mere sight of them, a bantering, conceited, happy mob. The faces of Yvonne and Antoinette, standing among the crosses, were wet with tears and convulsed with rage. Hatred was so clearly visible in their eyes that the faces of the Germans grew hard and stiffened as if they had been given a slap in the face. They pass, they are gone, and now the prisoners are coming. They seemed to have made up their minds to accept the situation. They were hot, and talked among themselves in a low voice. The officers drove in a jolting car, motionless and spent. We could not see them very well, but we could distinguish the stripes on the Captain's sleeve, and then the cart disappeared from sight at a winding of the road. The way was open; we went home, and when we were alone, Geneviève and I fell into each other's arms, and without saying a word wept again inconsolably. Towards the close of the day the garden tempted us. It is a dear old garden, full of shade and of old-fashioned, sweet-smelling flowers. It is about four yards above the level of the street, and if you sit on the wall, as large as an easy-chair, you can see all that goes on in the street below. Like souls in agony, we dragged ourselves along the alleys edged with box, doleful and weary. From the wall we observed the four points of the compass. Not a Prussian in sight. So we began to talk to little Mme. Laineux, who looked out of her window just over the way. Close to her stood a young girl about fifteen years of age, whose head, framed in a handkerchief tied under the chin, was the most exquisite ever seen. Raphael might have drawn her fine features, her clear eyes. Even her hands browned by the sun were pretty; even her waist was elegant in spite of an unbecoming frock. O France, you are rich in all treasures, and that sweet little maid is not the least of them! The grocer's wife confided her sorrows to us in a bitter tone. Two old men passing by stopped in the street to condole with her; then a third person, shabbily dressed, joined in the talk, and from the very first proved interesting. He was a soldier, escaped from the yesterday's fight, and he told us his adventure in detail.

"Tuesday," he said, "we slept in Arden, a small place we had reached at five o'clock in the evening. The horses were not tired, and we might have marched on. At least, we ought to have been up at three, instead of which we set out again at six o'clock, and were not bidden to make haste. We did not know that the enemy was treading in our steps. About nine we approached this place, quite easy in our minds, when we heard the people cry: 'The Prussians!... To the right-about! Quick! Quick!' Convoys like us are not looked upon as fighting men, do you see; we ought to be a few miles behind the front. We were but scantily armed; some of us had a revolver and no bullets, the others bullets and no revolver. What could we do against the cannon, which peppered us from the top of the hill? We were ordered back.

"The drivers made what speed they could, when, just at the turn of the road, one of the carts managed to tumble down; those that followed at full speed were thrown down upon it, and thus made a barricade, which held up all the rest. The guns fired without ceasing. Our Captain came up: 'Nothing to do, my lads; we are caught. Be quick, get a white flag.' We looked for a white flag.... There was none. At length a white handkerchief was hoisted on a stick. And then a troop of horsemen cantered down upon us. 'Lay yourselves in the ditch,' we heard. The horses pawed our backs, and I assure you the Prussians did nothing to hold them back. I will show you."

And the man, taking off his jacket, bared his bruised and swollen back.

"Still lying in the ditch, I noticed close to me the opening of a gutter-stone stopped up with mud and grass. I tried to pull it out; it gave way. I got into the narrow passage, and cried out to my companion: 'There is room but for one.'

"'It is one safe and sound,' he answered, and stopped up the opening of the pipe again.

"For twenty-six hours I lay in there, with the Germans overhead. Never in my life did I think of my wife and children as I did then! About eleven o'clock, when all the noise had ceased, I ventured out of my hole. People who were working hard by took me in, dressed my wound, and gave me civilian clothes. I hope to escape to the woods and join the French army again."

And so saying the man went away. We called him back to slip some biscuits and chocolate into his hand. With a smile he pointed to his full pockets, and said, "I am well stored, you see. I will share with the others." Alas, he was not alone! The convoy amounted to 800 soldiers. About 15 had been killed, 350 taken prisoners, and the rest were hidden in the woods. The boldest or the luckiest might reach the French lines. The others would probably wander about, like wild beasts who hide themselves, would suffer cold and hunger, and then after weeks or months of this wretched life they would be caught and sent to Germany ... unless they were shot.

Our thoughts were mournful as death when at nightfall we climbed a second time to the hay-loft. We could not sleep, our anxiety was too great. Were the Germans still gaining ground? Would they sweep onward, like a cloud of insects, towards Paris, whose splendour and renown dazzled and attracted them invincibly? Oh, may they burn their wings there and be carbonised to the last one! The next day we went to see the place of the skirmish. The fields on both sides of the road were all covered over with things the soldiers had thrown away. In some places the grass was heaped with knapsacks, papers, clothes, and arms. We tramped on; the road wound its way through meadows and woods, and then got into a funnel-shaped valley. Here had been the thickest of the fight. The cavalry came up from behind; there were the guns on the rocks to the right and left. Alas, the convoy had really been caught in a trap! The three carts still stood in the middle of the road, and the meadows were thickly strewn with soldiers' things, papers, and discarded arms. Colette discovered a beautiful sword hidden in a bush; she quickly put it back again, that presently she might come and fetch it. It would be so much gained. A passer-by gave us some other details. There was a body here, another there. It was to be feared that a few more dead soldiers were hidden in the wood. On our way back we picked up all the letters, books, and papers which we found, hoping we might later on forward them to the soldiers' families, and at the same time tell them news of the unfortunate convoy. We passed through Neuville, and there we saw the ammunition captured the day before, heaped up in a yard. Another Cerberus, adorned with a spiked helmet, watched over mountains of bullets and boxes of cartridges. There was seven million francs' worth, said the peasants.

Returning to the village, sunk in despondency, we heard the sound of a drum, and we arrived just in time to listen to the proclamation which the rural constable read aloud:

"Arms and clothes, belonging to French soldiers, must be gathered up, and brought without delay to the Mayor's house.... By order of the German authorities," said the reader, a small hunchbacked man.

And tears rolled down his cheeks.

At Mme. Laroye's we found a change for the better. The refugees had set out homewards, and the friends from Laon, by taking leave, enabled us to live once more after the fashion of civilised people. With pleasure we stretched our limbs, which three nights had stiffened and tired out, in a comfortable bed.

From that time Fate proved merciful, and for a few days spared us new troubles and violent emotions. Of course tears always trembled on our eyelids, if some incident happened to revive our wounds; but after so many mental pangs the surrounding peace was a solace to our minds. Life sprang up anew in our hearts, and with life, spirits. Many a time—was it a reaction?—we burst out laughing, broke into mad, inextinguishable laughter. Liza more than once set us in a roar. Liza is Mme. Laroye's maid,—a maid who has land of her own, who possesses a mile away a house, a horse, a dog, and, in ordinary times, a husband. But, as the times we live in are by no means ordinary, Zidore—for he is called Zidore—had joined the army, to make war against the King of Prussia.

Was Mme. Laroye alone? Liza would discharge with assiduous attention the duties of her place. Had Mme. Laroye friends or relations to entertain? Liza went home again, and reappeared only to give herself up to her menial duties. Liza is a tall woman, clumsily built, with a funny Hun-like face. Her small eyes, her high cheekbones, prove that a drop of Asiatic blood runs in her veins. Have I not hinted, in a former chapter, that Attila may have sent a reconnoitring party down here? But if Liza has inherited her strong frame and her snub nose from her ancestors, the Huns, to whom does she owe her restlessness and her pusillanimity? No doubt to her great-grandmother, the Frankish woman, who had to submit to the wild Asiatic. For Liza was not brave; Liza did not dare face the Prussians. From Laon, Morny, and other places, people fled to Chevregny. It was then an additional reason for Liza's fellow-villagers to run away farther too. The women had made up their minds to go. As soon as the enemy was descried from afar, Liza's horse—Mouton—and Mme. Laroye's horse—Gentil—would be put to, and both fiery steeds—as fiery as their names—would take their mistresses to a safe place.

But, alas! man proposes.... A cry arose: "The Prussians!" Liza heard it, snatched up a big loaf in bewilderment, and went full gallop towards the forest with her dog at her heels. After her galloped a troop of her companions just as bewildered. They went down the road, struck across the country, cleared the hedges, and plunged into the forest. In the heart of the wood they stopped, blessing their star which had led them to this wild and safe spot. At that very moment they became speechless. The report of a cannon resounded in the air, then a second one, and a full volley followed. The poor wretches had thrown themselves headlong into the valley, where the convoy struggled against its foes, and the grape-shot fell upon them without mercy. The harmless troop, however, lifted up its suppliant arms towards Heaven, which did not see them at all, for the foliage was too thick, and muttered hollow prayers to some sylvan divinity which heard them not, for the cannon was too loud. Then they ran away and cowered under the bushes. Shells bespattered them facetiously with moss and earth. They crouched in a hut that happened to be there. A malignant cannon-ball carried off a corner of the roof. They stuck close to the trunk of a tree. Merely to tease them bullets tore off its leaves and its branches, which rained gently down upon their heads. The unfortunate fugitives, at last gloomily resigned, sat in a circle, and waited for the end in the calm of despair. Then all sounds ceased. They opened one eye, then the other, stretched themselves, got up, counted themselves, and discovered with the greatest amazement they had lost neither one hair, save those which they had torn in terror, nor one button, save those which panting fear had burst from their corsage. These refugees of the forest had no thought of leaving their precious shelter. They ate the provisions which in their prudence they had brought with them, and Liza's big loaf proved a great success. They spent the night in the hut, and slept with one eye open, raising their unquiet heads whenever they heard the tramping of a Prussian horse on the road. In the morning nothing was to be heard. I do not know who was courageous enough to poke her nose first out of the wood; I expect it was the dog. At last, however, our villagers plucked up their courage, and with common accord went back to their native hamlet. Mme. Laroye did not receive Liza exactly with open arms, but with that gentle irony of which she has the secret:

"Well, well, Liza, I understand. 'The old lady is too slow,' you thought, 'she will disturb us. She had better stay at home.' And so you scampered off."

Liza protested, and we laughed, and Colette pointed the moral of the adventure.

"It is very funny, Liza's story. But don't you think it is just like ours?"

The Prussians had forced open most of the houses, and had anticipated the taxes which they hoped to levy. Fowls, pigeons, geese without number, and even plump pigs were absent. At Liza's house the ravishers had shown a certain modesty. A sack of flour, a few pigeons, one or two ducks only had disappeared. But the intruders had turned the room topsy-turvy. Did they look for treasure? And, by a sad whim, they had seized upon two photographs, whose red plush frames were the ornament of the mantelpiece—Liza in the garb of a nun, and Zidore in a soldier's uniform. For what purpose had they torn up these precious pictures?

"And Zidore had it taken the first day I saw him!" So the enemy had destroyed the fond keepsake of a happy day!

Really, the age we lived in was hard, and the Prussians heartless! All the world was so firmly convinced of this that everybody stayed indoors as much as possible and ventured reluctantly out of the village, for fear of dangerous encounters. No one was bold enough to risk horse and cart on the road, since the first soldier that came might requisition both. Happy indeed was the owner who was not compelled to turn back and drive the Prussian to a far-off place. Thus it happened that many a villager, who, having gone out with team and horse for a few hours, came back home on foot and alone three or four days later. From this you may see that communication was not easy, even between places at no great distance from one another. An old lady, seeing the Germans arrive in Chevregny, died of the sudden shock, and for several days it was impossible to send the sad tidings to her son, who was no farther off than Laon. Indeed, we knew not what was happening in the neighbourhood, still less at Morny. "The country is overrun with Prussians," we were told.

So the emotion was great when it was rumoured that flour ran short in Chevregny, for Chevregny fed two other hamlets and a great many refugees. Every morning the baker's shop was carried by storm. Every morning the housewives had to wait their turn for an hour to get a loaf. It was a heart-rending sight to see how the baker toiled; his wife did not know which way to turn; his boy knew not what to be at. At this rate the flour sacks would melt away like snow in an April sun. We had to find other sacks, or famine would break out in the village. One morning, then, Liza announced: "My horse is required to go and fetch flour at Pont-Avers."

In the country the word "requisition" does not exist. You are "required"— that is all. Mouton, then, was required to go and fetch provender. Very well. He could not tempt the greed of the Germans, being well stricken in years, and somewhat lame.

"But who will drive Mouton?" asked Mme. Laroye.

"Well, I don't know, perhaps me," said Liza.

"You don't say so, Liza," her mistress cried out. "There are men enough left in the village to do that. Now a woman has to stay at home, that is her right place."

In the afternoon Liza came back, and said in a triumphant tone:

"The blacksmith is driving to Pont-Avers. I have told them it was not a woman's job."

The good creature was delighted with her saying, and repeated over and over again:

"I told them so ... it is not a woman's job."

Alas, how many things women had to take charge of which were not "women's jobs"! How courageous and hard-working they were, the women of the villages! The men had gone to the war, and left the harvest ungathered. "The work must be done," said the women, and, without a moment's rest, they bent in toil to the earth. We, too, did our share. Perched upon steep ladders or hazardous trees, we picked thousands of small blue plums, which Liza crammed into big-bellied casks. After mysterious treatment the fruit was expected to turn into an exquisite brandy, pronounced by the well-skilled old gossips a cure for every ill. Better than that, we shut up with our own hands Mme. Laroye's hiding-place. For who would have believed it? Her house was not in order! She had buried a cash-box full of golden coins in her garden, but we thought she had better remove a great many other things just as valuable as money. Besides, she had a hiding-place. It was not a fanciful hiding-place like ours, but a serious hiding-place, contrived by a workman, a past-master in digging and masonry. The cellar opens into the arched entrance of the house. In a corner of this cellar is a trap-door which, lifted up, leads to a break-neck flight of steps hewn out in the rock. At the foot of the steps is a smaller cellar, which is the hiding-place. We took down the other silver, linen, fine old shawls, at which we gazed with envious eyes, and then the wine.

"Not all the wine, dear cousin, not all. They will never believe you have no wine at all."

When the trap-door was closed, we carried down with great trouble a few barrowfuls of earth, which a skilful hand raked over properly. Then we stamped upon it, swept the cellar, scattered grey dust over the fresh earth, and put old boxes and tubs in the corner. Shrewder than a Prussian would he be who saw anything here! Alas, it was a beast who brought our fine work to nothing! In the course of time we heard that Uhlans on their way through Chevregny put horses into the cellar. The horses, as they are wont to, pawed and scratched the ground.

"It sounds hollow!" cried the Prussians.

"It sounds wine!" they went on, in a fit of inspiration, and then discovered they had been cheated.

I do not know what became of the other objects, but I know perfectly well the way Mme. Laroye's wine went.

In spite of these interesting occupations, we were bored. And yet we had discovered in Bouconville, three miles off, a well-stored shop which supplied us with cotton, wool, and stuffs to give work to our idle fingers. In spite of Mme. Valaine's anxiety, we went, two or three together, and brought back in triumph what was wanting. But we never ventured into the wood, and on our homeward journeys we cast sidelong glances at the "sand-pit," whose green shade always allured us. Such is the name of a few acres of wood, belonging to my mother-in-law, where I hope some day to install my household gods. There a brooklet murmurs, and hard by shall be my house, with a willow charming and majestic, an ash lofty and elegant to give me shade. There I shall live happy on milk and honey—goats and bees will be mine—with my husband and the children which I trust God will grant me. We shall be once more in Arcady.

Thus I mused on my way home, when suddenly some German troops appeared on the horizon to dispel my dream of Arcady, and sent me home in haste to the shelter of the farm.

I have said we were bored. Life was chiefly unbearable for want of news. What was going on? For two days we had heard an echo of the guns. Was there a battle? The first Germans we had seen had told us with a sneer:

"Parisse, Parisse, within dree tays we are in Parisse!"

Had the progress of the haughty boors been stayed? Hope trembled at the bottom of our hearts; hope, which dared not grow, and which we dared not avow.

Ten times a day we left our needlework or our book to run to the garden. We listened. A kind of rumbling was all we heard. Was it to the east, the north, or the south? Was it a singing in our ears or was it cannon-shots?

"What if we placed our ears to the ground?"

And so we lay on the grass like so many dead bodies, and concentrated our whole souls in listening.

"There certainly is a rambling." This conviction filled our hearts with joy and anxiety, and the whole day long we fidgeted about the house. Besides, we could not stay for ever in Chevregny. We had to make up our minds.

"Since the Germans are here, there, and everywhere," I said, "we had better go back home, where at least we are comfortable and at ease."

In Chevregny, to be sure, comfort is unknown. For instance, cleanliness does not hold a large place in the people's life, though we had transformed the bakehouse into a very decent bathroom. Every evening Pierrot was washed at the pump, and pretended to throw the water which deluged him to the bright and passionless moon.

As long as the weather kept warm it was pleasant enough, but all the same home would be better. But before taking so long a journey, we thought it well to think over it at leisure. A word from M. Lonet settled the matter. "There is no danger," he wrote; "some one ought to come back; the house might be occupied."

If one of us went, then we would all go. Union is strength. Boldly we had come to Chevregny by night, nine in number, including the dogs. Nine in number we would go home by day. We had spent a week in Chevregny.

On Tuesday we had Gentil put to. Liza huddled our luggage into the cart, helped Mme. Valaine and Pierrot up, and sat on the box. In a few feeling words, one and all took leave of our kind cousin, and we followed on foot.

We walked on without hardihood, casting suspicious glances before and behind. The mere shadow of a helmet would have put us to flight. Besides, the horse might be requisitioned, and Liza left us at Bièvres, and drove home as fast as she could. In Bruyères we met with a big dog almost as alarming as a Prussian. Percinet is fond of fighting, and he cannot bear the sight of his kindred alive. Two days before he had satisfied this thirst for blood by killing two dogs. At the entrance of Morny we passed three riders on the road, dressed in green, booted and spurred, with their helmets on. We did not think them mere gendarmes, as we heard afterwards they were. They contented themselves with gazing at the dusty, weary group that went by. At length we got home. Dear little house! it had not altered! Its white walls were still there; so was its grey roof. The Virginia creepers shook their branches like arms to wish us a hearty welcome. We threw the gate open. The dogs rushed into the stable at a cheerful bound.

Leaving the luggage in the lobby, we dropped into the dining-room chairs, and gave a deep sigh of satisfaction.

CHAPTER V

We were at home again! This was a set-off for the misfortunes with which a wretched fate had loaded us. The house was as snug as we had left it, and we had but to return to our old habits. So we did and exactly! The cake we had left, at our flight, was still lying on the table. As we were hungry we each snatched our share, and ate it with ravenous appetite. It was a bit hard, but all the same delicious. We wandered through the house with joy. We were at home again! How many of those who had fled from the invasion had renounced the pleasures of home for months or even years? Some of out friends at Morny had not yet come back. Yet could we pity them? A thousand times no; at least they would never endure the trials to which the conquered are exposed, and which, after a momentary calm, once more had depressed us. The presence of the Germans, quartered in the village, seemed unbearable.

Ah, poor, poor snails that we were! In spite of our efforts, the flood had overtaken and submerged us. The tree we tried to climb was too low; the inundation covered everything; and we could not foresee the end of the nightmare. How long should we have to groan and struggle in that all-devouring water? We besought God to deliver us, and God seemed deaf to our prayers and blind to our tears. We called to you who were on the mainland over the mountains, insurmountable as the great wall of China. Our hearts called to you, and no one answered. For a fortnight the floods had been out, and already we were losing patience.

Morally drowned as we were, we still had a physical need of food. A household of seven persons and two dogs must furnish its larder and cellar with abundant provisions. The grocers of the village had but empty shops; our neighbours were unhumbled, because each was the owner of a plot of ground. Less favoured than the poorest of the poor, we had no crop at all. What would become of us? I have said we had no crop. I was wrong. We even had a superb crop. The pear trees, even those which these last fifteen years had yielded no fruit at all, had deemed it a point of honour to do their best, in hard times, and were all laden with huge plump pears, which made your mouth water. They were not ripe yet; but, determined not to tempt the green-uniformed marauders, we made up our minds to gather them. For two days we picked them, and filled basket upon basket with pears, long or round, green or yellow.

Then there was the problem to solve, where to hide them? We laid our heads together, and by unanimous consent decided upon the deserter's attic. On one side, the attic was full of faggots; on the other, behind the chimney that comes up from the wash-house, there was a floor-space, about eight feet square, and there we laid our beautiful pears amid shreds of paper instead of straw. To conceal their retreat, we heaped up at the entrance old boxes, hen-coops, and a garden roller in elaborate disorder. Nobody would ever have thought that this innocent pile of rubbish was a treasure-hoard. But we, who knew, put one foot here, another there, and at a bound we were on the floor in the very abode of the pears, where cunning paths allowed us to visit our friends and choose the juiciest among them. We never made these visits without a groan, for we always forgot the existence of a big cistern, fitted up in the roof, and constantly knocked our heads against this iron ceiling. But the shock itself kindled our imagination, and struck out a flash of genius.

"Suppose we put the wine into the cistern!"

We thought we had given all our wine to the French soldiers, and then we discovered in the bottom of a box about thirty bottles, which we resolved to hide from the Germans' thirst. I must admit that our sobriety equals the camel's. We drink hardly anything besides water. A bottle of wine a week satisfies the needs of the whole family. But, all the same, we did not want our wine to moisten German throats. So through the yard, up the ladder, over the boxes, the bottles went their way. Not too well poised on a tottering scaffolding I wriggled into the narrow space between the beam and the cistern. I held out a groping hand, into which was placed the neck of a bottle, and little by little the receptacle was filled. We went quickly to work. My sister-in-law carried up the bottles with care; I laid them down with a gentle hand. For it is well known that a Prussian ear detects the clinking of bottles a mile off, and of course the Prussian, contiguous to the ear, being forewarned, rests not until he has secured the too imprudent bottles. But all of a sudden I was aroused by a loud shout, instantly hushed to a discreet silence.

I jumped down from my scaffold, leapt over the pears, scaled the boxes, tumbled down the ladder, and found myself in the midst of a perplexed group.

"Grandmother, what is the matter?"

Yvonne and Colette, prying in the cellar, had discovered a fair-sized keg, which gurgled when it was shaken.

The treasure-hunters thrust in the bung with an effort, inserted a tap, drew out a glass of the liquor and brought it to me.

"What is it?"

Unctuous, yellowish substance. Was it oil, or syrup? I looked at it, shook the glass, smelt it, even tasted a drop with the tip of my tongue, and then announced:

"It is glucose."

Glucose! glucose! and we had no sugar left! Every morning we drank milk and coffee unsweetened by honey. Mme. Valaine declared my diagnosis right, and we leapt for joy like marionettes.

There was no more meat, no butter, and eggs were uncommonly rare, but sweetened dishes take the place of everything. Baskets full of pears! A keg of glucose! Thirty bottles of wine! Who talked of dearth? For truth's sake I must say glucose did not answer as well as we expected. When I tried to sweeten the milk with it, the milk turned sour, and with it the experiment turned also, to my shame.

On the other hand, by stewing the beloved pears with glucose and wine, I obtained an unforgettable dish, over which a jury of cooks greedily licked its lips. And every other evening, for two months, our scanty menu was thus composed: soup, stewed pears, bread at discretion, fresh water at will. The glucose went to keep the wine company in the cistern, except for a few bottles of either liquid, which we craftily concealed in the garden, and in case of need we had but to cry out:

"Pierrot, go and fetch the bottle that is in the reeds or in the blue fir ... or in the big yew...."

It was much more amusing than simply to go down into the cellar.

Thus our life was not uninteresting, but our chief occupation was to watch the horizon, east and south, where our soldiers were fighting. The guns were coming sensibly nearer; we heard them growl day and night, and when it grew dark we saw shells burst above the hills. We spent many hours in the garden looking out for these illuminations, hoping we might understand something from the way they went. Then came the gleam of an explosive, striping the sky with a flash of lightning or with a slow trail of light. The better to observe, we got up the ladder, and sat on the wall. To the casual passer-by we might have resembled a flock of crows at roost waiting for gossip's tales. Mme. Valaine had no taste for these perilous exercises, and contented herself with the stories we told her. For us the only spectacle we thought worth while was that very one which almost rent our hearts. How eagerly we wished for the shells to burst nearer, nearer, to set the house in a blaze so that we might be set free from our chains!

About the 25th of September took place the first shock between us and the German army. It was nearly eight o'clock in the evening. The supper over, I went into the garden, and was peering at the dark sky, heedless of the cold wind which caused my hair and my shawl to flutter, when a frightful uproar broke the silence. Gruff voices cried out vociferously; heavy boots kicked at the gates; the angry dogs barked till they choked.

"Good Heavens! what is happening?"

I threw myself down the ladder, fled through the garden—those days were full of wild races—got to the house, and saw Geneviève hasten forth, a key in her hand.

"They want us to open the gate," she said, "and we must."

Yvonne seized the dogs by the collar and dragged them in. The gate was hardly unlocked when those without threw it open, and at the same time overran the yard. They were furious, and one of them shouted out in bad French:

"When the Germans knock at a door, it should be opened immediately."

"You think so, do you, you Boche!"

On hearing us speak fluent German they softened, and looked at us in amazement.

They all had the same round faces, which the lantern of an under-officer lit up.

They wanted a lodging: barns, stables to shelter men and horses. All that was difficult to get!

"There is room but for one horse in the stable."

"Well, that will do for two horses and two men."

"And here is the wash-house."

"Six men will sleep there."

The others withdrew to look for a lodging somewhere else. The remainder, who seemed to be harmless blockheads, were convoys. We heaved a deep sigh, but hardly had a mouthful of air reached our lungs, when the yard was already swarming with a new mob. Standing on the steps I engaged in parley with the *Feldwebel*.

"The house is chock-full, and eight soldiers are already lodged in the outhouses."

He was young, big, and stout, and his hard-featured face was deeply scarred.

Of course he did not allow himself to be prevailed upon.

"It is all the same to me," he answered; "make room for me if you have none."

He ordered me to open the coach-house, but when he saw it crammed up with all sorts of things, he made a wry face.

"And up there?" he asked, pointing at the deserter's attic.

Good Heavens! the pears! the wine! I was trembling with fear, and was at a loss how to answer when the man altered his mind:

"I would rather have a bedroom to myself," and so saying he opened Antoinette's door.

"That will do," said the person, and waving back the silently waiting soldiers he kept but two of them with him. We began to remove a few things from the room, which Antoinette had always kept for herself, and before the sergeant's taunting eyes we carried away clothes, books, and knick-knacks. The door we had left ajar was suddenly thrown open, and a little coxcomb of an officer came in and cried out in a cheerful tone:

"Oh! oh! Two at a time!"

That was more than we could stand, and leaving blankets and coverlets we ran away.

At the corner of the house a brutal arm stopped me, and a soldier I hardly saw in the night muttered something I did not understand about money— five francs. I tried to break loose from the man's hold, and answered at random we were no shopkeepers and sold nothing.

"If you are busy," he said, "another lady would do."

In the dim light of a glimmering window I caught sight of a Slavonic-featured, black-bearded, sneaking-eyed face that belonged to one of the stable-dwellers—a perfect brute. He looked so strange, his voice was so peculiar that I suddenly understood the meaning of his words. Frightened, I shook my arm to get it free, set off running, and got so quickly out of sight he might have believed I had been swallowed up by the night. I rushed into the house, banged the door, turned the key in it, pushed the bolts, and even then I was not sure I was secure. I wished for padlocks, bars, chains, to protect us against such creatures. We thought we would never dare go to bed.

With Mme. Valaine I went through the house to test the wooden shutters. In the street the carts of the convoy stood close to the house; here and there we saw a lantern glimmer. Lying under the awnings the drivers tumbled and tossed, and from time to time uttered heavy groans. Those carts reminded us of monstrous beasts, hunch-backed and mischievous, which squatted at our door to watch and threaten us. The yard was pitch dark, all seemed to be in a sound sleep, but for the horses, which kicked and pawed the ground of the narrow stable. The men were snoring; the dogs shut up in the lobby whined gently. We talked in a low voice and went on tip-toe. In our own house we felt beset with dangers and cares. Without taking off our clothes, we laid ourselves down, our eyes wide open, our ears attentive to all outside sounds, our nerves on edge. So we waited for the break of day.

The Germans got up at the first glimmer of a misty sun, and we watched them through the trellised shutters. They had cooked a potato soup, a grey and sticky stuff, to which they added some brandy, and which they ate without conviction.

For hours together they peeled vegetables, hummed tunes, whistled, dawdled up and down; but they never drew a drop of water from the pump, and they seemed wholly unacquainted with the fact that a human being ought to wash. Then they began cleaning their arms most carefully, and deluged them with petroleum and oil. Our amazement was the same which the sight of wigwams or niggers' cabins might have roused, seen for the first time. Their guns, leaning against the gate, confirmed this impression. Real savages' arms, the bayonets were about a hand's breadth, and notched like a saw. At the mere thought of the wounds such teeth would make in the flesh, an icy chill ran through our veins.

About nine, after half an hour's monotonous shouting, the convoy filed off, and soon after vanished from sight. As soon as they were gone we rushed out. The street swarmed with people, like an ant-hill which a clumsy foot has trodden on. Well! well! German boots leave traces. The High Street of Morny had never before witnessed such filth. On all sides lay dirty straw, muddy rags, formless scraps of iron. The horse-dung looked clean compared with the rest.

As to ourselves, we cried with horror at the sight of our poor yard, into which we could not put our foot. Oily pools stood here and there; the pavement, bespattered with mud, was covered all over with dirty rags, greasy papers, vegetable peelings, and, overtopping all the rest, what Antoinette pompously called "human dejections." And yet in a corner of the garden was a closet formerly intended for the gardener.... But such people....

Disgusted and bewailing, old Tassin spent the whole afternoon in cleaning the yard, and made more than one unpleasant discovery, such as about 40 lb. of rotten meat concealed in the straw. The "small room" was in a sorry plight. The pandours had emptied the ink-pot into a work-table, scribbled the walls all over, broken a vase, taken away a woollen blanket, an eider-down, and a door-curtain. As to the mattress and the spring-mattress, we could not have touched them with a pair of tongs, covered as they were with spots of grease. It is agreeable to receive Germans!

Antoinette instantly made up her mind to change her room, and easily transformed one of the attics.

We went roundly to work, and the "small room" was soon as empty as a Pomeranian's head. We had made up our minds that the creatures should bring straw with them if they required hospitality a second time. To the King of Prussia himself we would have grudged a bed, lest he should leave it in as bad a condition as his men.

The convoy came back that very evening. Our guests of yesterday went back to their lodging. Only the inhabitants of the "small room" did not return. Perhaps what was left them of conscience reproached them with theft.

Early in the morning the carts went off, and after three hours' work old Tassin declared he had removed all traces of their second visit. The whole village complained that the rascals had not only dirtied whatever they approached, but had stolen what they wanted, wasted provender and oats, and had thrown down whole sheaves of wheat for their horses to lie on.

In the first weeks of the occupation the invaders bled the country to death. In Morny they took thousands of fowls, hundreds of pigs and sheep, and I don't know how many horses and cows. M. Lantois' black bull, which his ravishers had tethered to a cart, and then abandoned in the middle of the road, protested in a wild, fierce, and fitful roar that he repeated every other minute for hours together. The farmers dreaded marauders still more than official requisitions. For what was requisitioned they obtained, if they insisted, a note of hand, often scribbled in pencil and almost illegible, but at least proving they had been deprived of something. The soldiers of course took an unfair advantage of their victims, who knew not German, and cheated them in every way. We were often asked to translate such I.O.U.'s as had been composed according to the writer's own fancy. "Paid and carried away a horse," wrote one requisitioner who had but paid with lies.—"Exchanged two horses of equal worth," another pretended, when a broken-down hack had supplied the place of a good mare.—"Received 40 lb. of bacon." And the honest customer knew he had gained 450 kilog. on the pork-butcher.

In spite of all, the country people attached great importance to these notes of hand, and the marauders gave them none. They went two or three together, got into the houses when the people were working out in the fields, searched them from top to bottom, and laid hands on what pleased them. They stripped the hen-houses and dovecots; they would drop in unawares when the people were about to sit down to dinner, and then divert themselves by seizing and feasting upon the dishes before the balked peasants' very faces. Thus eaten out of house and home, the village would soon be starved. The Mayor of Morny and M. Lonet resolved to go to Laon and seek some protection against the raiders. The answer they got from the Germans was that, first, rural matters were no concern of theirs, and secondly, that the people were expected to give everything the soldiers asked for.

A word to the wise is enough.

Those who have not known the evils of invasion cannot imagine the rage and despair which filled our hearts at being thus enslaved and ground down. Impotent wrath, overwhelming despondency took hold of our souls, at once humiliated and revolted. Like true civilised people, we could not understand why we were forbidden to claim justice, to seek redress; why we were expected to yield to brute strength. And there was no use to cry out for help, to crave assistance. It seemed to us that we were forsaken by God and men.

But was the trap shut tight? Were we, for instance, whose interests, life, and dearest affections lay on the other side of the front, without means to break through the enemy's barrier? Were we actually prisoners?

My mother-in-law made up her mind to go to Laon in order to consult competent judges. I was to accompany her. This poor Laon, which I had seen but a few weeks ago bright with French animation, in what state did we find it! We saw a few civilians only, with hard and hostile faces. On the other hand there were a great many grey-clad Germans in the streets with their helmets on, bustling about in the best of humour. They seemed at home everywhere, and masters of all the houses. Most shops were shut up. I tried to get into the only one I saw open, but nobody was in it. Only in the recesses of the back-shop a big hand was busy about a saucepan, and heavy steps shook the spiral staircase. It is easy to understand that I had had enough of it, and that I hastened out with all possible speed. The sight of their forsaken shops would have rent the hearts of the owners had they been gifted with second sight. One of them, I suppose it was a grocer's, had been smashed to atoms. Glass jars, drawers, looking-glasses were but things of the past, and the floor was covered all over with a litter twenty inches high, of biscuits, sweets, macaroni, rice, and odds and ends of all kinds. We went to see the Mayor, and asked him the questions which we were anxious to have answered. Were the Germans to settle in the country? Was it possible to go to Paris? His answer was like a death-knell.

Nothing was to be done. The Germans were not likely to clear out. He deemed it folly to try to go away. I left the room heart-broken.

We arrived in Morny just in time to see some German infantry march through the street. They came from the front, and their ill-looks filled us with joy. They trudged along with weary faces, and were all muddy, and bent as if with old age. "Just look at them," we said. "Where do they come from? Surely they are beaten men. Is the French army advancing?"

Colette, hidden behind the curtains, never failed to throw her wishes after the Germans as they passed through the village.

"Die, die, die. Die, you nasty red-haired fellow. Die, you fat brute. Die, you young whipper-snapper. Oh, a wounded man! Die too, poor wretch; die, die, die"; and the litany drew to a close only when the regiment had filed off.

"That is to help the French," said she.

Many an adventure befell us in the month of October. I can merely refer, for instance, to a certain officer who at eleven o'clock one night wished to lodge "twenty horses in our barn"; or to four requisitioners who dragged us out of bed at five in the morning, and forced us to dress in haste, merely to prove we had no pigs. These same soldiers delighted to talk German with French women; tried to convince us that England was responsible for the war. "The whole world is against us," they said in a sulky voice; "the French, the English, the Russians, the Belgians...."

"But you are so numerous."

"Not so numerous as all that."

I remember also that we were once awaked by two drunken soldiers, who insisted upon our opening the window, and who at our refusal threatened and vociferated for an hour, promising to come back and set fire to the house.

On the other hand, listen to the tragical, horrific history of one afternoon—it was a washing day; the charwoman had forgotten to close the gate. Two or three of us were in the yard, when a sergeant and four men made their appearance. Horses were waiting in the street. The sergeant was of lofty stature, stupid, grave, blue-eyed, and dark-bearded. He asked us if we could furnish lodgings for "Herr Mayor and his ten men." The honour was not tempting. We pleaded want of room, we wrapped up our obvious ill-will in a mass of words. Antoinette carelessly pointed at the "small room," and hinted that we had no other left. The men withdrew, the horses rode away, and we sang songs of victory.

But the following morning, about seven, I heard a noisy knock at the door. I hastened out, and reluctantly admitted the visitors of yesterday. From the top of his head the sergeant announced that "Herr Mayor was very cross, furious even, that we declined to receive him." He had sent the ruffians now to see how many rooms we might place at his disposal. I felt sure anxious ears were listening behind every shutter in the house. The alarm had been given, and the sluggards were making what speed they could. The fellows entered. The family gathered together, scared and haggard. A few of them were dressed; the others were in dressing-gowns. The Germans examined the rooms whose morning disorder had been hastily concealed, went up to the attic and down to the cellar. The sergeant then pronounced judgment in a solemn voice. We might have offered five bedrooms to the German army.

Five bedrooms! And we had but five rooms, containing five beds! Where should we have slept? On straw with the dogs! That was a happy thought!

"And you would have offered Herr Mayor that small room overlooking the yard! Herr Mayor!"

As a matter of fact we had offered Herr Mayor nothing. But the poor wretch was as much shocked as if we had proposed to lodge the Crown Prince in a pig-sty.

Well, then, to punish us and to teach us the respect due to German officers, we were condemned to take into our house Herr Mayor and his ten men.

Death-like silence. A thunderbolt had fallen and struck us dumb. The soldier went on:

"Get dinner ready at half-past twelve—a table for one in the dining-room, for men in the kitchen."

At last we found our tongues.

"You talk of dinner! But we have no provisions to cook. Meat is not to be had at the butcher's...."

"You will be provided with meat. We want wine—champagne."

"Champagne!" We laughed in the face of the man.

"There is no wine in our cellar. We drink nothing but water."

"Anyhow, mind you do things properly."

This was said in a threatening voice, and we made no reply.

The sergeant had executed his mission, but he thought fit further to admonish us on his own account.

"Are you aware that the Germans are unwilling invaders? They did not want to make war. Who wished it? Can you doubt? It was England."

"Was it? Oh, really!"

"And the civilians should be kind to the soldiers, who are very well-behaved. For instance, we ourselves all come of distinguished families. A private soldier is not necessarily a scoundrel."

"I know that," Geneviève answered. "My brother is a soldier. But as patriots yourselves, you should understand that we are patriots too, and that it is painful for us to receive the enemy."

"The enemy! The enemy!"

The sergeant, bounding with rage, struck the pavement with the butt-end of his gun.

"No, we are not the enemies of women and children; we know how to behave ourselves...."

While he discoursed, one of the young men of "a distinguished family," standing on the staircase, caught sight of my husband's shoes on a shelf. He seized a pair and put one shoe into each pocket. Turning round he encountered Yvonne's looks, and hastily replaced his spoil. Twice, thinking himself unobserved, he recovered the shoes. But being too carefully watched he gave it up as a bad job, and his superior officer concluded his speech in these words:

"If the French went to Germany the civilians would receive them kindly."

Indeed! I was pleased to hear it. But if the German women are ready to give a hearty welcome to our soldiers—and that is quite easy to understand—it does not follow that we ought to deal in like manner with their sons and husbands. We have never pretended to govern ourselves by the fashion of Berlin!

At length they went away, and we had but to yield and prepare our saucepans. We would rather have given a dinner-party to Gargantua and his family than prepare food for a German officer and ten men just as German. We went to Mme. Tassin in our extremity. She would surely come to our help, in spite of rheumatism. The meat—about half an ox—was duly brought; half of it was for soup, half to be roasted. In the wash-house, Mme. Tassin made a gigantic soup, flavoured with a thousand vegetables. In the kitchen we peeled mountains of potatoes, and prepared two bottles of French beans, which a soldier had brought in, stolen I know not where. Antoinette, uncorking one of the bottles, broke its neck, and cut her finger.

Her blood poured upon the beans. Hurrying to help her I tore off a bit of my finger.

"Never mind! get on with the potatoes!"

At length the work was finished.

Huge and lean, wall-eyed and mouthed like a pike, Herr Mayor arrived with happy nonchalance, and seated himself at the table. His attentive servant for very little would have served him on his knees. Dinner done, Herr Mayor required tea, and, being presented with a teapot, he demanded a liqueur, to flavour the tea. A few drops of rum were all that was left of an old bottle which happened to be in the dining-room. I took it in. As distant as Sirius I saluted the intruder. With a smile Herr Mayor made a low bow. Something like intelligence lit up his pale eyes. He cleared his throat, and faltered out:

"The ladies ... would be ... safer in Paris ... than here...."

I gave the rum-bottle to his servant, removed a hundred miles off, and answered:

"Certainly, sir."

I withdrew.

In the kitchen the ten men seemed to be rather constrained; they talked in a low voice, but did not lose their appetite for all that. My mother-in-law stood by, thinking that too many things might have led them into temptation. At last they went away; Herr Mayor too. His servant informed us that he would come alone to supper, and that he desired eggs and pancakes. With slow steps the officer went down the street. Behind the buckler of our blinds we burst out into bitter invectives:

"Be off, you old cut-throat! you old scout! You grind the weak; you bully women! You have eaten my finger-tip and have drunk the blood of Antoinette! Cannibal! Man-eater!"

The cannibal came back in the evening, ate a small *pâté*, was pleased with the poached eggs, and satisfied with the pancakes. Then he smoked his cigar at leisure, and all the while remained unconscious of severe eyes watching him from the garden. Yvonne and Colette made a wry face. "The sight of him is enough to make you sick. Fancy! I saw him put a whole egg into his mouth! His glass was covered with grease when he drank. Ugh!"

The next day after, another tune was played.

At twelve, precisely, Herr Mayor arrived, and calmly declared that, as his servant was out on urgent business, we must have the kindness to wait upon him ourselves.

"A pretty request, truly!"

Mme. Tassin was nowhere. The omelette, done to a turn, was getting cold in the kitchen. Meanwhile Herr Mayor was waiting in the dining-room. It was high time that the dish should make the guest's acquaintance. I made up my mind.

"I will take his dinner to the man."

"Never! You wait at table!"

"And upon a Prussian!"

"He did it on purpose, of course."

I persisted.

"I assure you I shall not deem myself degraded. And I promise you the man will feel uneasy sooner than I."

So beneath Herr Mayor's haughty nose I put the omelette *aux fines herbes*.

To the same nose I presented the roast veal with boiled potatoes, which is dear to all German hearts, and thought I might rest on my laurels. Then I saw that I had forgotten the sauce. Herr Mayor was chewing dry veal, sunk in melancholy. I put the sauce-boat on the table within reach of his hand.

"I had forgotten this; I am not in the habit...."

What did I say? Herr Mayor looked uneasy. He nearly begged my pardon.... "Indeed, I am afraid I disturb you...."

Ah! you deign to notice it? And you might as well have dined at the village inn? But you don't think that you and your ten gormandisers have reduced our stock of vegetables to nothing, and swallowed up our last egg!

But you have not always an officer at hand to give you information, and so I thought I might improve the occasion. "What is the cannon," I asked, "which thunders day and night in the south?"

"We have been fighting in Craonne for the last ten days," said he; "the battle is said to be coming to an end. Just before we were in Fismes."

Herr Mayor pronounced Fismesse. In a doleful tone he bewailed the evils of war.

The regiment he belonged to had suffered forty per cent losses since the beginning of war. He himself felt very ill. He had slept in the open air seven rainy nights running. Had I any kinsman in the war?

"Of course, my husband; and I get no news at all from him. That is the worst of all privations."

Herr Mayor nodded assent. These partings were cruel. Frau Mayor, too, would have given a good deal to accompany her Mayor. As to ourselves, our situation might change for the better. It was, for instance, to our interest that the Germans should advance. The front would then be removed farther from us. I answered that we should welcome no such change for the better. But suppose that just the reverse happened? If the Germans were driven back, the front would also remove farther? Wouldn't it?

"Oh! no, no.... Really, this war was stupid. England delights in making mischief, and the French are mad to enter into an alliance with the English, when another country was so eager to come to an agreement with them. France and Germany would get on well with each other. What, then, prevents a thoroughly good understanding?"

"A mere nothing, sir; a grain of sand.... Alsace-Lorraine, sir."

Herr Mayor shrugged his shoulders. He had forgotten Alsace-Lorraine.

His lunch was over. I asked if he intended to come and dine at our house.

Again he seemed at a loss what answer to give.

"H'm, h'm ... I am not sure. I will let you know."

His grey cloak streamed in the air, and Herr Mayor went away never to return.

Some days after I met him on the road. He bowed very low, and with a smiling face inquired after my husband. The double-faced fellow knew only too well I had not heard from him, but in common politeness I was fain to inquire also after his health. Herr Mayor was better, much better. In a week he would be back at the front, and if he happened to hear from my husband's regiment, he promised to send me the news.

And with many a bow Herr Mayor smiled himself away. His face was not ever smiling. The peasants were terrified at his way of carrying out requisitions. On the other hand, it was rumoured that he believed himself sprang from the thigh of Jupiter—I beg your pardon—of Wotan, and spoke to no one.

The family did not fail to exercise its flippancy at my expense. They asked for the recipe of my philtres to charm Prussians; they urged me to write a treatise on the art of training Germans, and prophesied a fine future for me as a tamer of tigers.

I did not mind being scoffed at. Too many cares claimed my attention. Besides, Barbu and Crafleux had just appeared in our orbit. But I am anticipating. Our chief anxiety was commonplace enough. The food problem was hard to solve. Fortunately, in spite of direful predictions, bread did not run short at the beginning of the war. Milk we had every day. Though Mme. Lantoye had been robbed of several cows, and though children were provided for first, she always gave us some. We had almost forgotten the taste of meat. Butter and cheese, hard to discover, were extravagantly dear, and eggs were as scarce as in Paris at the end of the siege. We had laid by a small provision of rice and macaroni, articles of food no more to be found in the shops; but we had decided to keep this reserve for extremities, in case, for instance, a bombardment kept us in the cellar. We all agreed to live from hand to mouth upon what we could come by. My reflections were profound when, after half a day's search, I found one egg, from which I had to concoct a dish for the whole family. You laugh? A proof that you lack imagination. With a single egg, as a base of operations, you can make pancakes, or apple-fritters, flower-fritters, or bread-fritters, or any fritters you like. By the way, I advise the use of nasturtiums. Rose leaves, on the other hand, are rather tasteless. But here is something better. You make some pastry, then beat up your one egg with a glass of milk, a few crumbs of bread, a bit of cheese, if you have any; then you pour the mixture on the pastry, put the whole in the oven, and when it is baked you will find a dish that will feed six women. Oh! we made no complaints; not yet, at least. Really when a *menu* consists of a potato fricassee to which laurel and thyme have given a zest, artichokes with melted butter and chervil—butter, replaced by grease, alas!—fresh salad, and juicy pears, who would not pronounce himself satisfied with such a meal? Marmontel, who loved good cheer, Marmontel in the Bastille, where he so highly appreciated the fare, Marmontel himself would have been delighted with it.

The want of light was the worst of our evils. Petroleum was no more to be had, and candles were hard to come by. Linseed oil and modest night-lights grudged us a glimmer by which we gloomily went to bed. Therefore as soon as the night fell the fiend of melancholy seized upon us. The dull light spread a gloom over the room we sat in, and from the black corners dark thoughts seemed to rise and grow upon us. So we would rather walk in the garden, or even look out of the window, when night fell, than sit at our work or our writing-table. How many hours have I spent leaning out of the window in a nightgown, and watching the shells burst. In September and October, just after the Germans' arrival, there were beautiful moonlit nights, worthy to be worshipped on bended knees; yet I felt an inclination to imitate Salammbô and cry to the moon with arms uplifted:

"O moon, I hate you. You are deceitful, unrelenting, and cold, and even the pale glimmer you send us you steal. There is nothing true but the warm and cheerful sunbeams, which give us light and life. You fling your silver arrows where you please, and throw what you choose into the shade. You slip your sly rays into closed rooms, through cracks and chinks; no secret escapes you. You favour illicit love, unpunished crimes, acts of violence, and foul deeds. All those things you feast upon, O moon! But your light is never so pleasant, your caress never so soft, as when you shine on a battlefield, on places where men kill one another. You take pleasure in the sight of dead bodies, shrivelled limbs, wide-open mouths, features distorted in the weird horror of death. You play on bloody weapons, on dark-mouthed cannon; you pass by the wounded, crying for help, by dying men whose death-rattle is unheard, and you smile yourself from the charnel-field, glad to leave the victims in the unfathomable shades of night."

Moon, I hate you! Everywhere and always you have looked on murderous battles, unbrotherly contests, man maddened against man. You saw the formidable army of Xerxes contend with the Greeks; you saw the Roman Empire quivering at the onslaught of the Barbarians. But can any sight you have ever witnessed be compared with that which you look down upon to-day? Europe in arms, cannon spreading death everywhere, thousands of men killed in the marshes of Poland, on the hills of Galicia, in France, on the plains of Flanders? Are you pleased, O moon?

Moon, I hate you!

To shun the moon, to shut out the sound of the guns, I close the wooden shutters, pull down the window, draw the curtains. The cannon are not silent. Chilled with cold and horror, I fling myself on my bed, bury my head in the pillows, creep under my blankets. The cannon still roars, and shakes my bed. I wake up, and the cannon roars louder than ever. To have lived, and have been sometimes careless and merry, we must have been as mad and as blind as the moon herself. But we cannot attain to the moon's insensibility, and that is why our laughter often turns to tears, and humour ends in a sob.

CHAPTER VI

Morny being near to the battlefield, we naturally saw many soldiers. The village sheltered four convoys at a time within its walls. Officers and non-commissioned officers were billeted on the inhabitants, and we had to bear our share of the common misfortune. And thus Barbu and Crafleux fell to our lot.

Barbu and Crafleux were two Prussian officers, escaped from a toy-shop, and carefully wound up before they were let loose from Germany. They always arrived side by side, with the same automatic stride, the one tall, thin, and—bearded; the other short, stout, and—*crafleux*. I must explain that *crafleux* in the popular speech of Laon means a misbegotten, rickety creature. The name was not well chosen, for the man was solid, though ugly; but his round, clean-shaven face, his pig's eyes sunk deep behind white lashes, well earned him the nickname. And Barbu himself was no Adonis. He had a small head, with regular features, a pointed beard, an aurified smile, cheeks seamed with scars. His style of beauty is not that which I commend. But what matters the want of good looks? Barbu and Crafleux revealed to us beautiful souls; they were two model Prussians.

One morning, then, the village constable brought in a smart sergeant, who seemed to have been taken out of a bandbox. All bows and smiles, the young man asked for rooms, and we dared not refuse him. The contest with Herr Mayor had been a warning to us.

"This will do," he said, entering Geneviève's room, "and this," passing on to Yvonne's and Colette's. He withdrew, still with a smile on his face, giving us full liberty to prepare the rooms and to rail as we chose.

"Alas!" groaned Geneviève. "Never again shall I like my room, after I have seen a Prussian loll on my bed."

"To begin with," I said, "you won't see him. And secondly, I have a just and clear conception of a Prussian's method of repose. He stretches himself out as if he were on duty, and his head on the pillow is carefully adorned with a helmet. He is just as proper to look upon as his photograph would be, taken after a review."

We hung tasteless chromolithographs in the place of pretty water-colours; we took away all the books, the knick-knacks, and the papers. Here and there Colette pinned up peacock's feathers—"to bring them ill-luck," she said. Then both rooms waited with a grim air for the unwelcome guests. Presently the orderlies came in, brought heaps of baggage, got everything ready for their masters, and withdrew. An indiscreet curiosity prompted us to take an inventory of the riches deposited with us. Yvonne and Colette spat, like two angry cats.

"Look here! Isn't it a shame? For a single man, two boxes! five bags! portmanteaux! Well, if he wants so much to go and fight...." Crafleux was more modest, but Barbu had certainly imported a whole dressing-room from Germany. The day after his arrival he showed off heaps of small brushes in small boxes, small creams in small pots, small scents in small bottles, and photographs and photographic apparatus, electric lamps and re-fills for these lamps, sporting guns and india-rubber cushions, soft blankets and uniforms without number. But he was chiefly remarkable for his befrogged pyjamas of sky blue or Chinese flesh colour! The sight of him must have been affecting when he had on his helmet by way of nightcap! So Barbu and Crafleux installed themselves downstairs, and we upstairs. Yvonne settled down in a tiny attic, and Colette slept on a couch in Antoinette's room. I gave Geneviève a share of my own bed in the room which already sheltered the youthful Pierrot. We were not very comfortable, and what was worse, we suffered from the cold. This requires an explanation. Some time ago a direful rumour had spread about: "They have requisitioned a great number of mattresses in Vivaise." Now Vivaise is a village not far from Morny. "You may be sure they will do the same here," said the well-informed. And so, in all houses, the beds were only half as high as before; and he was cunning indeed who could say what had become of the missing part. We, for instance, have plenty of mattresses: large, soft, elastic mattresses which would make you wish to be ill and keep your bed—and should the enemy of France rest upon them? That shall never be, we declared. By the unanimous exertion of the whole family, climbing, pulling, pushing, toiling, we succeeded in hoisting up most of these useful objects, and hiding them in the loft under the roof. Every bed was left with one only. When Barbu and Crafleux intruded themselves into the house, we were hard put to it. One of us made shift with a palliasse, while Geneviève and I slept on a hair mattress. This plan is not to be recommended unless you choose to mortify your flesh, or to copy the fakirs of India. We could have put up with our uncomfortable bedding if, to add to our misfortune, the cold had not seized upon us. Our present guests laid their hands upon heaps of blankets, their predecessors had stolen two, and so we had just enough, and nothing to spare.

We went to sleep as straight as arrows, one on each side of the bed; we woke up in the morning twisted into knots, one against the other, like two shivering cats. Despair drove Yvonne from one extreme to the other; either she lay half-smothered with heat under an enormous eider-down, or benumbed with cold under a thin cotton blanket. The authors of our hardships tasted the honey-dew of sleep upon beds of down; they knew not that threatening fists were shaken at them upstairs, and that bitter invectives vowed them to execration. Yet I think that when logs unexpectedly tumbled down, and pieces of furniture joined the dance, they gave a start and felt uneasy. But on the whole, as quiet as Vert-Vert at the Visitandines, they led a happy life, got up between nine and ten, saw about their convoy, fed well at the village inn, often went shooting, or, if they had a mind, drove out to Laon, came back home to rest a while and dress for dinner, and then about ten, eleven, or midnight, got back into their rooms and their comfortable beds.

I hinted that war, conducted in this fashion, was not disagreeable. Barbu knew that I was laughing at them.

"But our comrades ... who are fighting...."

"Do not lead such a pleasant life ... I am sure of it."

"And I think ... French convoys take their ease too."

"Well, I hope so."

But really, Barbu, it was only right that you should live in comfort, for none knew better than you how to appreciate it!

One day, going in to return a newspaper he had lent me, I surprised this lover of comforts seated in an arm-chair, his feet on the fender, his head resting on a cushion, his back on another, a book in his hand, a lamp behind him. He looked a perfect picture of self-satisfaction. But such delights cannot last for ever. "The present convoys are going to the front," some people said. Do you hear, Barbu? You will go to the front. You will change your carpet for the mud of the trenches, your pleasant fire for an icy fog, the studious light of your lamp for the red glare of the shells! You will go to the front!

They did not go to the front. They were to pass one or two nights in our house, and they stayed a month!

The village groaned under the reign of the invaders. Every morning the housewives on their way to the baker poured out their complaints.

"Have yours decent manners?"

"Oh, mine are very hard to please!"

And the gossips began to tell their grievances, for many of these undesirable guests were in truth very hard to please, and their manners were detestable. They wiped their filthy boots on the beds and arm-chairs, deluged the carpets and floors with water; they burnt the furniture and linen with their cigars. They came back very late at night, generally tipsy, went to the kitchen, searched the larder and sideboard, and cooked an extra meal with the stolen goods. The mistress of the house deemed herself very happy when she was not aroused from a well-earned sleep and ordered to go and rattle about saucepans and kitchen ranges. Of course, Barbu and Crafleux would have repudiated such methods with disgust. Barbu and Crafleux piqued themselves on their gentlemanly manners. Barbu and Crafleux were two model Prussians.

For truth's sake I must admit that occasionally they came home after midnight amiably drunk, and—I am a credible witness—danced a jig in the yard. But these are venial sins, and our watch-dogs themselves, who from the first day had been hand in glove with the officers, looked indulgently upon such gambols. Gracieuse was even accused of cherishing a guilty passion for Crafleux, having once been discovered, curled into a ball, upon the bed of the gentleman aforesaid-a most improper act for a lady dog brought up never to enter the house. Another fault was ascribed to Barbu. On the officers' arrival, we had held a secret meeting to discuss the question of lights. At length we decided to give one candle to each man, having laid by a box in case of emergency. The next morning we discovered a scandal unheard of. Barbu ... his candle ... a virgin candle, a white, shapely candle! The criminal had burnt it up in a single night! A huge candle which in the present state of things was worth its weight in gold! A few waxen tears, still hanging to the socket, bore witness to the poor thing's death. We put in its stead a dumpy one, whose loss we should not feel so deeply, and after that he must provide others for himself. He must provide his firing also. As a matter of fact he did. One day the officers demanded fires in their rooms.

"Very well, the charwoman will look after it. But ... fuel runs short."

Barbu wrote at once a note of hand, gave it to the smart bustling sergeant, and the day after ten sacks of coal were brought and discharged in the coach-house. We gazed at the black heap with envious eyes, for we used to do our cooking and warm our rooms with a poor faggot of wood.

The officers very well knew that we lacked all kinds of stores, and Barbu asked me once in a roundabout way if they might offer us some petroleum and sugar.

"We have just received an abundant supply," he said, "and shall be enchanted if you will make use of them."

This was worthy of reflection. We answered at last that we would gratefully take their proffered goods, on condition that we might pay for them.

My sisters-in-law made a great outcry against this proposal.

"Never," said they, "will we receive presents from Prussians!"

"Gently," I replied. "To begin with, we pay in cash for their 'presents'; then our hospitality, forced as it is, is worthy of some recompense. And, indeed, it is ridiculous to speak of 'their' merchandise. Is it not stolen goods? Does it not come from our bonded warehouses and stores? Besides, is it not a good deed to help in exhausting their provisions?"

So petroleum and sugar, flanked with coffee and rice, reappeared in the house, and were highly appreciated by all, in spite of their Teutonic origin.

But when the officers carried kindness so far as to offer us a hare of their own shooting, they embarrassed us sorely. Though we were not tempted to accept the gift, we thought a denial would offend our dangerous guests.

"We have too many," Barbu said artlessly; "yesterday we have shot a roebuck, seven hares, and twelve partridges in the wood of Bucy."

In our own wood! Very well, we accept the hare; it will not pay for the rent of the shooting, so we feasted upon jugged hare, and found the very French flavour much to our taste.

Barbu and Crafleux were two model Prussians. I do not unsay it. I even think I have proved it. But a Prussian is always a Prussian, and the best of the brood will never understand certain things.

"Is your piano dumb?" asked Barbu one day.

A few dances might have cheered up the house, he thought, and the roar of the guns and the clatter of German feet in the street would have been the best possible accompaniment. Another day, this same Barbu—to tell the truth he talked to me with his pipe in his mouth, but you cannot expect much from men brought up in Heidelberg—this same Barbu asked me if I would not go for a drive to Laon with him and some fellow-officers.

"It will be a good opportunity for shopping," he said. "No? The other ladies will not either? Last week I dared not ask you, our carriage was too modest, but to-day we have one of the Prince of Monaco's coaches."

Barbu still wonders why we refused. Then something still better happened. When the officers had settled themselves in our house, we made up our minds that the Germans should not catch sight of us in the passage, and the order was given, "Disappear"; and the Germans never saw the pretty faces which swarmed about us. But since I am a married woman and proficient in German—my mother-in-law does not understand a word of it—I had been appointed spokeswoman to the officers in case of need.

But one day I suppose the intruders caught sight of a golden head in flight, and Barbu asked me:

"There are young girls in the house?"

"Yes, my four sisters-in-law."

"Really, we had not the least idea of it."

The next day I happened to go into the drawing-room. The blinds were down, and the door was open into the passage. An unaccustomed object was lying on the table. Bless me, it was a box of chocolates! Delicious sweets, no doubt of it! And on the cover Barbu had written in his neatest hand and best French, "Sacrifice to the invisible spirits." Every one came and contemplated the gift and the autograph with laughter. Then we allowed the poor chocolates to get damp in the dimly lighted room. They disappeared three weeks after as mysteriously as they had come, the day of "our Prussians'" departure. May they lie lightly on Barbu's stomach!

At last the convoy left Morny. On the morning on which they were to start Barbu plunged us into an ocean of perplexities by asking us:

"You do not mind my taking a few snapshots of your house, do you?"

"Certainly ... not, sir."

"I should be very happy if one or two of the young ladies consented to sit at a window."

And nobody had prompted him in that! In vain I objected that the hour was early, and that my sisters-in-law got up very late.

"Oh, it does not matter," said he. "We will wait for them. Ask the ladies to get ready, and we will come back in half an hour."

Think how nice it would be in a year or two in Berlin, or Leipzig, or Heidelberg, to show a few photographs! "Here are a few souvenirs of our victorious stay in France! In that house we led a very happy life. The young ladies whom you see were reluctant hostesses, but the French, breathing revenge, were obliged to welcome us!"

The whole family was in a fury of anger.

"Of course, it is out of the question to comply with all the wishes of these wretched Prussians!"

Two days before Barbu had invited his brothers-in-arms to dinner. Upon this occasion he asked us for a table-cloth, a large table-cloth.

We took out of its dark hiding-place a damask cloth and eighteen napkins.

"Is that what you want, sir?"

"We wish vases also."

"Will these do?"

"And we desire flowers."

"Take some asters from the garden."

And then:

"May I take a photograph of your house?"

"Sir, I cannot prevent you."

"Will you put a smiling face at the window?"

No, no, a truce to jesting. Give him a flat denial. But how? On taking leave the Germans would certainly try to shake hands with us, that is their way, and we were determined not to shake theirs. Would they take it amiss?

More than once it had proved hazardous to irritate these dangerous guests. Mme. Valbot in Lierval saw her house plundered. Why? She had refused to sew on a button for the officer who lodged in her house.

Old Vadois, the confectioner in Laon, was listening to the tales of "his Prussian."

"The people are not kind enough to the soldiers," the officer said. "The French are better received in Alsace-Lorraine than we are here."

"So the French are in Alsace-Lorraine!" the old man cried out, with a blissful look.

"Soldiers, take this man into custody, he speaks ill of the Germans," roared the officer. And they threw the poor wretch into a dungeon, where he slept on straw.

Our neighbour Polinchard, who is something of a simpleton, was pruning his pear-trees one day, when he saw his enforced boarders making fruitless endeavours to open a fastened door.

"Not through this one," he cried, waving them back with a motion of his pruning knife, and pointing to the usual entrance.

"What now!" cried the soldiers. "He threatens us! He threatens Germans! Away with him to prison!"

The culprit was condemned to two months. That is why, on reflection, we hesitated to offend Barbu and Crafleux. They had been kind, well-behaved men, certainly, but in the village they were looked upon as haughty, violent, and hard-hearted.

"What will Barbu say," we wondered, "if, when he holds out his large paws, we put our hands behind our backs? Will he send us to prison, and put us on bread and water? Will he fasten us to the stirrups of his horse and drag us to Laon all six in a line? or will he give some such order as this to the commandant of the village: 'Should an opportunity come, billet fifty men on these people'?"

A pleasant prospect! The moment was critical. I made up my mind to brazen it out. There is always—I had quite forgotten this—a chord, or rather a cable, in all German hearts, and this chord or cable is sentiment. Let us, then, proceed by sentiment.

I advance. My countenance is that of an angel; my eyes are full of melancholy, my voice is honey-sweet, my hair ... no, it is not dishevelled, or at least only morally dishevelled. I began to talk. Of course my mother-in-law had no objection to their taking photographs of the house. But they would permit us not to appear at the windows. The gentlemen would understand our feelings. They were men of heart and intelligence. They had been very kind to us, and we were very grateful to them, but ... I became animated. "But we are at war with you ... we cannot help seeing in you the invaders of our country, and I am sure you are aware that certain things are painful to us! You know how hard it would be to your wives and sisters to receive strangers. You cannot wonder at our dealing with you as with adversaries. And I must tell you that every time I see you I think with an inward thrill of terror, 'This man may kill my husband.'"

I had done. I wept with emotion. Crafleux was gazing at his boots with a shake of his head. Tears stood in Barbu's eyes, and through this sentimental haze he saw his wife receiving French soldiers. As to myself, I felt I would soon have to blow my nose. My mother-in-law beheld the scene in silence, waiting to know the effect of my harangue. It proved effectual.

"Madam, believe me, we understand and respect your feelings. We have now only to thank you for your hospitality, and to assure you we shall always remember it."

They bowed themselves out of the room, bowed again from the threshold, bowed again in the yard. We heard the gate close behind them, a silence while they took a few snapshots, and then the rolling away of their carriage.

They were gone! Gone for ever! And no hindrances had stood in the way! They had gone leaving behind six sacks of coal.... They had gone even leaving a letter of recommendation for the officers who would take their place!

God forbid I shall ever revile the memory of Barbu and Crafleux!

CHAPTER VII

After the convoy's departure Morny was empty. The only Prussians left were those who held the lines of communication and a few soldiers at the sugar factory. We walked abroad without meeting the enemy at every turn; in brief, we felt at home again. We were all like people crushed by a landslip, who recover their breath, and take on again their former shape as the earth disappears which overwhelmed them. But, alas, it was out of the question to forget the past! Empty barns, stables, and poultry-yards deprived of their inhabitants bore witness to the passage of the scourge.

Other things also proved that the wind was blowing from the east, whence came the all-devouring grasshoppers.

One morning, as I came back from a quest after milk, I stood still, struck with amazement, and followed the example of the dairy-woman in the fable. I looked at the village steeple, and could make nothing of the time it proclaimed to the four points of the compass. Old Tassin happened to pass by.

"Well, Mme. Valaine," said he, "what do you make of this? It is German time up there. We are Prussians now!"

I lifted up my eyes to the sky, and, seeing the sun, felt easier in my mind. No change there; it was eight, not nine o'clock. Yet they had made fruitless attempts to set the sun by the German time I was sure. That is why I saw officers cast reproachful looks at the sun, which dared tell the French time in a territory occupied by Germans! That was playing them false. That was treason, and the sun would rue it bitterly.

A certain regiment, passing through Morny, chanced to trust to the village clock, and did not reach its goal at the appointed time. The delay was the cause of a failure, which put some big-wigs with helmets on into a rage. In short, the village constable was ordered to put the machine right, the German time being the only right time under the sun.

However, the departure of our guests set us at ease, and the whole village along with us. As the village might not revictual itself officially, it revictualled itself by fraud, and as much as possible. Now there lives in Morny a sympathetic drunkard named Durand. Fond of quarrelling as he is in his cups, when in a sober state he is a good, kindly soul. He had been invalided, because his hands were twisted by gout, and this infirmity rendered him equally unfit for the work of the fields; so he became a tradesman. He deals usually in rabbit-skins, scrap-iron, and rags. His business and stock-in-trade consist of a box set up on two wheels, and drawn by a good-natured yellow dog. Scrap-iron may hide a good many things, and with a view to present circumstances our friend contrived to extend his import trade. Far from me to hint that Durand, in ordinary times, snaps his fingers at the gendarmes and laughs at the laws, practices as common in our border departments as unseemly everywhere. But he improvised with the war a wonderful cunning, thanks to which he smuggled all sorts of necessary things into Morny, under the Germans' very eyes. In his surprise packet were concealed butter, grease, chocolate, sugar, to say nothing of candles. The housewives scrambled for the provisions, which rose almost to the usual level. The weary dog put out his tongue and laughed, for he knew well that we were getting the better of the Germans.

He was not the only one to laugh. The peasants, too, laughed in their sleeves when they saw the Germans stock still in "the mountains." At the first moment of invasion, the people were struck with dismay. The arrogant enemy, sure of victory, seemed to meet with no obstacles. "Handsome men, well armed and equipped. Ah, there is no reason to laugh at them!" said the old women. They thought the situation hopeless. But now it was whispered about, "They won't pass 'the mountains'; they won't cross the Aisne." At this conviction their hearts rose, which yesterday had been filled with bitterness. Evidently the invaders had been stopped; they knew not how, but the fact remained.

One morning I encountered a knot of gossips in the street. They talked of a new attack on Soissons. Mme. Tassin assured us that William had said they must pass, and pass they must. Without stopping in my walk, I interjected: "And General Pau said that they won't pass, and pass they won't." It was reported that a French prisoner had spoken these words in Laon. Whether General Pau had really expressed himself thus I don't know. But the Germans gained no more ground; we were sure of that; but it was no less certain that we were caught in a trap, that we could not stir a limb. We had good hopes the trial would not last long. All the same the situation could not be helped, and we resolved to accept it. In the village, things were going tolerably. While the baker's wife, gallant soul, made her bread, the work of the fields progressed slowly. They left the beetroots as long as possible in the earth, expecting that "our French" would come back before the harvest, which was superb. At length they had to submit to fate and bury the precious roots in vast silos. With us the days crawled by like centuries. It is true that the housekeeping entirely rested with us; it was no use looking for help in the village; women who had not a good many children to look after were working out in the fields. Only Mme. Tassin consented from time to time to come and help us. But how many hours, what long evenings, remained to fill for six women shut up in a house! What, indeed, can you do at home but dream if you are a hare, and sew if you are a woman? We sewed.

After Barbu's stay a little petroleum was left, which we used with miserly care. At dinner we contented ourselves with a night-light, and when we worked only our heads were allowed to come within the circuit of the lamp.

We made sets of baby-linen for poor little ones who took it into their heads to be born into the world, when their fathers had gone off to the war, and had left larder and purse at home empty. We competed with one another in the making of caps and shirts. Yvonne is amazingly clever, and when she has a mind to sew works no end of wonders in a trice. Our ambition increased with success. We fashioned web-like laces, and our embroidery might have aroused the jealousy of the fairies. Generally we kept silence. Sighs frequently answered the guns, and if we talked we poured out plaints of pity for those who fought, or called up remembrances of happier days.

"Just think, there are people who get letters!"

We moaned at the thought of our deprivation.

"Lucky people! They know if their relations are dead or alive."

"At this very moment there are some who read the papers!"

"Oh, rage! oh, despair! oh, hostile blockade!"

"And there are some people who know the truth! When shall we see a newspaper again?"

"At this very moment some are enjoying ... nice things to eat!"

"Oh, for a tea at Rumpelmayer's!"

"Oh, for chocolates from Pihan!"

Such memories did but sharpen the thorn of our hunger. And yet we had not lost all the pleasures of life. For instance, do you suppose we had given up having tea in the afternoon? By no means. It is highly important that women should swallow something good and hot about five o'clock. Simple toast was the only dainty we allowed ourselves. Well-buttered toast with a well-sugared cup of tea is not to be despised. Hold! Toast, yes, but no butter! The little we had was jealously salted and reserved for cooking. And tea? Do you think tea a native of the department of the Aisne? Tea was no more to be had. Sugar was so scarce that we never ate a single lump without a family council to decide whether it was the proper moment. Fortunately I found a recipe of my grandmother's at the bottom of my reticule. I requisitioned all the licorice in Morny. Mme. Lantois' walnut-tree provided us at little cost with a basketful of green shining leaves. Walnut leaves are like good women: in the long run they may lose their beauty, but they retain their virtue. These leaves then, boiled with licorice, gave us a delicious drink all the winter, which had nothing in common with the pale decoctions we nowadays moisten our throats with at the end of a dinner-party. I had been careful to say negligently: "This tea is excellent for the complexion. Regularly taken, it would greatly improve the skin, and give it a matchless bloom."

No one ever missed the afternoon tea. This ceremony, indeed, was often transformed into a great patriotic meeting, vibrating with despair and lamentations, or with enthusiasm and hope, according to the news of the day. For news we had, though I said we got none, and it was commented upon with passion. Our news of course was all unofficial, and evil or good rode fast. It spread throughout the country; it floated in the air; it came from every quarter. When I left Mme. Lantois' dairy with a can full of milk, my pocket was also full of news; likewise if we went to the baker, or if we called on M. Lonet.

The initiated came back in a hurry, called the whole family to gather round, and feverishly told the news. We ended by putting a bell in the dining-room, known as "the war bell." If one of us heard anything fresh, she rushed into the room and frantically rang the bell. From the garden, the attic, the bedrooms we flocked, allured by the hope of good tidings.

"What has happened? What is going on?"

Marvellous things always happened.

Periodically—at least twice a month—neighbouring towns were retaken by the French.

"You know, that cannonade ... so violent ... simply meant that our soldiers recovered St. Quentin."

Noyon also was reconquered I do not know how many times, and La Fère retaken with bayonets. Once the news really seemed worthy of belief. The Germans had put it up in Laon: "La Fère has been in a cowardly manner retaken by the French." We thought it true. Really, now, who would make up such an adjective? The Germans had certainly used it. On inquiry it was found that the adjective, like the news, had been invented, and the bill had never existed at all. Glorious feats were just as frequent on the front near us.

"The Route des Dames ... you know?... The French have held it since yesterday. And to-night they have carried the village of Ailles."

"Really, I thought they took it last week."

"Last week it was a false report; to-day the thing is certain."

And the Allies! Think how they worked!

"Seventy thousand Russians have just landed at Antwerp. The English are shelling Hamburg. Our Northern army is advancing, yes, it is...; deliverance will come from the North."

Ah, the secret of making legends is not lost! Popular imagination invents hundreds of them. But nowadays they cannot live long. Books and newspapers cut their wings as soon as they are hatched, and the poor things flutter an instant, and then die. But imagine a corner of a country like ours, perfectly isolated from the rest of the world for some ten years, and deprived of all news, all writings; suppose the peasants should be questioned long after upon the events of the present war, from their statements you might compose the most beautiful epic poem ever heard. As in the good old time, its title would be, "The Gestes of the French by the Grace of God."

Frenchmen, my brothers, I know you were splendid. You fought like lions, like the heroes that you are. Your glorious feats are too numerous to be counted. It was our despair not to know them. But, in revenge, we invented feats for you, fresh ones every day. Once, for instance, the French, masters of the stone-quarries of Paissy, made good use of a secret passage, and leaping unexpectedly from out of the ground, flick, flack, flick, spread death and dismay among the Germans; then, like jacks-in-the-box, they disappeared as if by magic. Struck with consternation, the Germans would have thought themselves dreaming had not too many proofs testified to the reality of the brief apparition. And what do you think of the *chasseurs à pied* who, behind a hedge at Malva, planted a forest of poles with a cap on the top of every one, and then, when the enemy with loud cries were in the very act of rushing upon this trap, shot them down to the very last man?

And don't let us forget the Africans. Ten negroes from Senegal—you understand, ten—sprang out of their trenches on a night as black as ink— of course we did not know whether negroes were or were not in the trenches—noiselessly crept along the ground through brushwood and darkness, and shouting their war-cry bounded forward into the village of Chamouille. Panic-stricken, the German soldiers fled, while the officers— seventeen in number—not one more, not one less—let the Africans cut their throats like so many lambs. The ten negroes lay down once more, flat on their faces, and crawling along on their hands and knees, went back to their trenches without a tassel missing from their caps, without a rent dishonouring their large breeches. These anecdotes were our daily bread. Innumerable were the villages taken by surprise, the convoys seized, the batteries triumphantly brought in. We were always breathless; every one of us lent a half-sceptical ear to everything that was said, and tried to detect a little truth among all this fiction. Who invented or transformed the news? It was difficult to know. Many a time Mr. Nobody-knows-who had confided it to Mrs. So-and-So, who told it to Mr. Everybody. But generally the information came from the best sources. If M. H., the Mayor of Laon, had really said all that was ascribed to him, he had done nothing else but commit the secrets of our army to the office-porter or the fruiterer over the way. On the other hand, it is hard to conceive how many secrets our countrymen extracted from their German guests. Speaking of the officers to whom they gave hospitality they assumed a mysterious air, and hinted that, walking delicately, they had elicited from them avowals as mortifying for their pride as encouraging for us.

But there was another origin, quite modern, for the news no one wanted to take upon himself. It was no difficult riddle. The news came from Heaven. Aviators dropped it. Letters had been picked up here and there, said rumour; some of them were evidently home-made, and were but laughed at—this one, for instance: "Friends, take courage; reinforcements are coming." A touching contrivance of some ingenious liar to cheer up his neighbours!

Other messages, written in a kind of official style, were so precise that they seemed worthy of attention; and one of them, known throughout the country as the message of Magny, was for a long time looked upon as authentic by the most competent judges. Oh, we were very credulous, and you laugh at us, all of you, who read the papers every morning at your breakfast. We were so cruelly crushed by the invaders, so uneasy at hearing nothing, so eager for news which might have been bones for our anxiety to gnaw that we greedily snatched at all the falsehoods we came across, and found our mouths a minute after full of sand.

Was there no means of encouraging us? Floods of sentimental ink were wasted elsewhere upon our fate, but the smallest drop spilt in the Vernandois or the Laonnois would have done us more good.

We had not deserved thus to be forsaken, for we were admirable. I maintain, laying aside all useless modesty, I maintain that we were admirable. Our persons and properties had been given up as hostages. A line was chalked out on the map; it was the part to be sacrificed. In this part we were shut up, bodies and souls, with no possibility of shaking ourselves free. We not only suffered it to be so; we agreed to the bargain; we resigned ourselves to hunger, misfortune, oppression. We submitted to see our houses plundered, our forests levelled with the ground, our lands destroyed, so that the rest of the country might be safe, the metropolis undamaged, that France herself might be free to recover her power and to prepare her vengeance. Exposed to violence, requisitions, even to reprisals, we did not give way; we wished for victory, never for peace; we thought of France, not of ourselves. But what unbearable pangs did we bear! We laboured under "the hope deferred that maketh the heart sick," as the Bible says. Sometimes we seemed to think the burden too heavy for our strength and impossible to be borne any longer. What became of us when, in the last days of October, the Germans arrogantly announced that they had won a victory at Soissons, that they had broken through, and that they were going on to Paris...? "Parisse!... Parisse!..."

We were heart-broken by it, sunk in desolation, and when thereupon came the welcome message of Magny, full of excellent things, although scandalously false, should we not have believed it true? Rather than not to have believed it, we should have framed and hung a copy in every house!

The message of Magny made its appearance on All Saints' Day. On coming back from the cemetery we watched the shelling of a French aeroplane, which laughed at its assailant, and the smoke of the shells was like small round balls gilt by the sun. The cannon rolled furiously in the direction of Noyon, and we thought: "If they have passed, it is not over there."

In the village we heard the good news that every one whispered in his neighbour's ear: "They haven't passed; on the contrary, they have been soundly beaten at Vailly. Besides, aviators have dropped a letter near Magny, copies of which are passing from hand to hand."

They have not passed! They have been beaten! Oh, joy! how lovely is the day! And how near is the Capitol to the Tarpeian Rock! Yesterday we lay on the ground broken with the shock; to-day, lively and drunk with joy, we rush with a bound towards the regions of trust and hope!

Our best source of news was Mme. Lantois'. The kitchen of the farm is a large, gay, bright room, whose painted walls, black and white flags, glittering copper saucepans, and cages full of song-birds, are pleasant to the eye. A select society was to be met there about five in the evening. To find a seat you had to disturb one of the cats which lay enthroned on all free chairs. To upset a cat is high treason. To remain standing would have looked uncivil. I used to get out of the scrape by taking on my lap Gros-Blanc, Yé-Yé, or Belle-Limace, who seemed to approve of this arrangement.

All tongues were let loose.

First, we exchanged and commented upon the news of the day. What troops—infantry, cavalry, artillery—had been seen in Morny and its neighbourhood, whether there were many of them and which direction they took, whether the trains were loaded with soldiers or ammunition—

these were the questions asked and answered. Then we were told what wounded soldiers and prisoners had been brought to Laon, and heard what motor-cars had traversed the village. Twice the Emperor himself was seen within our gates in an iron-plated car, preceded and followed by two cars occupied by soldiers armed to the teeth. Upon this occasion the Prussians of the village posted on both sides of the road had bawled themselves hoarse to such a degree that they had been obliged to run to the next cellar in order to moisten their gullets. Hundreds of pairs of eyes, moreover, had watched the sky and discovered aeroplanes—English or French—which had been fired at by such and such a battery. The German flying machines had been disporting themselves here or there. The captive balloon—"William's sausage"—had perched above certain points. How many of us had, the night before, observed the signals that came from Laon or glittered in the "mountains"?

The ears had just as much to do as the eyes. Guns had been fired from this quarter and that, German cannon or French, ordnance or fieldpiece. In one direction a mine had been fired. In fine weather we heard the sound of rifles or the crackling of mitrailleuses. One stormy day the workmen declared that they had heard the French bugles sound for a charge. What a fine harvest of news we gathered every evening! What would we not have given to be able to hand it on to those who might have turned it to good account! When we had gone all over it again there followed a warmly conducted debate; we drew conclusions as to the successes or reverses each side had met with, or as to the positions they occupied.

But as it is impossible always to be discussing strategy, and as we could talk only of the war, we fell to telling stories. And many of them touched upon our general flight before the Germans and its failure.

M. and Mme. Lantois, with their son René, a big lad of eighteen, had tried to run away too—not, like ourselves, on foot, but in a cart drawn by two stout horses. The prudent hands of the farmer's wife had heaped up in the bottom of the vehicle two sacks of flour, a keg of wine, a barrel of salt pork, two hundred eggs, and even thirty bottles of petroleum. No matter whither they would have to go, they were thus prepared for any events. The first hours all went well, but near Nouvion-le-Vineux the fugitives were overtaken by the French army. They were ordered to draw up on the roadside and wait. Night fell. The soldiers kept on advancing. A cannon happened to break down and got somewhat injured. So the weary farmer went to sleep leaning against a post, while his wife, lantern in hand, gave a light to the poor gunners, who, cursing and swearing, did their best to mend the damaged wheel. The stream of men flowed on uninterruptedly till the morning. The good people, who had kept out of the way all this time, thought the moment propitious to resume their journey. They put the horses to, and were about to move forward, when they were startled by a loud shout. Fresh soldiers were advancing, and ... they were Prussians.

"I am sure," Mme. Lantois said, "that at this point they were not three miles away from our rearguard."

Horses, cart, provisions, and even petroleum—ogres turn up their noses at nothing—were swallowed in a mouthful. The three fugitives, despoiled and abashed, came back on foot to Morny, all whose inhabitants returned to their houses sheepish and downcast.

In other places the Germans were not even put to the trouble of despoiling the people, who of their own free will sacrificed to the new-comers. They mistook them for English soldiers. In Festieux, for instance, not far from us, the urchins of the village cried out:

"The English are coming!"

And the peasants crowded about them. They had already stripped themselves for the French, but all the same they were eager to welcome the Allies. And they poured out wine and coffee, they offered fruit and biscuits. The woman who told us this story, after she had shared a whole pail of lemonade among "those poor boys who were so hot," went to the tallest of the band, a man with gold lace, and, in a very loud voice so that he might understand French the better, said to him:

"Well, as a reward, you will bring us William's head!"

The man spread out his face in a broad grin, and, wiping his mouth with the back of his hand, answered:

"We no English, we Germans...."

Tableau!

This comical scene had its tragic side. In the same village were still two French foot soldiers. A kindly soul ran to call them.

"Come quick, there are English soldiers here! We are all brothers."

Smiling, the soldiers came up.

"You idiots!" they cried, "they are Prussians!"

And, climbing upon a carriage which happened to stand there, they opened fire upon the invaders.

The Germans replied, a refugee was wounded, the women screamed, all fled and hid themselves. Of the two courageous soldiers, one, alas, was killed, and the other taken prisoner.

More than once we heard accounts of the fighting from eye-witnesses. M. and Mme. Robert, large landowners of Ailles, told us how their village had been occupied by the enemy. Every day German patrols had been seen in the place; but one morning the French came back. All fell into raptures, kissed one another, marvelled at the return, dug up their treasures, and kept the day as a feast. In the evening the youths of the village went for a walk with the Zouaves, listening to the warriors' tales, and the fiddler of the village played madly the sole tune that he knew.

The next morning, about half-past five, Mme. Robert, looking out of the window, said to her husband:

"Look, some one is trying to get in through the orchard gate."

In truth, some one was coming in. The Germans had arrived in great numbers; they sprang up from all sides.

Our soldiers were ready. A close fight took place in the orchards, in the gardens, in the barns, and chiefly in the big yard of the farm. At the outset of the skirmish an officer had pushed the inhabitants into the kitchen:

"Stay there, don't go out."

The defenders of the village had to fight against fearful odds, and yet many Germans seemed to play their part reluctantly. Some of them took refuge in the barns, and hid themselves to avoid the scuffle. Then a captain came up, armed with a kind of whip, the leather thongs of which were weighted with tiny leaden balls, and with this he vigorously lashed his soldiers until they returned to the hottest of the fight. The Zouaves fought like lions, but they were only 250 against an enemy ten times superior in number, and in spite of their efforts at last gave way. Another German officer, noticing civilians in a room, cried aloud with anger, and shut them up in an empty cellar. For a long time the prisoners heard the noise of the fight going on above their heads, and little by little it became less violent, and then ceased completely. Only the third day, in the morning, were the poor people taken out of the cellar, half-dead with hunger and cold. M. and Mme. Robert were still dressed as at the moment of the surprise, their naked feet light slippered, he with a night-cap and white ducks on, she in a morning-jacket and short petticoats. They were not even allowed to go in for a minute to eat a bit of food and take clothes and money. It may be supposed that the German soldiers, always thrifty, had safely put into their pockets all that was worth stealing. Accompanied by soldiers, the poor people had to go on foot to Laon, half-naked and starved.

"Going through Chamouille," said Mme. Robert, "I was so hungry that I ate the potato peelings I found in the street."

In Laon, the prisoners were set at liberty, and they went to relations of theirs, who did their best to comfort and clothe them.

"Such rich people, too!" concluded the scandalised narrator.

Discussions and stories were not the only things that allured me to the farm. I had a secret there, the mystery of my life. I realised a dream cherished since my girlhood—I learned to milk the cows. At nightfall I jumped out of my window, fled to the warm stable, and there strove hard to draw milk from Lolotte's distended udders. She was a splendid large-horned cow, which has since been requisitioned so that her milk might be reserved for his Excellency the General So-and-So. The good animal mistook me for an awkward calf, and, looking at me with commiseration, endeavoured to lick me tenderly. Oh, we acquired many talents we never had dared to aspire to before the war. We sawed wood, we dug in the garden. And everywhere it was the same; all tried to make up with their imagination and their work for the many things that were wanting. René Lantois contrived an excellent blacking with soot and wax. Our neighbours grated and boiled their beetroots and so made treacle that they used instead of sugar, while a grocer manufactured sweets which were a great success among the urchins of the place. And the forest saw more women cutting wood than ever it had seen men.

When we were dissatisfied with the local products, we went off to Laon. I think that a longing for movement peculiar to all captive animals chiefly drew us to such adventures.

Laon may be small and provincial, but while you are there it gives you the impression of a town. You see tall houses, narrow streets, and policemen just as you see them in a capital. Booksellers, chemists, and dentists smile at you at every corner of the streets. These institutions, which civilised people cannot do without, are scarcely to be met in Morny. Therefore, and despite the uncertain times we lived in, we rarely let a fortnight pass without organising an expedition to our county town. Two or three of us went off, accompanied by the anxiety and good wishes of the family, and returned home in triumph, bringing back good news, balls of thread and worsted for our needles, and on lucky days a few pounds of provisions.

Thus it was that Yvonne and I went once to Laon on foot—the only method of travelling at our disposal—with our neighbour Mme. Lantois. Our shopping done, we could not help going in the direction of the "Agence," a big building, a sort of agricultural Exchange, in which French soldiers were being nursed. Of course we were forbidden to visit the prisoners. But by good luck, two hundred and fifty of them were just starting for Germany, and we had but to wait a moment for them. We saw them go down the flight of steps, limping and looking piteous and ill. They fell into line on the foot pavement. Oh, what sad happiness it was to see once more their dear caps, their red trousers, their lively faces, when we had met only wooden heads for nearly two months. Many were too weak to stand, and they dropped on benches, or on the steps of the staircase. A Turco sat down on the pavement with a far-away air. "Mektoub!" As they were going away we wanted to get something to give them. Not a shop was open save the chemist's over the way. We went in to buy cough lozenges of all kinds. Owing to the circumstance the chemist let his whole stock go at the lowest possible price, and his wife loaded us with piles of handkerchiefs. So we divided our poor gifts right and left. A big dark-haired lad felt the fine linen with pleasure.

"A handkerchief! Think, these last two months I never had one!"

Their guardians did not prevent us from talking to the prisoners, but when they caught sight of an officer they sent us rudely away. Most of the captives had been wounded and taken in the neighbourhood of Craonne, Berry-au-Bac, and La Ville au Bois. They did not complain, said they had been pretty well treated, but they were unanimous in adding:

"The English are most wretched; they are tormented in every possible way."

Presently we saw the English prisoners get down the steps in their turn, half a dozen big, thin men with worn countenances that moved our pity.

A stout German under-officer thought well to give us his opinion: "Here are the English!" said he. "Look at their pigs' heads. They ought all to be shot; not the French," he added, to be agreeable, "only the English." We wanted the poor Tommies to have their share too. As I was threading my way through the crowd and they were stretching out their hands, their guardian, with a blow of his large claws, swept away the boxes of sweets and put them into his pocket, amid the laughs of his comrades. It was too late to make good the German's mischief, for the soldiers were already moving forward. The less injured limped quickly away, a car drove the others to the station, into which no civilian was allowed to penetrate, and after many salutations we watched them go to captivity with a sad heart.

Our visits to the county town were not all marked by such incidents. One day, Yvonne was copying—in order not to lose a word—the official reports, in which we read: German victory here, Prussian success there, Austrian army advancing this way, English forces retreating in that one, and, believing nothing of it, she burst out laughing as she traced the news with her ironical pencil. A stern-looking sergeant came up and announced:

"You not laugh, townspeople, all that true."

But we laughed all the same. Every one laughed at those reports, the sincerity of which was doubtful, which appeared to us still more false than they were, and which yet were the only threads which connected us with the rest of the world.

Fortunately, the benevolent Germans resolved to keep us informed of what was going on, and published a weekly paper at Laon, the *Journal de Guerre*, which appeared for the first time in November. The purpose of this publication, we were told, was to let the invaded know the truth about the war. Oh! a German truth, of course, carefully dressed up, for their self-respect prevents our enemy from showing us unveiled so indiscreet a person as Truth. And the people laughed more than ever. They laughed from Sissonne to La Fère, from Anizy to Marle. I must say that the newspaper was—according to us, if not to the authors—ludicrous both in matter and manner. It was written in a language closely connected with the French. With a knowledge of philology and some application you managed to make out even the obscurest sentences. Thus, after a little practice, we succeeded in reading the new idiom quite fluently, if we were still unable to appreciate its niceties.

The first number of this precious periodical was a real poem. It was addressed to "the high and chivalrous sentiments of the true French nation." Its authors did not despair of explaining to the French nation that its Government and its Allies had shamefully deceived it, and hoped that it would soon see who was really responsible for the war, what humane and disinterested part Germany had borne in the whole affair. In another article peace was openly hinted at, and the author set forth the advantages which France would get if she listened to reason, that is, if she abandoned the Allies and sided with gentle Germany. And then, forgetful of all reserve, the Germans added that, in case of peace, the Government, far from requiring a contribution of war, would probably be inclined to "build a bridge of gold to France"—what a good promise we had there!—as Bismarck did in '66 to Austria. "It seemed weakness," the profound politician added; "it was strength." If the learned members of the German Universities had but attended a common school in France, they would have learned that which our La Fontaine wrote: "If we force our talent, we shall do nothing with grace." Maybe they had understood that sweet manners are not congenial to their nature, that the voice of the cannon alone suits their temper. We should not see them propose to France with bows and smiles the fate of vassal that Austria had accepted in '66. On the second page, the *Journal de Guerre* magnified the capture of Antwerp, and described its consequences in pompous phrases. Then the author of a small and acid article concerning the relations of France and Russia concluded with this sentence, as witty as it is nicely turned:

"Varus, Varus, give me back my millions and my billions! If Russia listens to that! It is very doubtful!" This is a literal translation.

Indeed, we laughed. Not a Homeric laugh, of course, stifled laughter maybe, a tittering rather than a hearty laugh, a catching laugh which the enemy might have happened to overhear, a real laugh all the same. We should have felt doubly prisoners if we had not made fun of our jailers, and to be prisoners only once was quite sufficient.

As we knew German, we fell upon the papers we came across and bitterly enjoyed the high praises they bestowed on their high deeds. They pleasantly jeered at the "parti-coloured army" of the Allies, at the negroes who, according to them, "tremble with cold like a leaf tossed by the wind," which, the Prussian libellers added, must produce a bad effect in a battle.

A number of *Simplicissimus* completed our edification. The proud German Michael was represented spitting his seven foes on his mighty sword. The Cossacks, bullying women and children, turn up the whites of their eyes at the sight of a single Uhlan, and fall on their knees. In Lorraine the German soldiers, by way of a change, leave off firing at the French: "Let us keep a few of them to kill with bayonets," they say. In conclusion, an Englishman helps his little Japanese monkey up the noble oak-tree where the German eagle is perched: "Go on," he says, "try to pluck some feathers from his tail."

CHAPTER VIII

The literature of the day, then, gave us little comfort. And every week the *Journal de Guerre* played the very same tune. Yet about the end of November we read in its columns a proclamation from the General-Governor of the place, which every one was bound to acknowledge interesting, if not agreeable. This proclamation brought us the orders and prohibitions of the almighty authorities.

"It is expressly forbidden to give assistance and shelter to French or Allied soldiers. Owners of arms of all kinds, telegraphic and telephonic apparatus, and bicycles, are ordered to bring them to the military authorities.

"It is expressly forbidden to keep live pigeons of any breed.

"It is expressly forbidden to go without passport from one place to another."

The tyrant who issued the orders concluded with these words:

"The population have nothing to dread as long as they submit to the laws of war and comply with our orders."

With our orders! With this you may go far, and they went very far.

The general regulations did not concern us nearly. Unfortunately we never met wounded or straggling French soldiers; we possessed neither bicycles nor telephonic or telegraphic apparatus; we owned no pigeons whatever, and we were content to assure our neighbours of our sympathy, when, not without groanings and great sorrow, they slaughtered the inhabitants of their dovecots. This massacre aimed at the suppression of all carrier-pigeons, and in many farms the application had not waited for the law. At Mme. Lantois', for instance, an under-officer and two men had dropped in unawares, strangled and taken away as many pigeons as they were able to carry.

"Don't take the big white ones," besought the farmer's wife.

Naturally, the Germans are too wise not to be suspicious; those French people might be cunning enough to disguise their carriers as big white feather-legged pigeons.

One night, old Leprince heard a noise in his out-house. Half undressed, he hastened out, and met face to face four soldiers, who in broken but energetic language ordered him back to his mattress. The old man watched the intruders go away, went to his dovecot, and by the light of his lantern saw the floor bespattered with blood and scattered all over with pigeons' heads.

But after the proclamation the slaughter surpassed any previous raids. It is easy to imagine the emotion that spread among the cooing tribe, famous for their attachment to family sentiments and home life. How many young ones just hatched were killed! How many loving couples severed from one another! Bewildered, the poor things fled in bands throughout the country, and made common cause with the crows, pecking corn in the fields. If a Prussian happened to pass, he lifted his gun to his shoulder and fired at the white birds. If the frightened flock sought refuge on a roof: "The deuce take the pigeons!" the angry peasant cried out; "am I going to pay 1500 francs because two dozen birds have alighted on my house?" Then stones were thrown and off went the birds. The order was explicit; for every pigeon saved, the owner was subject to a fine of fifty francs. Therefore all dovecots were shut up, and no one dared give asylum to the proscribed. The race of bicycles, also persecuted, was equally bewildered. The helpful bowels of the earth swallowed some of them; the mouth of a well engulfed a few others. Some I know spent two months in a brook, and then let themselves fall to little bits rather than serve the Germans. True patriots were the bicycles. As to those which had not managed to escape the Germans' attention, they were taken to the mayor's house, and clearly showed they were out of temper by grating, creaking, gnashing the teeth of their wheels and screws the whole way long. This did not prevent the invaders from using them on the spot with great satisfaction.

Of the regulations as to passports we had a proof before letters, so to say.

On a certain morning of November, Yvonne and Antoinette, attended by Pierrot, went to Laon. For Yvonne a visit to the dentist was urgent; Pierrot wanted a Latin grammar. About five in the evening we began to feel uneasy. The night and the fog fell in concert, and the travellers had not yet returned. At half-past five Mme. Valaine and I ventured out, ready for anything, and at two miles' distance from the house we saw the little group, walking along very fast, and with a candid air.

"Why, here you are! Frightened not to see us back? There was no reason at all! Look, we have got the *Journal de Guerre*, a pound of chocolate, and some sweets!"

We dined with a good appetite. Three days after we heard a loud ring of the bell, and two German officers, attended by the Mayor, were shown in.

"The young ladies who lately were arrested at the level-crossing live here, don't they?"

We looked at one another, struck with amazement. Yvonne and Antoinette alone seemed to be acquainted with the circumstance, and modestly acknowledged they were the young ladies in question.

"Well, they are to be at the Commander's office in Laon at two o'clock. You need not be afraid, thanks to the Mayor, the affair is already settled."

At two o'clock! It was now past twelve. There was not a minute to lose. We were ready in an instant, and on the way to Laon the offenders told the truth.

"Oh," they said to me, "we have been so frightened! You know, we did not want to worry mother, but you can imagine that we ourselves were terrified."

"We were already late," said Antoinette, "when at St. Marcel we discovered that we had lost Colette's ring. We went back to the town, found the jewel half-crushed, and hastened once more on the way home. It was about half-past four, the night was rapidly falling when we got to the level-crossing.

"'Passports!' we heard.

"'But we have none ... they have never been required.'

"'Then go back to Laon, you are not allowed to pass.'

"'Impossible! We have no house in Laon; my mother is expecting us at Morny.'

"'Wait a minute,' said a voice, and, riding on a bicycle, an officer, attended by two men, came out of the fog. We explained the whole thing in our best German, for he did not speak French at all. He was courteous, and seemed inclined to let us go, when he was struck by a sudden idea:

"'Are you English?' he asked.

"Yvonne understood, 'Do you speak English?' and answered:

"'Yes.'

"'So, you are! Then you don't go. Come into the house.'

"The soldiers gathered round and looked curiously at us. One of them carried a lantern, which made all faces red. Our hearts beat violently.

"'Sir, please let us go home. We are not English ... my sister mistook your question.'

"You will explain this to me; come in first."

"The door was thrown open; I stood on the threshold, when Yvonne caught my arm:

"'Don't go in, don't go in!'

"I looked around me. We were alone among these ten men, whose looks seemed very strange to me. Around us nothing but the lonely fields, the darkness, and the fog. In front of us a row of untidy beds; on a broken-legged table a wretched lamp completed this picture of a disreputable house.

"'Oh no, I pray you, let us go away; let us return to Laon.'

"'If you don't come in, and quickly, I will shoot you.'

"And the officer snatched up his revolver.

"Out of despair we went in, the ten men pushed us and rushed in after us.

"'You pack off post haste,' the officer said.

"The soldiers disappeared, except one to guard the door.

"'Well, you were wise to come in,' said the officer, 'or I would have ordered my men to fire at you.'

"To exemplify his officer's words, the facetious guard pointed his revolver at us. Pierrot chose that very moment to shriek with terror:

"'Oh, I am so frightened, so frightened!'

"We were frightened too, I assure you; yet we did our best to comfort the poor boy. I explained our case to our judge, and produced the twisted ring, the cause of our being late.

"'We live in Morny, were born in Morny, our anxious family is waiting there for us. Here are our papers; you see we are French students, and not English.'

"At last the interrogation was at an end. Pierrot's tears were still falling fast when the officer—a small, dark-haired, Roman-nosed nervous-looking man, more like a Meridional than a German—allowed himself to be convinced.

"'Well, I permit you to go on my own responsibility. It was a piece of good luck you met me here, or you would not have reached your home. Never go out at nightfall without a passport. Now go.'

"We had but waited for his permission, and were off as soon as it was given. Pierrot trotted along, still shaken by his sobs.

"'Poor Pierrot, no more crying, it is all over. Take this chocolate. But you know you are not going to tell tales. You may have one sweet more. Don't say a word of what you have seen. Mme. Valaine might be worried about it. Keep these cough lozenges, you will eat them to-morrow.'

"He took the bribe, and, consoled in his mind, promised not to open his lips about the adventure. So we came back with our heads high, and without a tremor in our voices."

"You throw off the mask now! You had not relied on the solicitude of the Germans, who wanted to know if you had come home safely."

In Laon, the Mayor, red and merry, overflowing with fatness and self-importance, told us simply that the thing was settled, as our declarations had proved true. He was sorry we had been disturbed to no purpose. And we too. To walk for three hours at full speed in order to listen to such rubbish! I shall be believed if I say that ever since then we never felt inclined to travel without passport, which, besides, was soon afterwards strictly forbidden. The general regulations were increased by rules peculiar to every village, differing slightly one from another according to the local commandant. Those inflicted on Morny seemed to us the most disagreeable. They saw the light one after the other. At any time of the day you might meet the rural constable in the street, his drum by his side, a scrap of paper in his hand. He looked ashamed of his paltry function, being used by the military authorities to announce to the world all kinds of nonsense.

"Order to stop all clocks and timepieces in all houses."

Why? Who will ever pierce the mysteries of a German brain?

The kitchens of the farms seemed empty when the pendulums which for ages had animated the rustic oak clock-cases suddenly stopped, when in the best bedrooms the shepherds and shepherdesses who adorned the mantelpieces ceased their tick-tack. Yet in many a room a discreet murmur survived, and the owner was ever on the look-out ready to stop the unwonted noise if any search impended. Then came another commandant who did not care for the order, and little by little the people made their clocks go as before.

"Order to bring to the *Mairie*—now called Commandature—one lamp out of every two."

A selection was made, the best lamps were hidden, and the rest given to the invaders.

"It is forbidden to let dogs and *cats* go out."

Poor pussy was astonished at the obstacles put in the way of her nocturnal adventures, and it is said that every garden and field mouse danced three times in honour of the German Emperor.

But what seemed to us more ridiculous than anything was the latter part of this announcement:

"It is forbidden to let the dogs go out; it is forbidden to let them bark."

Who indeed had invented this fantastic order? Some old grumbler maybe, who was prevented from sleeping by a loquacious bulldog, and as we had relapsed into feudalism, this temporary lord thought that nothing should disturb him. I am surprised that he did not throw blame upon the frogs in the neighbouring marshes. As our fathers, armed with poles, were wont to beat the ditches by night, repeating, as they did it: "Peace, peace, you frogs, let his Lordship sleep," so their sons of to-day might have beaten the marshes, saying: "Peace, peace, you frogs, let his German Lordship sleep."

Prevent the dogs from barking! Really, now, we did our best, and for a few days, even for a few nights, we nearly reduced them to silence. In our house, Gracieuse, a chatterbox by nature, had a great many interviews with the cudgel, which worked well, and all about us the nights were still. It was but the cannon's turn to speak. In vain, for the moon appeared, white and round and fascinating. Her four-legged admirers did not bay to her in chains. You may imagine the poor animals, crouching down in their narrow kennels, fastened with too tight a chain and too tight a collar, lying squat in the dark, and thinking with terror of the new and inexplicable severity, or casting a sly look at the whip or the broom which the master snatched up if any sound came from their throats. This lasted about a fortnight. Then one evening a pug-dog stirred up the others to mutiny by yelping furiously. The shepherd-dogs followed, then the hounds. And the curs, plucking up courage, made their deep bass heard, until at last, their muzzles lifted towards the sky, their mouths distended from ear to ear, the whole canine tribe began to bay the moon.

"It is forbidden to go out after five o'clock in the evening and before six o'clock in the morning."

"It is forbidden to keep a light burning after eight o'clock in the evening."

"How convenient it is!" moaned Mme. Lantois. "The dairymaid does not live at the farm, and this will oblige us to milk the cows one hour earlier in the morning, one hour later in the evening."

But the dispensers of orders did not mind putting the farmers out, and every one had to submit. We consoled ourselves for imprisonment in our houses for thirteen hours on end by thinking that in case of a nocturnal incident, under every roof, from every garret-window would spring a head, with which one might exchange one's impressions. What was something more of a hardship was to veil our lights after eight o'clock in the evening. Most of our neighbours go to bed shortly after the sun, but to townswomen as we are it seemed impossible to sleep before eleven.

Our fruit, our crops, our wine were requisitioned; well, we understood why. But for mercy's sake leave us our evenings, for none can enjoy them if they are taken away from us. On winter nights rooms are comfortable and warm, furniture friendly, and household gods favourable. Ideas float in the air and may be turned into talk or dreams. I warrant, it is the vigil of thinkers that has civilised the world.

In the morning everything has a cold air, inanimate objects are hostile, a dull light reluctantly falls from the windows, and for some hours you strive hard to tame life again and make it bearable. I beseech you, let me live in the evening. The Germans did not allow us to live in the evening. More than once, when the bell had rung eight o'clock, we heard fists hammer on the shutters, and harsh voices cry:

"Go to bed; French no light, no light."

Yet it took some trouble to discover that we were not sitting in the dark. These people had to thrust their noses through the chinks of the wooden shutters to perceive that there was no light in the room. The window-curtains not being sufficient to mask the light, we set our wits to work in order to conceal it. Geneviève and I stuffed the shutters with two big cloaks; Colette established a cleverly contrived screen all around her lamp, and Yvonne hung up an extra blind. Every day, when the lamps were lit, one of us went out to supervise the windows, while those within waited for information.

"Is my window all right?"

"At the top, on the left side, there is a tiny bright spot.... Good, now it is quite dark."

"And in my room?"

"Just a small streak at the bottom."

Into the smallest details of our life the Germans had managed to introduce something vexatious.

Yet Morny being a quiet village, with a prudent Mayor at its head, we were not so much to be pitied during the first months of the occupation. It might perhaps be thought that we were too easily resigned to fate, that we yielded too readily to the enemy's orders. Of course a rebellion, followed by fearful punishment, would look well in a story. But to what purpose should we attempt what would certainly bring new harsh measures upon our neighbours? Ah, if the least of our actions might have been useful to the country we were burning to serve, how eagerly we—even the women—would have risked all to be helpful, and exposed our lives, our liberty. But, alas, we were persuaded that we were helpless, useless, even of no worth at all. We were mere ciphers, as unimportant to one army as to the other, just like clods of earth in the fields! I know that a well-placed clod may cause a man to fall, and you may be sure that when we found an opportunity we never failed to make a Prussian stumble. But it would have been downright folly to think of an open rebellion, and we knew it well, though we sometimes talked of it.

The German soldiers said:

"French women not bad; Belgian run after us with hay-forks." Alas, what a price poor Belgium paid for her heroism!

Soon after their arrival, the invaders took care to explain how they intended to be obeyed, and to insist that the community would be responsible for all individual acts. The Hussars were very near burning Chevregny while we were there, because some one—evidently one of the French convoys escaped from the fight, and hidden in the wood—fired at a battalion passing on the road. One man was wounded in the foot. Furious, the commander talked of setting the whole village on fire, and it escaped only because the priest proved that a soldier had fired the gun and not one of his flock.

At Laon, a German soldier was killed by a civilian—in a brawl after drinking, French witnesses said; while asleep, the German report declared. We have read the poster stuck up in Laon. The end ran thus:

"The house where the crime was committed has been set on fire, and the guilty man will be shot. If a similar deed occurs again, the quarter where it takes place will be burnt, and the town condemned to pay a million francs."

We did not require telling twice that it was not worth while. Bought one at a time, the Prussians were really too expensive. An invaded country could not afford them at such a price! Then all power of action had been taken away from us; we could but try to the utmost of our power to save as much of our goods as possible, to set bounds, with cunning, which is the arm of the weak, to the ravages of the scourge. If impotent anger often moved the women into tears, what shall we say of the men? How shall we depict the fate of thousands of soldiers ordered back home on the eve of the invasion? They are soldiers, they ought to fight for their country. They watch from afar the different stages of the battle, whose manifold din reaches them. They stand, panting, with clenched fists. They think: "This is going on, such a thing is happening. If I were with my brothers, I would fall upon the enemy, I would fight against the invaders."

Their blood is burning; they wish to kill; they will kill some of them. A sudden uproar, imperious voices are heard. Be quick! Prussians are at the door. They are shown in, even with a good grace. To refrain so long from murder, for which they would gladly have paid with their life, more heroism was required from our men—the natural defenders of molested women and famished children—than is necessary to rush headlong into the thickest of a fight.

I have already spoken of the regulations the German authorities had decreed. But what is impossible to explain, and what people can never understand who have not lived among the invaders, is the way the laws were applied, and the thousand vexations that came from them. We were constantly threatened with requisitions, inquisitions, perquisitions. We never saw two soldiers walking together in the street without thinking: "Where are they going? What do they want?"

Among those who were quartered in Morny during October, were a certain veterinary surgeon, pale-faced and red-haired, and a certain professor, red-nosed and dark-bearded, both with gold spectacles. The excellent fellows spoke French as if they had been born in Pontoise, obtruded themselves everywhere, and took a great interest in everything. They talked cattle with the farmers, flour with the baker, provisions with the housewives, and sweets with the urchins. They teased the young girls, and patted the dogs. After three weeks of such dealings they knew Morny just as well as the elders of the place, knew your income, your family affairs and secrets, better than you. They had a large share in the writing of a guide for the use of the invaders, and when every inhabitant had been duly analysed, both went away to their pleasant trade elsewhere. You may guess how useful this was for the Germans, if you consider what an advantage it would be to leeches to understand anatomy, and to know the disposition of the blood-vessels.

So much for inquisitions. As to requisitions, they were always going on, and the farmers never got up at dawn without thinking: "What are they going to steal to-day?"

So we continued to hide as well as we could all that we possessed.

Think of our anxiety the day we heard they were said to search houses!

One morning, about the end of November, the street was suddenly filled with soldiers. The word "perquisition" was hovering over our heads. How anxious we were for the cheese and butter we had the luck to get but the day before! If they happened to notice it they would be sure to come back and fetch it. So we rushed into the garden, and with all possible speed thrust the three pounds of butter and the five pieces of cheese, the hope of many a future meal, into the box borders. Everything was ready. On our features was a mask of carelessness. Then the bell rang; we opened the gate.

"Come in, gentlemen, and may it please Mercury, the god of the thieves, your patron, to let you pass close to our hiding-places without discovering them!"

A soldier guarded the door. Two other ones came in with a sergeant. As the saint, so the altar. From one room to another we followed the visitors. They were careful not to forget the drawers, which their hands searched and researched. They disturbed the dresses hung in the cupboards, to make sure that no French soldiers were hidden behind. They shook the *portières*, to scare the carrier-pigeons away. "Ah! this bed-curtain is swollen ... a French soldier ... the iron cross for me...." Flat down on his face lay the knave. Alas! no feet were to be seen beneath the curtain, nothing but the innocent frame of a picture forgotten there three months ago. They went upstairs, took a careful survey of the attics, pried into the heaps of logs. Then catching sight of the roof whose shadow served as a screen to our bedding:

"What is up there, then?" asked the under-officer.

"Up there? It is an empty space between the roof and the ceiling."

The man seemed satisfied with the explanation; the big boots got down again; they paused; they had found nothing. At length they made up their minds to go out; they disappeared from sight; they went to search the next house. A week after these operations the villagers still talked about them.

"Has your house been carefully searched?"

"Oh, dear! dear! they have looked even into the saucepans!"

"They have gone through the papers in my desk."

"They have climbed upon the beams of our roof."

The visitors seldom found anything worth while—one or two pigeons which their owners had hidden in the attic, and for which they had to pay fifty francs each. Other villages were less happy. For a trifle a man was considered suspect, and taken into custody. If a cartridge happened to be discovered in a house, the owner was arrested and sent to Laon, Hirson, or still farther off—and after the retreat of August what urchin had not a collection of French and Belgian cartridges?

A gentleman-farmer of the neighbourhood was put into prison under the pretence that he talked German too much! Another was arrested all of a sudden without any apparent reason.

"But why am I arrested?"

"Go on, you will know later."

The poor wretch came back from Germany a year afterwards, ill, worn out, done for. Only they had neglected to reveal to him why he had been imprisoned.

It is not difficult to imagine how these prisoners were hunted. A man was arrested in Barenton. A gun had been found in his bed, it would seem. He was confined for a time at Laon, managed to escape, and went right to Morny, where M. Dunard, his lifelong friend, hid him in his house. Did any one betray the runaway's retreat? I do not know, but two days after his arrival an under-officer and four men came to M. Dunard's, one from the street, the others from the garden, turned the farmer, his wife, and the maid out of doors, conscientiously searched the house, found the fugitive, and took him away. We saw the poor man pass between two gendarmes on horseback. He looked desperate; his hands, tied to one of the stirrups, were quite blue. But immanent justice, dear to the Germans, had a watchful eye. Here it was even imminent. A good citizen of Morny was just coming back from the forest, with his donkey put to a cart, loaded with wood. The ass saw a procession, which he thought unseemly, and proclaimed his opinion in the way usual to his kind. The horses, frightened by the loud hee-haw, reared and fell back. A military motor-car which was approaching could not stop in time, and gave a sudden lurch, followed by a general confusion. Horses, gendarmes, donkey, cart, and logs fell topsy-turvy to the ground. Oh, the poor prisoner with his tied-up hands! Well, he alone came off safe and sound. He alone, and the donkey of course. Gendarmes, horses, and driver got up lame to the right and left, and more or less injured. After some bandaging the Germans took their prisoner away all the same, but the interlude had given a few minutes of intense joy to many people.

For a long time we were afraid that the men of the village would be all taken away. We knew that in many northern places the male population had been carried off to fill up German prisons. When would they do the same in Morny?

"When the Germans withdraw," was the general answer.

And the expectation of this day filled us with a mixture of joy and dread. The day came, and the Germans did not withdraw. One morning all able-bodied men were summoned to the "mairie." They were taken in herds to Laon, and shut up in the citadel; for two nights they slept on the floor and had to eat a nameless stew. On the third day of their absence, towards evening, a joyful rumour spread in the village. "The men are coming back! the men are coming back!"

Women and children rushed out to meet husbands, sons, and fathers, and the noisy troop came back home, and stayed there.

We thought ourselves crushed with grief. What seemed to us most unbearable was the want of news. Every family had one or several of its members away at the front, and we asked over and over again, are they dead, wounded, ill?

And we knew no more of what happened in the invaded country, in Lille, St. Quentin, or Rethel, than of what happened in San Francisco, Paris, or Pekin. Every village was an island carefully isolated from the rest of the world, and kept up very few relations with the nearest towns. On the other hand, we can think only with compassion of the everlasting threats hanging over our heads, of the uninterrupted plunder, of the vexatious measures, which left us no rest. Yet all this was bearable compared with what we had still to support! First the bad season was coming; soon we should suffer from the cold, since fuel was rare; and even from hunger, since bread was scarce. One day Colette cried out: "Oh, mother, look! Winter is coming; the Christmas roses are in bloom." On the very same day we heard that the village had a new commandant. Until then Morny had given hospitality but to convoys and troops of the reserve. We should now have to deal with soldiers on active service. About a hundred Death's Head Hussars settled themselves in the big farm on the Laon road, and their lieutenant became the supreme chief of the commune. The invaders certainly organised their government. Every village was provided with a commandant, who grew more and more powerful. You can imagine how these people were puffed up with pride. Just think of a lieutenant, a small country squire, owning beneath the sky of Pomerania three acres of barren, unfruitful land, who all of a sudden sees himself absolute master of a rich territory of 1500 souls. It was enough to turn his head. Von Bernhausen was the name of the one we got. He was of an historical family, and gave himself out to be a rich cattle-breeder. He was a huge fellow—Geneviève and I reached to his waist—aged about twenty-six. Boldly cleft from heels to chin, he bore on his interminable legs a kind of shortened bust, a gallows head with small eyes, a little nose, still less forehead, a great deal of cheek, and still more of a thick-lipped and ever damp mouth. This ugly lieutenant was a thorough glutton, and the poultry-yards of Morny had many proofs of it. As he did not walk very upright, his coat, which was always greasy, formed in front a mass of horizontal creases that might have aroused the jealousy of an accordion. Two days after his arrival he was nicknamed Bouillot for short, a diminutive of Crabouillot, which means in the *patois* "dirty." Self-confident, conscious of the rights his title and name gave him, this lordly personage went to Laon, or received his superiors, without any change for the better in his dress. The peasants said he was the cousin of the Emperor. We shall be more modest, and be content with saying that his forefathers are very well known in Germany and other countries. His faults were overlooked in high quarters, and I leave you to imagine the benefit he reaped from his post and the way he understood comfort, good cheer, and service. To begin with, he requisitioned a capital cook of the place, and told her that she was to exert all her skill on behalf of Germany. A salary was quite out of the question. Early in the morning he was often to be seen in a poultry-yard, busy selecting his birds among the few geese, ducks, and fowls that were still there, and then: "I want this to be at the farm at ten o'clock." If the owner timidly asked for a note of hand, the officer turned short round and shouted in his face: "I told you to bring me this at ten o'clock."

Once he came to M. Lantois and said: "I want the carriage you've got; bring it to me." The farmer, after a moment's hesitation, dared to pronounce, too, the words "note of hand."

"I shall give none; you don't want any; your cart won't get lost."

Suddenly the man went into a regular rage, tore up and down the yard, uttered yells of anger, and bellowed:

"I am the commandant of this village! I can do everything I please! You must give me all that I want!"

He took the carriage away, and two days later it was lying broken in a ditch.

Thus we had nothing to do but suffer these exactions. We had marched straight back towards the Middle Ages. We were bondsmen, attached to the soil, as no one was allowed to leave the land. The mighty and powerful lords had re-established all feudal rights. They took toll for the shortest journeys, sold our own flour in common mills, from all men required villein service. They were careful not to forget certain prerogatives, and thought they had a double right to the favour of all women and girls, being at once lords and conquerors. Accordingly a house like ours seemed to them especially created for the pleasure of the King of Prussia's officers.

And yet how careful we were to hide ourselves! From the moment that the hussars haunted the country, Mme. Valaine did not allow us even to go and fetch the bread. The bakehouse was deemed too far off, and the garden sufficient for exercise. Mme. Lantois' farm, M. Lonet's house, a hundred yards to the right, a hundred yards to the left, were the longest walks we were permitted to enjoy. And before risking our nose in the street we took a rapid survey.

"No Prussian is to be seen? Good, I will risk it."

Despite these precautions, we were forced to receive frequent requisitioners or perquisitioners, and we soon heard that the soldiers called our habitation "the house of the pretty girls."

Fatal name! No sooner had Lieutenant von Bernhausen heard it than he despatched to us his second self, the sergeant Marquis, *alias* Sainte-Brute. For, as no one can doubt, Bouillot had about him worthy followers—this sergeant, Sainte-Brute, as much dreaded as his master, and a few other hussars, "he loved above all," as Victor Hugo says. Was it "for their great courage and their huge size"? I do not know, but for their ferocity in any case, their want of scruple, their hatred of France. Among them he reckoned "the Blackguard," a vicious lad with a pink and white complexion; "Rabbit's Paw," who looked like a degenerate fool, with a long bovine face; and the "Japanese," whose slanting, spiteful eyes were always laughing.

One evening, when all the inhabitants of the village had locked up their houses, a loud ring was heard at our gate. This made our hearts beat quickly.

"So late, O heavens! what do they want?"

We ran out, and soon showed in Sainte-Brute, attended by two soldiers. Like a conqueror he walked up the steps and entered the dining-room. He showed his best graces, his small moustache was curled up, his cloak put on after the Spanish fashion, his cap roguishly set on one side. A paper in his hands, he made a show of his fingers—he had well-kept nails, I must acknowledge. Mme. Valaine, Geneviève, and I stood and waited. A night-light illumined the scene.

"It is six o'clock," the under-officer announced. "Everybody must be at home. I want to see all the inhabitants of this house."

Come along, then! Let him count us; set the family in a row; it is fair-day; the Germans are amusing themselves!

The girls came in reluctantly with fury-flashing eyes.

Sainte-Brute thought the light too weak; he pointed his electric lamp at us, and one after another scanned our hostile faces; then he declared:

"The 'population' say that you often go to Laon without passports."

"If the population say so, it is lying. In the last ten days we have been but once to Laon, and here is the passport you gave us yourself."

"Hum, hum, the population...."

Sainte-Brute seemed to hesitate. The Blackguard plucked him by the sleeve:

"Come, come...."

"Mind, you have had your warning," the sergeant concluded by saying. "It is strictly forbidden to travel without leave from the military authorities."

Satisfied with his speech, the man withdrew. He took a careful survey of the lobby, opened the kitchen door, cast his light in every direction. He seemed to take a great interest in the copper of the saucepans. Yet he went out, followed by his acolytes. Their steps resounded in the street. We bolted the door, and an hour after had not recovered from the emotion.

What was the meaning of this visit?

The next day, under the pretence that he wanted to see what lodging we might give to chance soldiers, Bouillot himself came to see us with his train. At his heels was a big hound. Percinet did not believe his eyes. A dog in his yard! He flung himself on the intruder; a furious fight began; with his heavy boots the officer gave our poor collie many a hard kick, and at length knocked him down.

"Brute!" cried Colette, in an indignant tone.

Herr von Bernhausen replied with a smile. He was kind enough to believe the epithet was meant for the dog.

While Yvonne was taking away the poor limping beast, the lieutenant asked a few questions, then turned on his heels and went away. Once in the street, he lifted up his long arms, as if to say:

"There is nothing to do in this house!"

He had pronounced our sentence; the reign of terror had begun.

Were I to live a hundred years I should never forget the weeks of mental torture I owe to the Germans. Ten times a day terror sent all the blood of my veins to my heart, and made my legs shake under me. Ten times a night terror awoke me panting from my sleep, with my eyes swimming with tears.

Is any one coming in? Is there a knock at the door? Is the bell ringing?

For we had been officially chosen as butts, and at any time, under the most futile pretences, two or three hussars, or a troop of them, used to enter the house. They well-nigh forced the gate open, or broke the bell, and roaring out horribly one day required harness we never had, another maintained they would find in our garden their horses broken loose. Then, at nightfall, when our neighbours were all shut up in their houses, they would come back and stay in front of the house. More than once they arrived drunk, and all the while they made a frightful uproar, shouting, calling after us, kicking in the gates, knocking at the shutters with their revolvers, and trying to break them open. If from upstairs we asked what they wanted, they answered with threats, insults, and invitations to come down.

This life was a very hell.

For weeks we kept a ladder raised against the wall so that if the soldiers, more intoxicated than usual, managed to force a shutter open and entered the house we might escape. Thanks to a small pent-house built on the other side of the wall, we could in a few steps be in Mme. Lantois' orchard.

The farmer's wife had said to us:

"Do come in case of an emergency. The doors overlooking the garden are never locked, and if you were pursued my husband and son would take a hay-fork to defend you."

Colette, who now slept in the big room upstairs, had a hatchet nigh at hand.

"Oh," she said, "if they got up to my room, I would split two or three heads before I jumped out of the window!"

Of a certainty we had a very large share in the distribution of cares, yet the sun shone—or rather the wind blew—for every one. It is useless to say that the hussars were prompt of hand, and were not always satisfied with threats. One day Lieutenant von Bernhausen had a mind to go to Laon with his retinue. He sent for the Mayor of Morny:

"Make haste, I want three coaches put to at eleven o'clock. Be off!"

Bewildered, the Mayor hurried away to carry out the order. Where would he get three coaches whose wheels would hold together, three horses whose legs would not shake under them, whose backs would not be covered with bruises and scabs, when the farmers were all eaten out of house and home? Besides, the less sorry jades were out in the fields at that time of the day. By dint of researches and efforts, three decent coaches were got together at length. But it was half-past eleven.

For thirteen minutes the commandant had been making the air echo with the thunder of his wrath, and when he saw the Mayor red in the face and out of breath, he rushed towards him with a stick, and vigorously beat the shoulders of the unfortunate magistrate.

Such is the proper way to deal with French people.

Let us be just. The following day the same Bernhausen dusted the jacket of one of his own soldiers, who had ventured to kick a civilian. Yet it is worth remarking that the rascal did not get punished on account of the ill-usage inflicted on a defenceless person, but for the insolence he had shown by encroaching on his superior's rights. Gold lace alone empowers you to distribute hard thumps and blows.

One farm on the Laon road, being in a conspicuous place, had to suffer particularly from the plunderers and requisitioners who happened to pass by. One day Mme. Vialat could not succeed even in giving her sick child something hot. As soon as anything was ready the soldiers rushed forward, took it away, and laughed at the thought that they had played a nice little trick.

There remained in the house a certain number of sheepskins, carefully prepared, and not less carefully hidden. One day the hussars discovered and laid hold of the treasure. The farmer lost his temper, and tried to defend his goods. Too many things had already been stolen; he required a note of hand; but Sainte-Brute never gave notes of hand. Things were growing bad; the farmer could not keep down his anger, and gave the plunderers a piece of his mind. The soldiers threw themselves upon him; Mme. Vialat and her niece ran to the rescue.

"They might have killed him," the young girl told us. "I came and stood before him."

The brutes gave her a sound slap on the face, struck her aunt with the butt-end of their guns, and on their own private authority carried away the precious skins.

A young shopkeeper of the village, Mlle. Grellet, objected to a close search into her own linen. The soldiers had no chance of success, as they were looking for a missing wheel. But the sergeant pretended that no one dared withstand his will, and with a hoarse laugh he rudely knocked the girl about.

Indignant, she struck him on the face. She was directly knocked down, her features belaboured with clenched fists, and justice was demanded of the commandant. The poor girl was immediately sentenced to three days' imprisonment. We saw her taken to the "mairie," she was shaken with sobs, her bloody face all bruised and swollen. She was guilty of having inflicted serious ill-treatment on the person of the rosy, smiling, and triumphant sergeant who was accompanying her.

As to ourselves, the witnesses of these chivalrous deeds, we looked on, with our fists clenched, with our teeth grinding, with tears of rage in our eyes ... and never uttered a word.

It was no use crying for help. Our very prayers seemed to rise to an unrelenting God, and we could but murmur:

"Father, Father, why hast Thou forsaken us?"

It was the reign of terror.

"Ah, Madam," said a woman all in tears, whose husband owned a merry-go-round, "they have just requisitioned our mechanical organ. Ah, Madam, such a beautiful 'music,' for which we had given four thousand francs—all our savings! They have taken it to amuse themselves. And how furious they were! When they are well spoken I don't mind it so much, but when they look so angry I tremble like a leaf."

It was the reign of terror.

"When I see them coming," another neighbour declared, "it makes my blood run cold."

M. Lonet himself acknowledged that he never saw Prussians enter his house without an inward thrill of fear.

"Whom will they harm to-day?" we thought. "People, animals, or things?"

It was the reign of terror.

When the invaders alarmed strong and courageous men, I, who am not a thunderbolt of war, how could I put a good face on the matter? Geneviève, on the other hand, was more indignant than frightened, but, as to myself, I was frightened to death.

It was the reign of terror, terror, terror. And you do not understand the meaning of this, you who have not rushed to your light to blow it out for fear its pale glimmer would betray your presence, who have not stopped panting in the dark to listen to angry yells uttered close to your windows, to hear your shutters shake and creak under the assailants' blows—you who have not realised that you are a woman and weak, and that a dozen brutes will seek more than your life if they succeed in their design. You do not know what it is like, but we know it from sad experience, and if the horrors that have overwhelmed other places have been spared us, at least we have felt their envenomed breath, and our bodies and souls have not yet set themselves free from the poison.

CHAPTER IX

Thus ground down and sunk in grief we reached the end of the year. You must not think that we were as yet urged to desperation. The courageous inhabitants who, after hours' waiting, got a passport to go to Laon always came back with the most comforting information.

"The news is very good ... very good. I should not be astonished if the Germans went away in a short time."

The farmer's wife of the "Huchettes" who daily took milk to Laon—so many bottles were requisitioned for the Red Cross—mysteriously said with her forefinger lifted up:

"I have good hope, good hope, that 'our French' will be back before the 1st of January."

And the cannon was ever booming; its voice cheered us; we never got weary of listening to it and studying it. Once we even believed that it promised our deliverance. It was the 21st of December, at about eleven in the evening. Geneviève and I were gloomily reading books held quite close to the light, when Colette knocked at our door and appeared in her nightgown:

"Come, come, a battle is being fought just now, don't you hear the cannon? It is roaring louder than ever."

On tiptoe, for fear we should arouse Mme. Valaine from her sleep, we went upstairs. Colette's window was wide open; we squeezed together in the narrow space. Both Geneviève and I got upon the window-sill and leaned against the frame, whilst the others pressed against the rail in front. And there, half-dressed, unconscious of the cold, we eagerly watched the horizon. The action took place in the direction of Vailly. In fact, the cannon was roaring with a rage never yet heard. Its near or distant rumbling never ceased for a second, and the bursting shells succeeded one another uninterruptedly. When certain pieces of ordnance were firing off full volleys, we felt a quivering all about us, and on the writing-table the penholder jingled against the crystal of the inkstand. Our bodies, our souls thrilled with enthusiasm, and the battle awoke an inward echo. With our minds' eyes we eagerly watched the place where great things happened. Our hearts flew onward to meet those who seemed to approach us!... Oh, come, come!

Our eyes were riveted on the horizon in flames, where ever-renewed flashes showed a red undulation marked with blue spots, or streaked with the lights of five turning beacons. We saw the shells burst, above, below, to the right, to the left. The cannonade seemed to slacken. Listen! listen! A soft breeze brought us the thrilling sounds of sharp firing, the crackling of machine-guns. Then the hollow voice began again, and drowned the others.

"Oh," Colette cried out, wringing her hands, "to think that our brothers, our hearts' blood, are over there! They are fighting ... they sink to the ground ... they are wounded ... they are dying...."

We trembled, we bit our lips, we said in a murmur:

"If only they were going to break through, if only they came back...."

"Oh, come, come!..."

The whole village was wide awake. Through attic windows anxious faces were peeping; restless people stood at their garden walls. From house to house they exchanged impressions.

A young woman of the neighbourhood had rushed to her coffee-mill at the beginning of the action, and by the time her old father went to the garden to unearth a precious bottle of *marc*, she had ground all her small reserve, so that "our French" might have hot coffee on reaching the village!

Alas, our hopes were once more hoped in vain! Little by little the firing grew fainter, the cannon less audible; the flames and the lights died away; and suddenly silence and peace fell upon the village. The extinguisher was dropped on us again. Speechless and gloomy we went to bed at two o'clock in the morning, with limbs and souls chilled, and we did not even try to seek sleep.

The civilians were not the only ones who thought the French likely to come back. The hussars had spent the whole night on horseback, ready, if their brothers-in-arms withdrew, to go at full speed to the north: such were the orders in case of an alarm—at least they said so. Officers, under-officers, and soldiers were all the more grieved with the disturbance as they were going to feast and make merry all night in order to keep Christmas, and were looking forward to such a junketing as they had never dreamed of in the Marches of Brandenburg. The lieutenant had visited all the farms of the village, felt a hundred fowls, and chosen the plumpest and the tenderest. The feathered tribe were waiting for their last hour in an adjacent shed.

But now to whom would the inheritance come?

"My beautiful fowls," the officer muttered between his teeth, "my beautiful fowls! Who will eat them? How many a slip is there 'twixt the duck and the lip!"

The alarm over, Von Bernhausen had not yet recovered his serenity. At break of day he summoned his host, the farmer, the cook, and the cook's boy, ordered them to slay, pluck, and roast directly all that bore comb or webbed foot.

"At eleven," he declared, "we shall eat them every one."

They ate them every one. Crammed to the brim, greatly pleased with themselves, the hussars strummed on their paunches: "'Tis so much gained!"

There is no need to say that they began their feast again on Christmas Day. In order to celebrate this godly day according to old customs, soldiers of all arms and all localities had looked everywhere for fir-trees. They were not satisfied with small ones, and in our wood, near Bucy, they lopped eighteen beautiful Norway pines; they did the like in other private estates, and even in a public place of Laon, where the beheaded trees cut a very sorry figure, you may take my word for it.

Their Christmas Eve supper was very merry, at Morny at least, and till a late hour of the night we heard the noise of dances, laughter, and shouts, mingled with women's voices. We civilians spent a poor trembling Christmas, whose bitter sweetness was made up of fond thoughts of the absent, and sad remembrances of past years. Christmas ... peace on the earth ... Christmas ... all the pleasures of our childhood recurred to our memory.... Good-will to all men.... Christmas, the feast of the one that said: "Love one another." And the strong still grind down the weak, hatred and bloodshed prevail everywhere!... The irony of the day brought to our lips a bitter taste.

On the 31st of December every one had gone to bed as usual; the people were but slumbering as they were now wont to, when out burst a sharp firing accompanied by loud shouting. Every one sprang up, all windows flew wide open, cries arose:

"The French!"

"Listen...."

"Hoch! hoch!"

Oh, despair! they were but the Prussians cheering the New Year. Even when they enjoy themselves, these people are not harmless. Their guns were loaded with balls, which passed through several shutters; it was a miracle that no one was hurt.

If that New Year's Day was not a merry one, it brought with it hope that is inseparable from everything at its beginning. Deliverance! that was what we wished one another. And we not only relied on the New Year to bring it, but to bring it without great delay. Fortunately this assurance gave us a moral satisfaction, for our material rejoicings were very scanty. In most houses, in ours for instance, meat did not appear on the table any more than it had for many a day. Only a few farmers succeeded in putting a chicken in their pot without the knowledge of the Germans. For it was understood that all fowls were requisitioned. Their owners had a right to look after them and to feed them, but not to eat them. At the butcher's horse-meat was sold—coming of course from animals killed at the front—and sometimes some coarse beef, which was obtained by large bribes from soldiers employed at the slaughter-house. Rather than feast upon such unappetising and expensive meat, we preferred to eat boiled vegetables. Sometimes frogs' legs varied the monotony of our daily menu; some of our neighbours managed to buy venison, poachers being not rare in the German army; and soldiers there were who profited handsomely from roebucks, which they killed when the officers turned their backs.

But these few windfalls did not make up for the lack of many things, hitherto looked upon as indispensable. And what was our alarm on hearing once that bread itself would run short! On a certain Saturday the people who went to fetch flour came back with their carts empty; likewise the following week. No more bread! This bad fortune had been long foreseen, and to provide against it we had dried slices of bread in the oven, and thus filled many and many a tin. But seven persons are not long eating up a reserve of this kind. So by a recipe, which all the village knew, a dough was made of mashed potatoes and a little flour—every one had managed to lay by a few pounds of it—and these thin cakes, baked in the oven, bore some likeness to the food we missed.

Other villages were even less fortunate than ours, and had no bread at all—officially at least—for a very long time. The farmers who had contrived to hide corn had to grind it in a coffee-mill or with the help of a mincing-machine, and the ovens—long unemployed—were again turned to account when no Germans were present.

On the whole our village did not starve now, as it had starved during October and November. A few peasants had mysteriously dug up their potatoes, and sold them just as mysteriously. Besides, through the Mayor's clever management, the Germans consented to our buying from them a certain quantity of rice, salt, and sugar. These goods, we heard, were the remainder of provisions sent to the commissary of stores. They were sold on stated days, and every inhabitant was entitled to a kilo of rice, a pound of sugar, half a pound of salt, once a fortnight. It was a sheer pleasure to chaffer with the invaders; they demanded gold as payment for their scanty revictualling, but later on they had to content themselves with a sum partly in gold, partly in silver. They played hang-dog tricks on the middlemen. Once the Mayor was informed that such and such goods were to be had to the amount of three hundred francs. Greatly pleased, he paid in golden cash. He was kept waiting one hour, then two, then three. At length he was told that he had been deceived. The provisions were not nearly so abundant as they were first thought; there was scarcely a hundred francs' worth. The difference was to be given back to the purchaser. And, indeed, two hundred francs were returned to him, but the two hundred francs were paid in German notes!

For three weeks we had no bread at all; then the Germans vouchsafed us flour of their own, so much a day; a loaf made with this powder took the shape of a small, flat, brown and heavy crown, which gave us such acute pains that we often preferred being hungry to having our fill of this dough. We were all poor wretches and starvelings, but we were fellow-citizens, and we arranged to keep a certain level of the provisions. But a hundred times more wretched and starving were the refugees who, when their villages were burned to the ground, had been shared among the communes throughout the country. For months they had neither house nor home, and about forty of them had taken shelter in Morny, where they were huddled in one or two empty houses, lived but scantily, and slept on straw. Several died during the winter. Laon was also overrun with hundreds of those poor fugitives, and throughout the town you were assailed and pursued by small ragged beggars who made you think of Naples or Marseilles. The poor things moved your pity the more deeply as you were compelled to think:

"Such is perhaps the fate that is awaiting me."

Indeed, nobody was sure that a whim of the Germans would not turn him out of doors. It was seen more than once. So many things were requisitioned. First of all, the invaders laid the absent people under contribution, and as long as their houses had window-panes and furniture, they were sufficient for the plunderers. But afterwards? A large manufacturer of the neighbourhood, M. Vergniaud, had built a castle a few years before in the Renaissance style, and filled it with Renaissance furniture. When the rumour of invasion came, the owner took flight with his household. The first soldiers quartered in the villa knocked off the sculptures of the cupboards with axes, while others carried away what pleased them. We saw a china bath taken away to the trenches; it contained two small pigs. In the luggage of an officer who lodged in our house there were damask curtains, plates of old Strasburg ware, and even children's clothes, all of which came from that castle.

In the end what remained of the furniture was taken to the station, loaded upon railway trucks, conveyed from one place to another for a fortnight, and then sent to an unknown destination. To Germany or to the trenches?

Some officers, who lived in Laon, did not approve of the costly furniture about them, so they sent for three civil prisoners. The orders they gave them were simple: "Take the furniture into the garden and break the whole in pieces with your axes; it will serve as firewood." The house thus cleared, these gentlemen had but to look elsewhere for the wherewithal to furnish their rooms.

If uninhabited houses contained nothing useful, they requisitioned what they wanted from those who had stayed at home. Von Bernhausen soon discovered that he might find many things in our house of which he could make a good use. First, he was sure that such people as we are overfed ourselves. In fact, boiled potatoes, boiled carrots, boiled beans, boiled rice, barley coffee, and nut-tree tea are everywhere looked upon as choice dainties. So one day the street was ringing with drunken shouts. We kept silent, attentive to the least sound. "Will they go by without worrying us?" Oh no! An angry hand rang a full peal, whilst heavy boots beat rhythmical imprecations upon the gate. The key had hardly turned in the lock when Sainte-Brute rushed in like a madman, with two other hussars. Geneviève jumped to avoid the shock of the man:

"Oh, he is drunk!"

These words increased the fury of the non-commissioned officer:

"Drunk ... drunk ... I am drunk.... You dare say it again. It is an insult to the German army.... You will see ... you will see...."

Geneviève, with folded arms and head erect, as white as her woollen jacket, faced the non-commissioned officer. She looked at him with such an air of scorn and defiance that the maniac broke into a new fit of rage. Bending forward, his fists clenched, his eyes starting from their sockets, crimson-faced, he foamed at the mouth, he spat out: "Drunk ... you said I am drunk ... you will go to prison ... you will be put on bread and water ... sleep on straw ... it will serve you right ... drunk ... drunk...."

Around us stood the frightened family. The "Blackguard" sneered, and "Rabbit's Paw," when the madman ceased, took up the burden of abuse. All of a sudden the sergeant altered his mind and sprang into the cellar. His companions followed him, and we heard them upsetting empty bottles and shaking casks. "You may seek for wine, my fine fellows, and if you find a single bottle I will pour it out for you myself."

In the depths of the cellar Sainte-Brute continued to breathe forth fury, loading us with violent and obscene insults. Fortunately we did not understand much of his foul language. Then he came upstairs again in haste, rushed into the garden, and squeaked:

"Beans ... beans ... beans...."

Like one stupefied, he stopped and gazed at the lawn as if he had expected the beans to spring up at his call. There was no sign of them.

Then he turned round to me:

"Have you any beans?"

Good Heavens! There was a small sack of big white beans which we had bought last week, and out of which we hoped to get many a meal! If I deny that we have any, thought I, these people will go to the attic, and the first thing they see is the sack of beans, white and fruitful of promise.

"Hum ... yes, we have a small quantity of beans. But as we bought them, they cannot be requisitioned."

"How much have you?"

The answer came reluctantly:

"About twenty litres."

"Well, they are requisitioned; you are forbidden to use them."

The callers were about to leave, but the drunken man still wished to take Geneviève away.

"She must go to prison ... she has insulted the German army."

The "Blackguard," who was almost sober, pulled him by the arm:

"Come away, come away! These people will make a fuss, and it will be said that we are barbarians!"

Sainte-Brute was loath to let himself be convinced. At length his unsteady legs took him off, and his acolytes followed him.

"Ah!" cried Geneviève, passing her hand over her forehead with a gesture as of madness, "to think that all our life we have been respected, that we have met only polite and courteous people, and now drunken brutes may insult us in our own house! Why, they talk of putting us in prison, as though we were old rag-pickers found trespassing."

The neighbours hastened to condole with us, for the shouts of the soldiers had been heard a mile off. The next intrusion came the following day. They returned to fetch the beans. This time they were merry in their cups, they asked for their prey with smiles, and laying hold of it seemed vastly amused. On leaving they burst out laughing, and Von Bernhausen, who was waiting for them outside, roared with merriment as he weighed the sack of beans in his hand.

The Prussians are full of humour.

For three days running, no offensive. Then, one morning, the Hussars announced themselves, as usual, by shouting, kicking at the gate, and ringing violently at the bell. They walked in, went through the house, and right on to the bathroom.

"We want this bath."

It was no use protesting. The bath was taken away. Three days after it was lying smashed to pieces in the yard of an inn which the Hussars frequented, and serving as a dust-bin for the sluts of the place.

Then came the turn of the piano.

Some time before Christmas the non-commissioned officer who had previously searched the house presented himself very civilly:

"You have a piano; I want it for a few days; we shall bring it back to you after Christmas."

We could not say a word. Weeks glided by; the new year saw many dawns break; and no one brought back the piano. This harmonious piece of furniture was the finest ornament of a house which the *garde-voies* had made their home. You saw nothing but black coats there; no Hussars, no convoys. The *garde-voies* are territorials, elderly, sedate men, fathers of families, whose stoutness their uniforms cannot conceal. They smoke pipes as big as beer glasses, and drink beer out of glasses as big as kegs. They looked scornfully on those who stay at the farm, whose drunkenness and rakish habits are a cause of scandal to them.

Therefore they kept aloof, searched houses, and requisitioned goods for their own account, had their private rejoicings, and spent their evenings amid tobacco smoke and the smells of beer, while they listened rapturously to patriotic songs or even playful ditties hammered out on our good-natured piano.

One day a rumour spread. The *garde-voies* are going away. The sergeant is already off. In fact, the non-commissioned officer had left our parts, unmindful of the various pieces of furniture he had "borrowed" from the inhabitants. It was the moment to go and claim what belonged to us. The house was about to be cleared under the superintendence of a corporal, who kindly authorised us to have the piano conveyed home. He did not care for it any more; he was going away. And the instrument was put back into our drawing-room. It did not stay there for a great while. That very evening Von Bernhausen came round, greatly incensed.

"That piano which the *garde-voies* had? I hear you took it away, without asking my leave!"

"But it is our piano. It was agreed we should have it back."

"I want it; I will come for it to-morrow at ten. You had no right to fetch it without orders from me."

Bouillot withdrew, proud of himself. The following day he came back followed by a vehicle and eight men chosen among the strongest of the band. All flocked round the piano, pushing, pulling to no purpose.

"I think," said my mother-in-law, "that it would be better for the walls and for the piano if you passed it directly into the street by the window."

"Hold your tongue," answered the kind officer, "you know nothing about it. The piano will go through the passage."

It went through, and took with it much of the wainscot. The Hussars made a great deal of bustle, sweating blood and water. "Peuh!" Yvonne whispered in my ear, "those fellows have no muscles, they are but fat. Two years ago, when we moved to Passy, the same piano was carried in by a single, small, hunchbacked man. But look at that!"

Bouillot acted the busybody, moved to and fro, jested with his men, and by way of encouragement gave them sound slaps in the small of the back. It was easy to see that these people, or at least their forefathers, had tended the swine in the forests of old Germany. At last by dint of effort the instrument was taken out of the house, carried along the pavement, and hoisted into the cart. The Hussars served as horses. Gee-ho! They rushed forward, but in the courtyard the carriage gave a start, and the piano—with intent to commit suicide—bounded out and fell to the ground. After a few convulsions, and one last writhe of agony, it lay quiet.

"Oh! my beautiful Pleyel," cried Yvonne.

Some fragments of wood had been knocked off; Bouillot picked them up:

"It will be easy to mend." They gave the piano a lift, and made for the farm. All along the street we saw it skip along in its jolting car; the ravishers scoffingly waved their hands, and mocked at us until they were lost sight of behind a screen of snow.

Two days after a new joke of the same kind. Bouillot and his whole gang broke in noisily:

"I want two chairs."

"All right," my mother-in-law answered, "I will give orders for them to be brought down."

"No, I will choose them myself."

The Hussars, merry as schoolboys on a holiday, came tumbling one over the other into the rooms, meddled with everything, poked their noses everywhere. Von Bernhausen went right to the drawing-room. Those he wanted were two easy-chairs in the style of Louis XVI.—ancient silk is matchless for wiping filthy boots upon. This was carrying things too far. Now an officer had installed himself in our house that very morning, taking the place of Barbu and Crafleux. Could we not appeal to him as a last shift?

Antoinette rushed forward, and knocked imperiously at the door of the newcomer: "Sir, sir...."

She was answered by a growl. Then the door opened slightly, and a ruffled head appeared.

"Sir, an officer is there who wants to take our furniture...."

But at that very moment Bouillot approached in a whirlwind. He stopped short at the sight of his brother-in-arms. The two men eyed one another.

"Ah! hum! you here...."

They shook hands coldly. They were face to face, the one immense, the other small; both had the same rank, the same decoration. Our guest had been aroused from his afternoon nap. It was three o'clock, the right time for honest men to sleep. His eyes were swollen, his dress untidy, and his toes, vexed at being incorrect, wriggled about in his socks. Yet he undertook our defence. He did not refer, I need hardly say, to justice or to the Conventions of the Hague. He advanced a single argument, but it struck home.

"I am quartered in this house."

"Yet this house is one of the best furnished in the village; it is but right we should fetch here what is wanting."

"... These are my quarters.... I want the furniture that is here...."

At the beginning of the conference the soldiers became serious, and one after another vanished on tiptoe. Bernhausen at last resigned himself and went after them. It was our turn now to laugh at the Hussars, when we saw them go away crestfallen, and heard their chief stammer explanations.

A few days after, Lieutenant Bubenpech, whom our roof had the honour to shelter, was appointed commandant in place of Bouillot, by right of seniority. Thus ended the persecution of which we had been the victims for two months. The guests of the farm continued their misdeeds and their extortions, but they avoided our house, which sheltered a power the rival of their own. We even had the pleasure of seeing the "Blackguard" come to our house on duty, a bashful, blushing "Blackguard," and more than that, as polite as a chamberlain in presence of his sovereign.

However, in the beginning of February, we again had difficulties with soldiers, coming from the trenches. Twice a week they went through Morny with heavily laden carts. Oh, these convoys! Monday and Thursday, as early as four in the morning, the carts rattled through the village, and noisily shook their empty sides on the pavement. They stopped at the station where there were large stores of straw, and a few hours later went back to the front full to the brim. The farmers took great interest in these personages. Loads, drivers, and carts engrossed their attention.

"Whatever those lazy-bones do," cried an old peasant, "is badly done, and ought not to be done."

To tell the truth, there is an art of loading carts with straw. The first layers should be well placed and should make a solid foundation according to time-honoured rules. The Prussians' loads always stood awry, and threatened ruin as soon as they were erected. First one bundle tumbled over, a second followed, then at a turn of the road the whole pyramid sank to the ground, hurling the listless drivers headlong into a ditch. Nearly every time they came to fetch straw the loaders managed to let it fall, and we watched them rebuild carelessly another tottering heap, Of course these men were thirsty after their hard toil, and they stopped at every fountain to refresh ... their horses; as to themselves they drank anything but water.

Such is, then, the way fifteen soldiers happened to come to our house to draw water from our pump. Many buckets had been pulled up, and the men did not go. They went up and down, laughed, opened one door, then another, ventured into the garden, peeped in at the windows. Geneviève went to encounter them.

"Do you want anything?"

"Nothing at all. We are pleased to stay here because there are pretty girls in the house," answered the sergeant in very good French.

"Then, if there is no need for you to stay here, you had better go away; I want to lock the gate, we never keep it open."

And the men withdrew. Colette, who watched the scene from upstairs, said afterwards:

"It was very funny! You'd have thought that our sister was driving these fifteen big louts before her."

No sooner were they in the street than the Germans gazed at one another. Did it not look as if they had been kicked out of doors!

"Hullo! we are not people to be trifled with!"

They soon gave proofs of it. Suddenly they flung themselves upon the windows, doors, walls. We were forced to give way, and my mother-in-law opened the gate. This compliance with their wishes did not abate the assailants' anger. They rushed into the yard, and poured forth worse volleys of abuse than ever an Apache of Montmartre could invent.

"Ah," cried the sergeant, grinding his teeth in anger, "you are not tamed down here; you do not know what the Germans are! Come to Lierval; you will see there how the people have been curbed. They don't say anything now.... They hold their tongues, I warrant you...."

One of his men drew the moral of this discourse by aiming his gun at us. "Franzouss ... all shot."

They stayed two hours, strolling about the yard, muttering insults between their teeth. To complete our misfortune, the convoy spent the night in Morny. The men came back in the evening, and the commandant being away they made the most fearful row we had ever heard, from nine to eleven, and yet the Hussars were not bad at rough music.

They were not bad at many other jobs. They were acknowledged the most skilful hunters of hiding-places, and Sainte-Brute, with his acolytes, spent many a day in wandering through fields and gardens. They sought for holes that might conceal potatoes, corn, or—generally near to the houses—wine which they were so fond of. The Conventions of the Hague, it would seem, allow the invaders of a country to requisition wine, for the use of the "wounded"; so when the soldiers emptied a cellar or discovered a *cache* they declared with gravity that it was all for the Red Cross. I suppose the Germans bear a likeness to zoophytes, what one of them absorbs is profitable to the others, and when wine had been unearthed "for the wounded" the whole pack were drunk for days together. And these creatures took all—all. They destroyed systematically what they could not take away. After having despoiled us of our money, they seized corn, straw, vegetables, wine, milk, eggs. Poultry, cows, oxen, the very horses which the peasants had bought of them in a bad condition, and taken good care of, belonged to them, and they alone were entitled to dispose of them. All that was on the earth and beneath the earth, all that was growing and living—including the people—were their own property. They carried off the very paving-stones heaped up on the wayside to repair the roads. If they stay long enough they will carry away, cart after cart, the rich, fat earth of our soil, to spread over and fertilise the barren ground of Prussia. If they could find a means, with the help of their alchemists who have made a pact with the devil, they would take away our deep-blue sky in panels; they would drag along our bracing and mild air to purify the mists of the north.

As they cannot—despite their bargain with the devil—perform such feats of skill, they wreak revenge on us by spoiling our beautiful country. Our farmers were furious when they saw the Germans—the first winter after their arrival—plough up fields throughout the land, unmindful of the limits and value of the soil. And what splendid tillage was theirs! Their laziness turned up about ten centimetres of earth; they sowed seed, and put no manure; before they leave they want to exhaust the soil of which they are jealous, and which they would like to annihilate. They cut down nut trees to make butt-ends of guns, and fruit trees to amuse themselves.

In the forests they committed downright murder. Where it is worth while they cut down trees of reasonable growth at regular intervals; anywhere else they break off saplings about one yard from the ground. In the wood of Festieux I know an immense beech-tree. Its trunk can hardly be encircled by four men with outstretched arms. In its boughs a nobleman of the neighbourhood lived for several weeks at the time of the Revolution. As they found no means to fell this giant, the invaders have hewn pieces out of it all round, and cut off its upper branches. The poor tree will not outlive the invasion. On the outskirts of the villages, along the roads and brooks, the Germans cut down the beautiful trees, poplars, maples, chestnuts, which gave a poetical charm to the country. To spoil the land is the aim of our malignant foe. Truly, it will be long before songs and laughter are heard again in the wasted country. The nymphs of our groves seek in vain their verdant shades along the treeless rivulets, and flee away, sighing their elegies. Can anything be sadder than this? No epic could be more tragical, no ode could exalt our hearts more than this call, more than this immense wailing we are ever hearing. It is the very breath of our sullied, bruised, wounded country, and it will not cease until the day when her sons return, and striking her soil with their feet will say:

"Mother! O, mother! thy cause is avenged! We come back from the country of thy foes!"

PART III

"There is no one in the jungle so wise and good and clever and strong and gentle as the Bandar-log."

"We are great. We are free. We are wonderful. We are the most wonderful people in all the Jungle. We all say so, and so it must be true."—"The Monkey-People," RUDYARD KIPLING (*The Jungle Book*).

CHAPTER X

Herr Bubenpech had hardly been appointed commandant in Morny when the enemy took a new step in the organisation of the country. From that moment two or three spectacled scribes gathered together in a large schoolroom, labelled "Bureau" both in French and in German, and busied themselves with endless scribblings. They drew up lists of the male inhabitants of the village, who twice a month had to be present when their names were called over. They put in writing all the divers tasks required of the villagers. They kept an account of the allowance of food sometimes granted to the civilians. They distributed passports and they superintended requisitions. From the outset Bubenpech seemed eager to show he was hard to please. The rural constable was ordered to announce that gold was to be brought to the "bureau," where the owners would be given bank-notes in its stead, according to the simplest exchange, 100 marks for 125 francs.

Pieces of gold are not readily drawn out of the stockings. Yet a few of them had to come forth. I am afraid that since then the invaders have managed to empty them; but at that time they were only at the heel.

By mere chance Morny had as yet paid no more than the contribution of war which had been levied on the whole country soon after the invasion. Other villages less fortunate than ours had been overburdened with taxes upon the most ridiculous pretences. A poor hamlet, Coucy les Eppes, was fined six times during the space of a few months. First came the general contribution. Then a fine of half a million francs was imposed upon the canton of Sissonne, to which Coucy belongs, and every village had to pay its share. It so happened that in September some soldiers, coming back from Reims, drove their carts through Sissonne, and as their carts were loaded with bottles of wine, they drank all the way, and threw empty bottles behind them. Then came motor-cars, which punctured their tyres on the broken glass. Great scandal! The civilians were accused of having put a trap for honest Prussian wheels. Their protestations availed nothing. The canton was condemned to a fine; the canton must pay; and Coucy paid like the other communes.

When all houses were searched after the great proclamation of November, an old flint-lock, kept in memory of an ancestor, was discovered in Coucy at an old maiden lady's. It never struck the owner that she should have brought it to the Mayor's house, or hidden it. And suppose the old maiden lady had shouldered the ancient gun? It is enough to make you shudder when you think of the danger the German army might have thus incurred.

As quick as could be a few thousand francs were levied on the village which dared be subversive enough to conceal an old maid and an old gun. Even then the troubles of the poor village did not come to an end. A French aviator dropped a bomb on the station, and the bomb disturbed a few German carriages. The military authority knitted its brows.

"Why! This Coucy is talked of again! Let it have a good fine, and it will keep quiet."

For what reasons had this village to bleed itself and borrow from the town in order to pay the invader twice more, I do not know, but so it was. Morny's turn was coming. One night a barn of the farm where the Hussars were quartered took fire, and was soon in a blaze with the straw it contained. The whole village ran to quench the conflagration. We stood near-by just long enough to see the peasants put the fire out with all speed, while the soldiers folded their arms, and were pleased to be amused. Von Bernhausen and Bubenpech looked on at the spectacle. Then Von Bernhausen thought proper to rate the Mayor sharply:

"There are not people enough.... Go and fetch civilians.... Be quick...."

All the able-bodied men of the village were summoned, and they sweated while the Hussars made sport of them. The *Gazette des Ardennes*, which took the place of the *Journal de Guerre* to the very best advantage, does not relate such accidents in this wise, but I can only narrate what my eyes have seen.

Bubenpech rubbed his hands. He had found an opportunity to show his zeal. With all speed he sent a report to the Staff, upon which he depended, stating that civilians had set the barn on fire out of spite. He forgot to add that a few hours before the disaster the Hussars had burnt their dirty, lousy mattresses in the neighbourhood of the said barn, where, besides, soldiers had been seen smoking many a time with perfect serenity.

So stout gentlemen in full uniform came to Morny, and with reproachful looks stalked majestically through the streets. A chance was given us to atone for the misdeed. If within twenty-four hours information was lodged against the civilian who had set fire to the barn, the village might be forgiven. Should the contrary happen, a severe penalty would be immediately enforced. No denunciation, and for good reasons. The people were convinced that the soldiers had kindled the straw on purpose. The military authorities, grieved to the heart, imprisoned, without further delay, the Mayor and six notable persons. Then they deliberated upon the matter, and always regretfully imposed a fine of 16,000 francs on the village. They ordered the other prisoners to be set at liberty after three days, but kept the Mayor under lock and key for two weeks, ill fed and worse lodged. M. Lonet and another municipal councillor went the round of the village, and did their best to get the sum required. They managed to collect 12,000 francs, and the Germans had to be content with that for the present. They knew only too well that they would catch us again.

Besides other cares worried us. In February 1915 our houses were again searched from top to bottom. It was proclaimed that the inhabitants should declare the quantity of corn, flour, and vegetables they had in store, so that the provisions might be requisitioned according to the needs of the German army. And mysterious sacks, closed baskets, furtive barrows were seen in Morny. There was an air of haste; men passed close to the walls, went along out-of-the-way paths, up to attics, down into holes. When the day of perquisition came—the Germans believed their own eyes rather than the declarations of the natives—there were tears and gnashing of teeth. Treasures were discovered, potatoes and corn dug up. The Germans laid hold of everything; they even despoiled the very poor of their slender provisions. For instance, our neighbours, the Branchiers, a very young couple, whose joint ages were less than forty years, who had only an empty purse and about thirty kilos of potatoes, were robbed to the very last shred.

That they might not lose a single potato they carefully raked Mme. Turgau's shed all around, and seized forty, though the poor woman has four children, who do not live upon nothing. We, in our house, tired of the war, hid nothing at all. We had possessed for a fortnight four sacks of wheat, which we had bought from a farmer, who had mysteriously sold this secret hoard. Where, I beg of you, could you conceal four sacks of wheat in an honest house? Especially when you know from sad experience that the perquisitioners perform their office conscientiously. At Aulnois they had watered a cellar to make sure that the ground had not been newly dug. At Vaux they had not left twenty centimetres of a certain garden unexplored. After a long debate we decided to leave things as they were.

But if peace returns and I am able to build a house, it shall have hiding-places, wells, tanks, deep dungeons! Hollow walls shall open by means of secret springs, and two, three, five cellars shall be arrayed one beneath the other, which, in case of need, shall swallow up whole herds, to say nothing of a vast reserve of groceries.

Meanwhile, our goods being full in sight, Bubenpech, who, out of politeness, gave himself the trouble to search our house, visiting every cupboard and poking his nose everywhere, had been at no pains to discover them. He declared he was compelled to requisition the corn, but with a smile he left us our potatoes. Colette was indignant.

"Why! this fellow does not take our potatoes because he wants to be amiable! And our neighbours have been despoiled of everything! It is a shame! We must share with the others."

And we did.

A basket to right, a basket to left, a basket over the way, our provision well-nigh dwindled to nothing. After that we were in the same state as our neighbours. It is beyond doubt that some people had managed to save many things, and of course the Germans had surmised as much. Two or three days after the first perquisitions they dropped in unawares, and made very profitable visits. Mme. Turgau, for instance, had succeeded in hiding a sack of wheat, and the soldiers were hardly out of the way when she baked a loaf to celebrate her good fortune. The loaf, yellow and round, was displayed on the table, while on the ground lay the sack, saved from the wreck, and little Lucienne, a slender girl of twelve, as reasonable as a woman, was grinding corn in a coffee-mill. Near at hand a dish was already full of flour; after a second operation of the same kind it would be fit for kneading. The mother was out, the baby girl, Claire, was busy sucking her thumb, with her admiring gaze on her sister; the last-born was asleep in its cradle.

Heavy steps broke the silence, big shadows appeared on the door-sill. "The Prussians!"

The coffee-mill stopped short.

"Ah! ah!" the non-commissioned officer said, "you have corn; you stole it."

"No, sir, it is just a little bit I have gleaned with mamma."

"You stole it," replied the soldier. "Don't you know that everything belongs to the Germans? If you have corn you must have stolen it."

And the perquisitioners carried away in triumph the small sack, the beautiful golden loaf, and even the dishful of half-ground flour. On coming back, Mme. Turgau found Lucienne in tears, Claire weeping in imitation of her sister, and Jacquot, ever ready to make an uproar, screaming at the top of his voice. After these fatal visits we had still more holes to take in in our belts. Nothing was ever left on our table. The dishes, few in number, were immediately divided into seven parts, and every one thought when rising from table: "I could begin again with pleasure."

The question of light was another plague of our life. The last drop of petroleum, the last traces of linseed oil had been converted into smoke a long time before. We were obliged to use horse-oil like our neighbours.

Horse-oil! Oh! for ever and ever nauseous remembrance! Always half-congealed, brownish, sticky, stinking, it made its bold manipulators sick for an hour.

This oil was manufactured by a man in the village when he could procure a dead horse, not too lean; and as we could not get as much as we had wished, we had to be sparing of it. The villagers simply poured it into an old sardine box, and the wick, leaning against the metal brim, smoked, charred, smelt nasty, and gave as little light as possible.

In spite of our efforts, this half-liquid matter energetically refused to ascend in the lamp; and we were forced to let it burn openly in a receptacle of some kind or other, and to support it by an ingenious system of pins. In fact it was so ingenious that the wick was swamped in the oil every moment, and we were left groping about the dark room, whose air was infected with a smell of burnt flesh. Doleful evenings, still more doleful nights. We no longer slept as we had slept before the Hussars' serenades. In order to give a larger apartment to Bubenpech, Geneviève and I had to be satisfied with the "small room" which is on a level with the yard and icy cold in winter. A simple rush-mat covered the pavement; the stove was small, the fuel rare, our blanket thin—the Hussars had requisitioned two others. We went to bed shivering with cold; our hot-water bottle alone gave us a little life. As to sleep.... One does not sleep much in an invaded country; every moment some unwonted noise makes you start; and then the rumbling of the cannon disturbs you, and the thought of the absent sends a thrill through your heart.

And then you ask yourself: How long? how long? In February 1915 the end seemed to have been postponed. "Our soldiers will come back next spring," said the peasants. Resigned to fate, we all waited for their return, and long were the nights. I know people who went to bed at five o'clock, without a dinner, for good reasons, and got up at about eight o'clock. How many pangs and cares thus wandered in the darkness! Geneviève and I dreaded the shades of evening, and it was often midnight before we made up our minds to blow out the light. Many a nightmare startled us, keeping us wide awake for the rest of the night. Who shall describe the horror of the dreams dreamed during the war? The dreams of the conquered! Every night brought its own vision, but two came back with a most distressing obstinacy.

A landscape covered with snow, a great deal of snow, round-topped mountains, the wind tossing the branches of the fir-trees. It looks like the Vosges. Why? Posy, are you in the Vosges? How can the wind make such a noise through the branches? I see but one fir tree black against the gloomy sky. And I hear it thunder, yet the thunder never roars in winter. I see a crow whirling round and round before it alights. There is nothing under the fir tree. But I know something must be there. Here it is, it is black ... it is long. The crow hovers. I do not stir, my feet are sunk in the snow. Yet I come nearer, or rather the thing is approaching. Yet it is exactly what I thought; it is a dead body. Its uniform is untouched. Its face ... the eye-sockets are empty. Who is it? who is it? The crow has torn out his eyes! Yet we buried the scout in Chevregny. Who is it? Oh, God! he that is nearest to me in the world!

Posy!...

I shrieked with terror and I awoke, panting. The wind moaned through the trees of the garden, and from time to time ceased as if to allow its raging interlocutor, the cannon, to roar instead of itself.

It was impossible to try to sleep again. But we also used to dream wide awake. In the invaded country thousands and thousands of people are thus thinking in the dark. Their hands are clasped in prayer, or clenched, or convulsively pressed, or relaxed out of utter weariness. It is the hour when the absent are present. What family has not one or several members at the front? And for many months an abyss has grown between us which cannot be crossed. But at night they come back; in the dark we see the dear faces smile; we watch their familiar gestures, we hear their familiar voices. Shall we be allowed to see them again here below? Where are they? where are the strong arms that embraced me when I murmured, "Posy, I am cold."

Where are the beloved ones? The mothers are at prayers, the mothers are crying; sisters, wives, all that love shrink with horror at the sights that pass before their eyes. Where are the beloved ones? They have been dead perhaps these last six months. Their bodies may be rotting among barbed wire; they may have been blown to pieces by an explosion, or swollen by asphyxiating gas, or burnt in the flames, or crushed beneath earthworks, or riddled by grape-shot, or torn by balls. Their bodies which have been cherished, cared for, kissed! And we go on hoping for them, thinking them alive, safe and sound. When shall we know whether they are dead or alive, whether strong and healthy or moaning upon a bed in hospital?

Our souls, our eager hearts are longing for delivery, and the day it comes will perhaps bring with it the bitterest sorrows. Most families will have to mourn a dead one; the whole country will be sunk in grief: Rachel weeping for her children and refusing to be comforted. We shall be despoiled and stripped of everything; we live but for the hope of meeting again our loved ones, and how many will never come back! And while they die, we receive their murderers! They sleep under our roofs, eat the fruits of our labour, and reign over us.

The want of news, the presence of the Germans, such were the saddest things of our life. Oh, they were present, always present! It was impossible to forget them even for one moment. They pursued us in our dreams, they haunted us. How often I have found myself stretched on a road, on an icy cold road in a barren country. And men came galloping up with loud shouting, and I could not move, the cavalcade was going to crush me:

The Hussars! the Hussars!...

Once more I set up a cry; I woke up. Steps, voices resounded in the street. The officers' evening party was at an end. The key fumbled at the lock; Bubenpech was coming back. It was one o'clock, or two, or three. I heard the dogs patter along the yard, they wanted to identify the visitor. The cannon rumbled with a sluggish sound. The hours were slow, slow.

At breakfast, Antoinette often said charitably:

"Just mind what I say, mother, one morning you will see the whole of us come up singing, dancing, laughing, perfectly fit for Bedlam."

To be sure one would go mad for less. Our life was duller than any one's: fancy six women shut up in a house, having nothing particular to do, always engrossed by the same tiring thoughts. Leisure is an evil very difficult to bear in an invaded territory. You wait; you do nothing else; you seem to be in a condition that cannot go on for long. Work? To what purpose? For whose sake? And what work to do? Save the men whom the Germans have requisitioned, and who, of course, tire themselves as little as possible, every one drags out his days. The baker, the teachers, and the cobbler are the only persons of the village really busy. We envied them their occupations, as we had but our needles to fill up our free hours. Very soon we had darned our old clothes, set them to rights, and distributed them among the poor. There was a family of seven children, whose mother had just died, and whose clothes we kept in decent condition. But it was not enough. We, too, yawned our life away.

Ten times a day we cried aloud for the means of escape! Escape! To live again an active life, to see people who are not Germans, to know what is going on, to live!

A gleam of hope came: it was in the month of March, the garden was already strewn with snowdrops, primroses, and crocuses. Captivity was harder to bear than ever. One day the rural constable made an announcement. He appeared to our eyes crowned with a golden nimbus, and more dazzling than an archangel; his voice was sweeter than honey. He said:

"The persons who want to leave the invaded territory to go into other parts of France may have their names put down at the townhall with the exception of the men from fourteen to sixty."

This caused so great an emotion among us that we well-nigh quitted this life suddenly and simultaneously. We kept on the look-out for Bubenpech, when he should come home, to demand further particulars.

This Bubenpech did not please us at all. It is agreed that no Prussian could have pleased us. But on the dislike we entertain to the whole race was grafted a personal aversion to him. He was dark-haired, middle-sized, short-legged, with a solid torso, topped by a big neckless head. He had regular features, deceitful eyes, and looked something of a rake. He was said to be nearly related to a general, and he thought himself irresistible.

"How dissipated he looks," we said the first time we saw him.

And one of his soldiers whispered in Mme. Lantois' ear:

"Lieutenant, not bad! ... but many women, many women. That's not good!"

In fact Bubenpech led a most dissolute life. He soon brought confusion upon Morny, and his stay there was the commencement of a debauch that caused a scandal throughout the region.

With us he was at first all smiles. But our looks soon chilled him, and he was content with a short bow when he happened to meet one of us, which was rare, for we carefully avoided him.

"At least," we said, "he is not too dull-witted; he understands that we look sour at the Germans, and he does not want to have us punished for it."

We were candid. Bubenpech was not rude and unmannerly like Von Bernhausen, and therefore his methods were different.

All the same he bore us a grudge for having been insensible to his charms; only he looked upon revenge as a cold dish. But he swore that we should pay dearly for the scorn of the Germans, and he waited his opportunity. He was sure to seize it, even if it limped with a lame foot.

For the present, he encouraged us to go, and gave most comforting particulars about the journey, which would be an easy one. The trains would take thousands of people to Switzerland, and within four or five days at the farthest we should be in Paris. Would we go, indeed! Rather than stay behind we would have made the journey in a cattle-truck, upon our head, or on our knees. Five days to go to Paris, what is that! Even were we to spend them sleepless, even were we to starve, and be squeezed tight like sardines in a tin box!

"Who will go?" I inquired. There were some who held back.

"I stay here," declared Mme. Valaine. "Up to now the house has not been plundered; I want to keep it as it is."

"I stay here," said Colette in her turn. "Do you think I will fly before the Prussians again? Besides, I have nothing to do in Paris. I will keep mother company. I saw the French go away; I want to see them come back."

"Then," Yvonne decided, "I will stay too. Shall I go and study music in Paris when the Prussians are still here? Never. Since mother and Colette remain, I stay with them. After all, the French can't be long in coming back."

Mother and daughters insisted.

"Besides," they added, "living will be easier when you are away. If Mme. Lantois manages to give us one or two eggs or a bottle of milk, this windfall will not have to be divided into seven parts. For us, all that is left of our potatoes! For us, the provision of macaroni that is hidden in the canopy of the bed of 'our Prussian.'"

After a long discussion the thing was settled. We fell into one another's arms. Every one of us shed a flood of tears, and with feverish haste we made preparations for our departure.

At the idea that he was going to see his mother again Pierrot had turned as white as a sheet, and then had begun screaming at the top of his voice, "Mother! mother! mother!" He jumped, he danced. We had to tell him that if he were so tiresome we should be obliged to leave him in Morny, and he became as quiet as a lamb.

Our bags were soon packed, and with thrilling hearts we awaited our departure.

The announcement of the journey did not arouse the enthusiasm which the Germans had expected. Bubenpech had given us a grand and imposing picture of those evacuations *en masse*.

"We purpose," he said, "we purpose evacuating forty per cent of the civil population. Why should we go on feeding so many useless people?

"We shall but keep back," he went on, "large landowners and the workers we are in need of. At the end of the month, a train will start every day; volunteers will first go, then the necessitous."

The number of volunteers were very small. The people reposed no trust at all in the Prussians.

"Do you think," the women of the village whispered, "that they are going to take you to France? To a concentration camp rather. You may take my word for it. Some people have thus left Chauny, and now they are somewhere in the north ... out in the open country ... up to the knees in the mud...."

We laughed at them.

"But why should the Germans take charge of us? They would be obliged to feed us no matter how little they gave us."

It was all of no use. Nobody was willing to go, not even those who eagerly wished to escape.

The organisers of the convoys were amazed. They determined that certain persons should go by foul means since they would not go by fair means. The commandant of every village was ordered to eject so many persons. The number for Morny was fixed at twenty. There were two volunteers besides ourselves, an elderly lady, Mme. Charvon, and her granddaughter; both wanted to go back to Paris. Thirteen reluctant emigrants were then to be picked up among the people. Bubenpech chose at random a woman from Braye, her five small children, and her old father, then three orphan boys, and a family including an invalid father, a mother, and two little girls.

These had two sons, sixteen and eighteen years old, who would stay behind if the parents went. They raised an outcry.

"My poor boys!" the mother moaned; "am I going to abandon them like that? We beg nothing of the Germans! We want only to be left together."

She went to the "bureau," threw herself at the feet of Bubenpech, who scouted her demand with disdain, and had her kicked out of doors. The morning we were to start she pretended to be ill, and kept to her bed. The lieutenant despatched four men who took her out of bed, heedless of her resistance, and made her get into the cart, with a blanket as sole wrapper. We heard the poor woman sob while she put on her stays and petticoats in the jolting cart that took us to Laon. And the folly of it was that another woman of Cerny wished for nothing better than to go.

"Since my sister and father are sent away," she said, "I choose rather to go with them; I have no mind to stay here alone with my two babies."

It was not to be. Three persons eager to stay were forced to go; three others, nothing loath to go, were bidden to stay. Thus had our leaders settled the matter.

In other villages it was still worse. A man of Barenton set his house on fire and hanged himself rather than leave. Some persons were sent away because the Germans coveted their houses for one purpose or another. At Vivaise the wife of an adjutant was compelled to leave her well-furnished house for the reason that it pleased those gentlemen. So a blind woman and her invalid husband, both aged seventy-five, were banished from Verneuil. In tears they left their small house where they had lived happily for many a year, their garden, whose fruits were sufficient for their scanty needs.

Besides, they had a few fowls and a little money, and so they were not in the least a charge upon the Germans. Of course they expected everything to be plundered and destroyed, and, weak and old as they were, they saw no hope that they would ever come back.

We were volunteers, at one moment distressed at the thought that we left three of our own people in the lurch, at another mad with joy that we should soon be at liberty, or trembling with fear lest we should hear bad news of those whose fate was hidden from us.

About the end of March, after many tears had been shed, embraces and kisses exchanged, after the very dogs had been hugged, we found ourselves in front of the "bureau" with the other departing travellers. We all got into two big carts, and sat down on our luggage. The departures were somewhat delayed. We had to wait for the woman who did not want to go away.

At ten the carts set out.

"Good-bye, we shall see you later in Paris," Bubenpech cried.

It was the parting kick of the ass.

"Then you will come as a prisoner," replied Antoinette, laying aside all prudence. The officer broke out laughing and turned a deaf ear. With a great deal of jolting, the carts took us away, and we soon lost sight of the pale faces of Mme. Valaine and her daughters. Two gendarmes on horseback accompanied us. Thus we were enrolled among the emigrants. We alighted in Laon, and were shown into a huge hall adjoining the station. The little emigrants of Cerny were still screaming, the refractory woman had not left off crying. Pierrot felt uneasy, and hung on my arm; we dragged our luggage along with a great deal of trouble. The hall we were taken to was already crowded with hundreds of persons. From early morning the refugees had been arriving in great numbers. Long rough boards nailed upon four upright pieces of wood served as tables and benches. Besides the picture of the emperor the walls were chiefly decorated with vast inscriptions. "God with us" was not absent; nor was "God punish England," in letters three feet high. The shrieking of the urchins, their mothers' scolding overtopped the general noise. The old people looked scared, and did not know what to do. On the rough tables soldiers put platters of a sticky, greyish soup; a smell of burnt grease floated in the air. We were waiting for our turn to go to a small room where three nurses of the Red Cross were busy feeling, searching, undressing the emigrants as they pleased.

"No papers, no letters?"

At two every one had filed off before these searchers, and we were ordered to start again. So through the streets of Vaux the pitiful crowd wended its way to the station, about twelve hundred emigrants surrounded by soldiers. From their thresholds the inhabitants stared at us. Truly a more miserable herd never was seen. The Germans had chosen to send away the poorest among the poor of our villages—bareheaded women, ragged children, beggarly men, sick people, cripples, idiots. All were laden and overladen with parcels, baskets, and bundles. There were two or three carts to convey the heaviest luggage, but every one preferred keeping what was dearest to him.

We, too, were overladen. We made what haste we could among the grey crowd. We had walked a mile, I could hardly carry my bag any longer. At one moment it even dropped from my hands. I approached an officer, stiff and stout, who seemed to be the manager of the caravan.

"Sir," I besought, "please order a moment's rest.... I can't go any farther."

"No, no, no halt. If you can't carry your things, ask some one else."

Some one else! That was easy to say. I looked around me despairingly; the people were all as weary as I.

Pierrot stuck to my arm, Antoinette was somewhere in front, Geneviève was spent with fatigue. Near us a soldier seemed touched with pity.

"I am sorry I can't help you, but it is forbidden."

At length I caught sight of a big fellow who carried his fortune in a handkerchief. He was one-eyed, one-armed, but he was willing to take charge of my bag. I was then able to help Geneviève with hers. We were saved, we stopped every other minute, put down our common load, and taking it up again ran forward to fall into place.

Where were we going to? We went on, tramping through the mud, with the noise of a flock of sheep, and, to crown all, there came on a heavy rain, which the poor crying children received on their dirty little noses. We had left the suburbs, and the road now passed through the open country. At about three miles from the station we perceived an immense train of third-class carriages that was waiting for us. It was carried by storm. Each one settled himself. We were but six persons in one carriage, we and two ladies of Morny, the grandmother and the granddaughter.

We exchanged congratulations. We had been told that the journey might be difficult: one of the hardest stages was passed. We sat down to recover our breath, stretched our stiff limbs, and then looked around us. The carriages we were in had been used to convey troops; they were bedecked with inscriptions in pencil. Some without much expense of thought merely wished that "God should punish England!" Others clamoured for "the death to those pigs of Frenchmen!" Or stated that "French blood is good." Pierrot conscientiously rubbed out with his handkerchief as much as he could. After many manœuvres, marches, and counter-marches the train decided to start. It was about four o'clock. Oh, memorable hour! We saw the gate of our prison open a little! Was it possible that we were going away? Was it true? Could we say in our turn, "within four days, Parisse!"

We were made with joy; we kissed one another; then we thought it wise to put our things in order. This carriage would doubtless serve us as a shelter as far as the Swiss frontier, perhaps for two or three days. The first thing, then, was to make ourselves comfortable. Our feet were cold. Suppose we put on our slippers? No sooner said than done.

When our first joy had somewhat cooled down, and we were properly installed, we watched the landscape. The train went slowly through a dull country; the clouds seemed to crawl along the ground, and the mist moistened the panes of the windows. We had hardly gone an hour when the train stopped, and left half of its carriages in the station. Then we resumed our journey, and soon made a second halt. We could not read the name of the station we were at; we did not know even what line we were on. The engine was reversed, then stopped some time after with a loud whistle.

Soldiers went along the carriages and threw the doors open.

"Get down, all, bags and baggage."

Sudden change! In great haste we put on our shoes, tied our shawls and cloaks together, gathered our bags, and jumped out on the line. Many cries and calls were heard. At last the train emptied itself; there was a whistle, and off it moved. There we were, about six hundred of us standing on a steep bank, and wondering what was going to happen next. No station was to be seen, the country seemed deserted, pasture-land on the left, hills stripped by the winter on the right. The emigrants, uneasy in their minds, bustled about; women fell a-weeping; relations sought one another; an old man bent with age, and walking awry like a crab, moved to and fro. "My wife, I have lost my wife." Thus he moaned to himself, looking for the weak arm that would hold up his greater debility.

The babies cried with cold. A sharp wind pierced us to the marrow, the rain cut our faces, and our hearts thrilled with fear, while the night fell on the anxiety of the miserable herd moving in the fog.

CHAPTER XI

Under the bridge of the railway was a high-road. The soldiers directed the crowd towards it. "Get down, get down," they cried, gesticulating all the while. Narrow steps had been cut in the dark slippery ground. The bank was very steep, yet every one ventured down; the young people held the old ones; the nimblest carried luggage and infants; the children tumbled forwards upon all fours. On getting to the road we saw a few carts waiting for bags and bundles. We abandoned ours into the hands of the soldiers. Happen what might to our things, our courage failed us to take charge of them again. Who knew how many miles we were to walk?

"Go on, go on," our guardians cried.

And the sorry band, so much the more lamentable as they were drenched to the skin, bent their bodies, and trudged off again. "What does this unexpected halt mean?" we asked one another with a mixture of curiosity and dismay. The road with hedges on each side, after we had met with a bridge and a crossing, took us to a village. Standing in front of their houses, the people, moved with pity, watched our beggarly crowd go by in the twilight, dabbling in the mud, and not knowing where they were being taken to. We did not even know the place we were in. The name we read on a finger-post did not say anything to us. At the top of the street two gendarmes on horseback divided the herd into two parts, so many heads to the right, so many to the left. We were pushed on to the right, we went to the right. We had left the village, and went down a road bordered with high trees that led into the open country.

"They were right all the same, those who said we would be landed in the fields," moaned a woman. Then we took a short cut between two banks. We were all over mud. At length, on the slope of the hill, we caught sight of a dark mass, a very large farm with vast outhouses. We had reached the goal. The lower windows glimmered; a few guards were seen in a room of the ground floor. We entered the kitchen, where whole beams blazed on the hearth. The soldiers bustled about. It was no light matter to settle in a short time—350 persons crowded in together in the courtyard. And they hurried over the job: so many emigrants in the house, in the barns, in the stables, in the attics.

"Straw is to be had everywhere; do as you can."

The people did as they could. Moving about kept them warm; it was their only means. We were among the privileged; we had been presented with a small room at the angle of the house, on the first story. It was very scantily furnished: a spring mattress in an iron frame, a child's bedstead, two trusses of straw.

"Pierrot, your couch would be fit for a king."

We buried him in the straw with his clothes on, and heaped clothes upon him. He was not cold; he fell asleep.

But we lay, dying with cold, all three on the narrow spring mattress, and the draught chilled us to the bone. In vain we wrapped ourselves in shawls and cloaks; we could get neither warmth nor sleep. We had brought with us a candle, and we let it burn, not without remorse, since we expected many another night of the same kind. A change of weather happened opportunely; the wind suddenly rose and swept away the clouds; we thought there would be a frost. A cold, bleak wind was howling round the house; the weathercocks creaked, the boards in the half-ruined sheds cracked, and the 350 emigrants shuddered with cold in the freezing rooms of the farm and in the draughty barns. A mile and a half away, at the sugar-mill, 360 others were shivering in halls and cellars. In the guard-room downstairs the soldiers gave a straw mattress to a poor old man who had terrible pains in the back, and who did not cease to wail the whole night long. Upstairs, in the attic, there were forty persons, among them fifteen children of charity. There was no rest to their weeping, nor to the patter of their feet. These small refugees, rather than go down the steep, black steps into a colder, blacker place, relieved themselves at the angles of the beams, and we saw with horror a trickle come from between the joists and run down our walls. Twice heavy steps shook the lobby, the door opened, a voice counted us: "One, two, three, four...." The soldiers were going their round. Half-frozen, we ventured downstairs to go and warm ourselves in the kitchen. But it was already crowded with about forty women with their babies, either in front of the fire or squeezed together on the benches. The air was unbreathable, so we went back to our icy chamber. Benumbed with cold, our limbs gathered up together, our chins on our knees, our feet stuck in our muffs, with a sore throat and a giddy head we made up our minds to wait for the morning, to take stock of our situation, and to find out in what place fate and the Germans had deposited us.

In the whole Thiérache, teeming with lovely hamlets, I warrant that there is no other so pretty as Jouville. It is perched half-way up the hill on the high-road to Guise, and its houses, first set in a straight row along the road, soon take a short-cut, and then descend the vale, where they meet with the purling Serre. They dawdle there in small knots, and storm a second hill, topped by a white steeple-crowned church. This building is not in the least handsome, yet it sowed dissension among the inhabitants. Jouville-East-Hill laid claim to the pious edifice; Jouville-West-Hill got it. Jouville-East-Hill forthwith took to free-thinking, flung itself into the socialist party, and swore it would never cross the Serre to gratify the spiritual needs of its souls. On the other hand, Jouville-West-Hill took a most serious turn, swore only by holy-water sprinklers and stoles, and sang nothing but vespers and matins. Jouville, in ordinary times, gives itself wholly up to cultivation of apples, to cattle-breeding, and to wicker-weaving. Each occupation adds a feature to the village. The apple trees fill the well-kept orchards that hem it all around; those meadows that stretch afar off feed the cows, and the willows, which will presently be converted into baskets, form thick hedges and make a draught-board pattern in the fields. The village, indeed, is packed with osiers, cut, tied in bundles, placed upright along the streets, and watered by the brook. So they grow green, and are covered with catkins, just like their brothers that have not been cut. The houses of Jouville are small, red and white, beneath a slate hood; their windows laugh a roguish laugh. On their roofs are fantastic weathercocks, and in front of them small gardens, in which box-trees flourish, cut into shapes. In short, Jouville looks at once simple and smart, modest and satisfied, and its mere aspect should cheer up the way-worn wanderer. Though this rustic Eden pleased us, we had no mind to take up our abode in it. The day after our arrival, we managed to ask an officer:

"What is the matter? What are we doing here?"

"Oh, the departure has been postponed, the organisers of the convoy are not in agreement."

"But how long are we going to stay here?"

"Not longer than a few days; you need not be afraid."

Although we were forewarned, our simple minds would not believe in duplicity. We were reassured.... A few days would soon glide by. When a soldier talked of a whole week, he astonished us. The chief cook in the kitchen, where he was superintending a swarm of busy scullions, dared to murmur three weeks, and he was hooted at by everybody. In the farm and in the sugar-mill the emigrants settled themselves as well as they could. A pitiful place, in which straw was expected to do everything! The straw served as seats and mattresses, it served as blankets, it served as shutters and padding. Nothing but straw to preserve oneself from the cold. And the cold was terrible. I think that we shall never suffer from anything as we suffered from the cold in Jouville. It was the icy chill of the seventh cycle of Hell, the chill that pierces you to the very marrow of the bones; it was the chill of death.... For a whole week we tried vainly to warm ourselves. The weather was clear; the wind blew with fury; the frozen ground was as hard as stone; icicles were dangling from the gutters; and the emigrants' teeth were chattering. They bent their shoulders, thrust their hands in their armpits, and wandered up and down. Some had on only rough linen clothes. From the yard they went up to the attic, from the barns to the kitchen, in quest of a bit of warmth, and they looked so cold that the mere sight of them heightened your misery.

In the sugar-mill some people had the luck to lodge in rooms that could be heated. But what of those who dwelt in attics through which the wind was blowing just as it did outside, or in cellars where they sat in a perpetual draught? The manifold misery we were the witnesses of was beyond description. I remember a room in the sugar-mill where about fifty emigrants had been huddled together—men and women, old people and children, in ill health or in good. It was a long, icy-cold room, with a low ceiling, feebly lighted by two deep windows in the shape of loopholes. At the threshold the odour of sick and dirty humanity suffocated you; the children's squalling, the mothers' scolding, the men's rough voices stunned you. In the dimly lighted room you perceived a path opened through the straw, spread out on both sides, on which you saw creatures crouched or lying. You stumbled on baskets, kitchen utensils, and bundles, had to shun wet linen and children's clothes, which the women had stretched out in the fallacious hope of drying them. When your eyes got somewhat used to the sober light of the place, you were able to single out the sick or the old people lying about the straw, the mothers suckling their babies, the men leaning against the wall. You saw their pale worn faces, their hands benumbed with cold, their thin clothes. And if you stopped to talk to them they told you many bitter, heart-rending stories. In a corner a girl of twenty was at the last gasp. She had but one lung left, and spat blood, while small children were playing about her. It was the hopeless horror of a concentration camp. Yet the commandant of the convoy, a lieutenant of the reserve, a good man after all, and the father of a family, did his best with the poor means at his disposal. Once even we saw a tear roll down his cheek at a distressing sight. The weather being inclement, he gave orders to have the greater part of the emigrants lodged in the village. The sick first, then the women and the children would be provided for. There was great excitement. A choice was made, and after three days and a good deal of writing, the farm and the sugar-mill had but a hundred occupants left, all huddled together in the few habitable rooms. The rest encamped in empty houses, slept on straw, a dozen in a room. At any rate they were under cover, and could warm themselves or accept the hospitality of the inhabitants of the village. Such was our case. Charming people gave us shelter, and placed two rooms at our disposal. We had beds. After we had spent three nights on a spring mattress and had shivered all the while, how pleasant it was to go to bed! But our apartment was not heated, had not been lived in for a long time, was impregnated with damp, and, chilled as we were, we recovered warmth only a few days after.

The life of the camp was organised after the military fashion. We were expected to obey at a glance.

In the morning, as early as half-past seven, the emigrants hastened to the sugar-mill or the farm, where each was inscribed in the place where he slept the night before. A grown-up member of each family presented the cards of those with him. In the two courtyards the emigrants filed past from right to left, and answered to their names mangled by the *Feldwebel*. Then came the daily allowance of coffee. Armed with saucepans, jugs, pots, and cups, women and urchins went to the kitchen to have them filled. They returned home, and at eleven o'clock, with porringers, pails, and coppers, they made again for the farm or the sugar-mill, to bring them back full of soup. Towards evening they wended their way a third time to fetch coffee for their supper.

About twice a week we were told in the morning that bread would be distributed at four o'clock. It was another errand to run. Every one produced his card, and received an allowance for several days. If the *Feldwebel* announced: "In the afternoon at three the emigrants will be passed in review," the whole village was in a flutter. It was no trifle to drag the old people and the babies out from their heaps of straw, to hold up the lame, to lead the blind, and to persuade the idiots. The ragged army, every day more beggarly, hobbled along to one of the rallying points. In the evening about eight o'clock the drum was beaten by way of curfew-bell. Every one shut himself up and blew out his candle, if he had one. Silence spread over the village; the emigrants, laying aside their cares for a while, fell asleep, and the night beneath its veil hid unnumbered miseries.

We were forbidden to go out of the village, and a pass was necessary if we would visit a farm half a mile from the hamlet. We were real captives, and no communication whatever was allowed with the neighbourhood. What an organisation, how many rules for such a short stay! Some people will think ... a short stay! One day followed another, and they were all alike, and always saw us in Jouville. "Next week the departure," the Germans said with unshaken impudence. Hope put us to the torture. One week followed another; we were still there. For two months, eight long and tedious weeks, we led this life of prisoners, thinking that the next day would set us free. Every morning, about eight, I left our lodging to answer to the roll-call. I was generally behindhand, and ran along the path that led to the farm every day with a hope which sank and withered. Shall we get news to-day? I hardly dared believe it; yet, my feet being frozen, my face cut by the wind, I made haste. In April the weather grew no milder, but the approaching spring was visible. A few flowers ventured to show themselves along the hedges, and the birds sang at the full pitch of their voices. Thus, while I ran along, the blackbirds in rapturous joy whistled each and all: "Fuit, fuit ... she had faith in the Germans!"

The tomtit ruthlessly and unceasingly twittered: "Sol, sol, mi ... sol, sol, mi ... you mustn't trust any one ... sol, sol, mi ... and still less the Germans ... sol, sol, mi...." And the wind jeered at me from the naked branches, and the bryony's small golden stars laughed in my face, spreading its wreaths along the path. I reached the farm, and the women gathered at once round me. If they caught sight of Geneviève or Antoinette, it was the same thing: we were taken by storm.

"Madam, madam, have you heard any news? When are we going?"

"Alas! within four or five days the officer said, but you know if he is to be believed."

A strain of protestations showered down:

"You will see, they will leave us here."

"Ah! we shall never go to free France!"

"They will take us to Germany. And we can't go on living here! Our brats have no more shoes; their clothes are in rags; it is no use to darn them, they fall in pieces."

"But the worst is that we are hungry. We could stand it, but our children, our little ones, are hungry."

And it was only too true, we were hungry, every one was hungry. What! Did the Germans not feed us? Of course they did! And on what! Twice a day each emigrant got a bowl of coffee. A bowlful or a dishful as you liked, this lukewarm beverage was not given out with a niggard hand. Lukewarm it always was, and thin too—stimulants ought not to be misused,—and blackish with a smell of mud. It was without sugar or milk, and there was no danger of feeling heavy after you had swallowed it. If the children fell a-weeping in the night, after having swallowed one cup of this coffee for their dinner, their mothers knew they were not going to have an attack of indigestion. We got bread. It was real, authentic German bread, kneaded and baked by Germans. Coloured outside like gingerbread, it was turtledove grey inside, and would have looked rather tempting but for the unbaked or mouldy parts. We supposed that rye-flour, pea-flour, and potato fecula were largely used in the making of it. Some pretended that they found sawdust in it too. I could not affirm this. I was rather inclined to think that chemicals had induced the heavy dough to rise. When new, this somewhat sour-tasted bread was nice enough, and we ate it without distrust the first days we spent in Jouville, as the bracing air gave us an appetite. Alas! it soon caused us pains in the stomach, sickness, inflammation of the bowels, in short put our digestive organs out of order. The emigrants ate it all the same; indeed they could not get enough of it. The first three weeks the Germans made a show of generosity: every person received a loaf every third day. The weight of one loaf was supposed to be three pounds, in reality it never exceeded thirteen hundred grammes. But the daily ration was sufficient, and nobody complained. Unfortunately the allowance became more and more stingy; during the last month every one received one pound every third or even fourth day. One hundred and twenty-five grammes—our daily pittance—do not represent a large slice, and the people began to clamour for food. We got soup. We were entitled to a ladle of soup by way of lunch. Shall I describe this mixture? Is it not already famous in both continents? Do our prisoners not feast upon it in Germany? It is a grey, thick substance which curdles like flour paste, whose chief ingredient is fecula. Each portion contained five or six tiny bits of meat, coming undoubtedly from over-fat animals, for we never saw a scrap of lean. A few horse- or kidney-beans, a little rice or barley, mixed with bits of straw, bits of wood, and other scraps of vague origin. Antoinette had once a real godsend. She discovered in her soup-plate ... she discovered ... how can I tell? Oh, shade of Abbé Delille, inspire me to paraphrases! She discovered one of those animalcules which ... plague take oratorical precautions! She found a louse on a hair, the whole boiled. This took away what was left of our strength, and we swore we would rather waste away, and slowly dry up, than eat such stew in the future.

"Look at this, madam, look at this hodgepodge," moaned the women. "At home we would not have given this rotten stuff to our pigs, and now we must feed upon it, and give it to our children."

M. Charvet, our host, cast a look of dismay at our porringers.

"As to myself, I should die beside this, but I would never taste it."

And yet the emigrants were obliged to eat it. From the first days of our arrival we set our house in order. Our bedrooms were at Mme. Charvet's, but we spent the whole day long at the rural constable's. The constable—a brave old man, wounded in 1870—gave up his large kitchen to us, and supplied us with wood at very little cost. In a corner of the kitchen stood a large four-post bed which received at night three of our protegées: a lady eighty-five years old, and her two grand-daughters aged seven and twelve years. Mme. Noreau, Mimi, and Miquette were respectively mother and daughters of a retired officer who lives at Coucy. Of course the officer and his two sons had not been allowed to go, and his wife had refused to leave them. But they took the chance of sending into France the grandmother and the little girls, who had greatly suffered from their life of privation. From the first evening, the sight of these helpless figures upholding one another had moved our pity. They gratefully accepted our proffered friendship and assistance. This is then the way we came to rule such a large household at the old constable's. A good oven served at once to heat the room and cook the food. For excellent reasons our stew was of the simplest. A few eggs, milk, sugar, and butter were to be had in the village, but as we had absolutely no other article of food—no meal whatever, no vegetables, no meat,—we were hungry despite custards and omelettes. I said we had tried to swallow the soup. We gave it up on account of the adventure afore mentioned after a fortnight of earnest endeavours. So much the worse, we said; we will live with empty stomachs. Many others were in the same plight. We were privileged beings, for only a few among the emigrants had a little money, enough to get something besides the usual fare supplied us by our jailers. I leave you to imagine the appetite of those who were reduced to bread, coffee, and soup in all. And remember that among them there were two hundred and eighty children under ten years who were not merely starved, but half-naked as well. The charity children were more miserable than the others. In the bitter cold weather they wound rags round their legs by way of stockings; their shoes were shapeless things, held together by string, their trousers were torn, their jackets had lost their sleeves, the girls' frocks were in rags. Their distress melted the people of the village to tears. Jouville has but four hundred inhabitants, and if their religious and political passions are lively, their hearts are none the less warm.

Jouville-East-Hill and Jouville-West-Hill showed themselves equally kind to the emigrants, and not only kind, but forbearing, and the emigrants needed forbearance. They were not the *élite*, and they were guilty of many a misdeed. M. Charvet well-nigh died of anger the day he discovered that his beloved fish-pond had been secretly rid of its finest inhabitants.

Another farmer was breathless with rage when he saw the potatoes he had planted the day before dug up in the morning.

Ah, you rascally emigrants! Of course some people will feel deeply shocked at such behaviour, and deem it a hanging matter—for instance, well-fed people, secure from danger, who afar off scowl at the Germans, the emigrants, and the typhus-smitten people with the very same feelings.

But I who was once numbered with those emigrants, who like them was a prey to hunger, I could not find the smallest stone to throw at them. And the inhabitants of Jouville, who were the witnesses of our life, threw no stone either. None of them caused our chains to be drawn tighter by complaining to the Germans. For the invaders of the north of France are very severe to the people who transgress the eighth commandment ... "Thou shalt not steal."

The Jouvillians did even better. From all quarters they brought to us and to the school-mistress of the village quantities of clothes fit to wear, if not new, and these were distributed among the raggedest refugees. We ourselves, with two others, did our best to clothe the orphan girls, and the poor things were extremely proud of their new frocks made up of shreds and patches. Some one gave them wooden shoes, and the bruised little feet could patter down the stony high-road without fear. The emigrants soon looked upon us as their private property, and thought us good for everything. An old woman would come to us, for instance, with an imperious air:

"I have been told that you are visitors of the poor, and then ..." some request followed.

The unfortunate visitors of the poor would sometimes have been glad to live on charity themselves. Well, this reminds me that we did once receive alms. We were following a path by the river, bordered with pleasant houses. It was a day of perquisitions, and the soldiers, having turned everything upside down, had left the quarter which we were traversing. A good old woman was coming from the river-side with a loaf in her hand, and the mere sight of the white, light crumb made our mouths water. The woman stopped, and said with a sidelong glance:

"You see, they don't want to know I have a little flour left. I hid my loaf in the hole of a willow tree."

She burst out laughing, and we chimed in.

I suppose she noticed our admiring gaze, for she said all of a sudden:

"Would you like to have some?"

She tripped along quickly, and, with short steps, went to her kitchen, came back with a knife, and cut off two large slices, which she held out to us. We seized the bread with an avidity hardly tempered with shame, and stammered out joyful thanks. This moved the compassion of the good woman:

"Fancy, they are hungry! What a pity! Such lovely girls!"

And so, jumping from one stone to another in the muddy path down the river, we burst into unrestrained laughter, and we devoured our bread which was the real bread, the white bread of France. We had, indeed, not a few windfalls. M. Charvet more than once presented us with one of those pretty round loaves, which he kneaded and baked himself.

We also were hand in glove with a farmer, who sometimes in secrecy let us have a few potatoes or a pound or two of flour, and thus gave us the means of adding something to our meagre fare. A few treats of that kind helped us to hold out! We looked like corpses, and we were, one after another, the victims of strange pains caused by the cold, the bread, and the continual excitement.

Most of the emigrants were ill. Eight of them died. We then had occasion to see and admire the way in which the Germans organise the sanitary service for the use of civilians. From the very first day an empty house had been bedecked with the title of hospital, and adorned with the scutcheon of the Red Cross. A large room directly opening into the street was chosen for consultations; two smaller rooms containing symmetrical heaps of straw served to receive the patients. There was a permanent orderly in the camp, and a doctor came daily from Marle. Emigrants, choose what sickness you like! You will be cared for!

And quickly influenza, diphtheria, bronchitis, inflammation of the lungs burst upon the emigrants. But we soon discovered that it was not easy to be admitted to the sick ward. I had to call four times on the officer before they vouchsafed to take away an old couple who, despite the Siberian cold, lived alone in a barn with big holes in its roof. The poor woman coughed pitifully, and her old companion could only bring her lukewarm coffee and heap upon her mountains of straw. She died two days after she had been transferred to the hospital. An old woman died, her body was carried away, and quickly another old woman took her place on the very same couch of straw. A dying woman, utterly unconscious, was left a week unattended to.

"I assure you the corner she was in was a very sink," said the man who took upon himself to clean it when the corpse had been taken away. "And my wife and children had to live in this infected spot!"

Our medical attendant was a young coxcomb, fair-haired, regular-featured, and harsh-looking. A glass was fixed in his eye. About half-past nine his carriage, drawn by a pretty horse, pulled up; carelessly he threw the reins to his groom; he alighted and penetrated his domain. His Lordship sat down in an easy-chair, crossed his legs, took a haughty survey of the patients who called upon him, and spoke in a curt and supercilious tone. He was soon held to be a villainous fellow.

"He is as wicked as the devil," a woman said, with a look of dismay.

A great many of them wanted their children to be examined by the doctor.

"I would rather die on straw than go to him for myself," a mother said ... "but, my poor little girl!"

But what was worse, the Prussian doctor did not care a fig for sick children! We had been told that every baby was entitled to a litre of milk, which one of the farmers of the village would deliver to the mother on presentation of a note of hand. But a child above two years was allowed to drink milk only if the doctor deemed it expedient for its health. A woman we knew had a little girl not yet three. Six months before the whole family had fled in a shower of bullets and grape-shot, and for nearly a month had lived in the depths of a dark stone quarry with hardly anything to eat. Since then the child had been as white as wax; she had no strength at all, and she was always staring straight before her as if she had beheld horrible things.

As she was penniless, the woman was forced to bring her child to this medicaster.

"Sir, you see my little girl ... I think milk would do her good...."

He had but to write a note, and she would have had it.

"Milk! I haven't any! I keep no cows in my house!" and the doctor burst out laughing, thinking himself very witty.

"Anyhow," the mother said with her teeth ground, "when he stays at home there is a brute beast in his house worse than a cow."

Another beggar woman had twins about two years old. One of them ate soup and bread, and throve like couch-grass. The other, who ever since the family had left their native hamlet had fed on indigestible things, and had nowhere to lay her head, had grown pale and sickly. She had ceased to run alone, took no food, and pined away visibly. Her mother brought her to the doctor.

"That child! What should I prescribe her? She is ailing on account of her being French. French children are all rickety and weakly. How am I to help it? Lay the blame on your race."

Before leaving, the little doctor sometimes gave a glance—a single one—at the rooms of the hospital, then stepped into his carriage, took up the reins, cracked his whip, and as harsh-featured as ever put his horse to a gallop.

However, some attention had to be paid to the sick. The orderly was there for that purpose. He was a big stout man, whose eyes seemed starting from their sockets. He did not like to be called up in the afternoon—he took a nap—and still less in the night. His remedies—the same for every sickness—were most economical: "Keep on low diet, apply cold compresses." Yet he understood his business well enough.

Our hostess, Mme. Charvet, a wealthy landowner, suddenly fell ill of a disquieting haemorrhage. No doctor in the village, not even in the neighbourhood. We ran in haste to fetch "Goggle-eyes."

"Oh, please, please, come!..."

"Goggle-eyes" lost no time in coming, showed assiduous attention to the patient, punctured her, and rode on a bicycle to Marle in order to fetch medicines. A few days after, a poor emigrant, mother of six small children, was attacked by the same disease. He was sent for in vain; and left her forty-eight hours without help. It was indeed a miracle that she did not depart this life.

This proves clearly that to the mind of a German, even though he be a *Sozial-Democrat*, the skin of a capitalist will ever be superior to the skin of a starveling.

The physician was not our sole caller. A few other ones came when the straw was still clean, and when we received a pound of bread a day. A stout commandant, and three days after, a thin commandant came to visit the camp. Both the stout and the thin looked extremely well satisfied, and seemed to say:

"What splendid organisation! How perfectly everything is getting on! Really, nobody but Germans could settle things like that!"

The thin commandant was escorted by the official interpreter of the camp. He never asked a question of the people, for many reasons, the principal being that he did know the language of Voltaire. The very first day he had given a sample of his talents by asking a youth:

"Hé ... vous ... combien hannées vous havoir?"

And the boy, stretching his legs and hands, stood there gazing, gaping at his interlocutor, and his whole countenance answered:

"I don't understand German!"

Therefore mimicry and loud cries bore a great part in the relations between soldiers and emigrants.

The stout commandant piqued himself on French. In one of the rooms of the farm he asked:

"You are comfortable here, aren't you?"

And the women, pickled in respect, answered all with one voice:

"Oh, yes, sir, yes!"

"You get good soup, don't you?"

"Oh, yes, sir, yes!"

"You get a lot of bread, don't you?"

"Oh, yes, sir, yes!"

"When you reach France you will tell the French you have been leniently dealt with, won't you?"

"Oh, yes, sir, yes!"

The stout commandant went away, proud of himself and proud of being one of those Germans who know how to organise camps for refugees.

"Rely on our saying how we have been dealt with," bantered the old women, the moment the officers' large backs were turned.

Another caller was a clergyman, who was quite different from the others.

The Rev. Herr Freyer was about thirty-five, he was tall, dark-haired, with malicious eyes and a turned-up nose. I must say he did his best to comply with our wishes and serve the cause of the emigrants. From the very beginning he told us that he was very fond of the French—yes, but the Germans are all fond of the French—and that his grandmother was of French descent.

"Why! then she had married a German?"

Well, let us go on to something else.

This man was certainly the cleverest German we had met, or rather the only clever one we ever met. We were all the more amazed to notice once more the abyss that separates the French from the German mind. An utter incomprehension of certain delicacies, a lack of sensitiveness, is peculiar to them. If they had fallen from the very moon, our ways of doing and thinking could not be stranger to them.

And in discussion, they are unable to cast out preconceived notions, which will ever get the better of reasoning and observation.

Herr Freyer certainly wished to show us kindness, and at every turn he told us things which set our teeth on edge. Yet he wondered to see us stand up for causes which he had looked upon as lost since a long time.

"How I pity France," he used to tell us, "poor degenerate France!"

And he looked quite scared when he saw our anger, and heard our vehement protestations. He was still convinced victory would be theirs. On the other hand, he once declared to us:

"There is a blemish in the character of the Germans ... they are kind-hearted to a fault. The German nation is thoroughly kind-hearted."

Owing to the circumstances we dared not say all that we wanted to, and were content to hint at Belgium....

"Oh, so many lies have been told! You ought not to believe such slanderous accusations. As to myself I know that what you are alluding to is false; the Germans are too kind-hearted to be guilty of the deeds they are charged with."

Such is our enemy's mode of reasoning. He denies what they cannot excuse. It is very easy.

"In Alsace-Lorraine we have been to blame in every way," said the clergyman to us.

He is making confession, we thought.

"Yes, we have been too kind-hearted, over-indulgent to the people. If we had had a firmer hand, everything would have got on much better."

This blasphemer had some merit, let us not be too hard on him.

Our leisure was propitious to gossip, and we spent many an hour listening to those who had seen the first tragical events of the invasion. Their simple, unvarnished tales were like so many nightmares. For instance, there were bargemen of Braye whose boat had been split in two by a cannon ball, and who had escaped death only by swimming and clinging to floating planks. There was the woman of Corbeny, driven by the Prussians from a village near Soissons. With several others she walked to Cerny at a stretch, with the Germans ever at her heels. The unhappy wretches had covered forty kilometres in the midst of a battle, spent with weariness, breathless, tumbling down, and trudging off again. Three of them were killed on the way. The woman who gave us an account of this carried her baby, aged eighteen months, throughout this wild race, and on the way the poor little thing was wounded twice in her mother's arms. Of Cerny were the poor creatures who were shut up in a deep stone quarry, and stayed there with scarcely any food for twenty-seven days. When they were taken out and brought to Laon they were pale, hollow-cheeked, and covered with vermin; they could hardly walk by themselves, and their eyes could not look upon the daylight. "The people wept as they saw us go by," the women said. During the first hours of their sojourn in the stone quarry, there had been a tragical incident. The fugitives were crouching in the dark when an officer broke in, accompanied with soldiers:

"Some of you," he said, "have harboured Englishmen. We discovered an English officer lying in such and such barn, in such a place. We have set the building on fire."

"Ho," said a man, "my barn!"

"Ah, it was yours! You knew an Englishman was hidden in it? Come on."

The poor man vainly protested against the accusation; he was taken away.

The following day he had not yet returned. His wife was greatly disturbed, and despite the danger made up her mind to go and try to see him. She took some chocolate out of the slender store of the refugees.

"They have thrown him into prison," she said, "and I am sure they will starve him to death."

The woman went. The village was half in ruins, and the ruins smoked. All was deserted. She summoned up her courage, went straight to her house, walked into the yard, and, close to the dunghill, his face fallen in the filth, his hands tied behind his back, saw the corpse of her husband. He had been shot twice in the head, and his side was pierced with a large wound.

The victim's brother and the niece from whom we heard this story, were not allowed to attend his burial.

From the same part were two ladies, a mother and her daughter, with a new-born baby, who were flung out of their house with only a dressing-gown and slippers on, and driven on without stopping at the bayonet's point, until they reached Laon, half distracted.

To Cerny also belonged those seven men who had been confined in the *mairie* of Chamouille, and who saw an officer come up and yell in a furious tone: "Your dirty French have discovered our presence here. One of you must have made signals. That's why we are getting a shower of shrapnel." The civilians denied the charge, and defended themselves. To no purpose.

"You shall spend the whole night in front of the house, and if you get knocked on the head, it will serve you right."

The men were drawn up in the street, and from evening till morning stood there within reach of their guards' revolvers. As if by miracle, the cannonade ceased, and during the night not a shot was fired upon the village. The next day the prisoners were sent to Laon.

Less tragic but just as remarkable, was the story of our companions Noreau, the grandmother, so small, so weak, that we more than once thought her death near at hand, and her darlings, with their pale faces and their eyes encircled with black. Major Noreau owned a large house in Coucy. It pleased the invaders, in their omnipotence, to take possession of eleven rooms, and to establish their offices in them. The owners had but the use of a single room, reserved for the sick father. Mme. Noreau, her four children and her mother-in-law, slept all the winter in a cold attic. Some of them slept on straw, but the old grandmother had, instead of a bed, ... a kneading-trough!

All the furniture had been carried away, scattered about the village, or over the trenches. To crown all, the family had suffered hunger almost unceasingly. Coucy had been still less favoured with provisions than Morny, and only the farmers had managed to lay by some few articles of food.

"One day," our old friend told us, "little Mimi picked up from the dunghill a lump of sugar an officer's servant had thrown to the dog. She knew her mother had had no food the last two days, and brought her this windfall."

The same little Mimi, after she had slept on straw for months together, forgot, for want of practice, her normal vocabulary, such words, for instance, as sheet, and the first evening she asked Antoinette, who had adopted her:

"What is the name of those things ... you know what I mean ... those white things one stretches upon the beds?..."

A great many emigrants were thrown out of their villages in September, when the Germans had been driven back. They had been pushed forward like cattle, had been penned up in the citadel of Laon, and left there for weeks, for months, sleeping on straw and starving. All these unhappy wanderers were stranded at Jouville. They had again met with their old companion Hunger. They were persecuted by the cold. Many lay groaning in the icy cellars of the sugar-mill, or in the airy attics of the farm.

And then suddenly came the spring. It came in one night. A light breath passed over the vale, which was soon like a nosegay. The meadows grew green, the hedges expanded their buds, the trees put forth tender leaves, the groves were embroidered with periwinkles. Beneath the thorn bushes came up lords-and-ladies; violets in tufts peeped out along the paths, and the meadows were strewn with primroses. Six small lambs in the keeping of a shepherd girl looked like six white specks on the slope of the green hill. The hedges were lively with songs and murmurs. The spring wondered much that it did not see the fresh idylls it was used to. Alas! Love had fled; Venus alone, a lewd and venal Venus, saw her altars besieged with a host of worshippers; but pure chaste Love had no faithful followers left.

Yet the spring bestowed with a full hand its gaiety upon all Nature. I met once with five small emigrants. The eldest was about eight years old; their clothes were all in rags, their feet walked naked on the stones. But they had flowers in their arms, and their pale faces were bright with the joy of the Spring. The joy of the Spring! Could we feel glad at it? "The month of May without France is no longer the month of May." This corner of France was no more France since we bore the yoke of strangers. In vain we lay basking in the sun, with outstretched arms. The sun could not, as once it did, warm and burn us, as if to make us die a voluptuous death. In vain did we listen to the watchful nightingale, whose song overtopped the noise of the water-gate. It expressed all the ecstasy and passion of mankind; it could no longer make us feel the sweetness of life. Our hearts were benumbed with grief, and had no taste for happiness.

Even the humblest of our companions, of our neighbours, understood this contrast between the sentiments of us all, and the joys which filled Nature. And we heard poor women say in a mournful tone:

"What misery! To think that we must live with the Germans in such fine weather!"

We lived with the Germans. In their train came all the ills—captivity, sickness, hunger. We suffered hunger more than ever since the ration of bread had been reduced almost to nothing. The women made loud complaints, and even talked of mutiny. The commandant of the camp—it was no longer he of the first days—replied to my complaints, lifting up his arms in a gesture of impotency and indifference:

"They are hungry! How am I to help it? I have nothing to give them. I had rather see them eat! It wouldn't disturb me in the least! Do you think I should care about it?"

A few women with their children and a cripple ran away, thinking they might reach their village. They were overtaken, some at five, others at ten kilometres from Jouville, were thrown into prisons without any further formality, and sentenced to wait there for the departure in which every one had ceased to believe. Two girls did succeed in getting home, but were likewise caught and brought back. These flights rendered our supervision stricter than ever. We had to answer to numberless roll-calls, and once, when the *Feldwebel* was in a bad temper, he called us all "a set of pigs!"

Our misery was alleviated at last, when the American-Spanish Relief Commission began its work. Jouville had already received some white flour. The mayor of the village interposed to obtain the same favour for the emigrants. He succeeded, and the last week of their quarantine the poor people got bread—white bread. The first day we went to the baker we saw a stirring sight. The children gazed in wonder at the golden loaves; they squeezed, they smelt their portion with joy, and without waiting broke off pieces which they ate eagerly. I saw women look at their share with staring eyes, and say weeping:

"Bread, real bread!"

This happened the last week of our sojourn in Jouville. Indeed the longed-for event was about to take place. There were endless reviews and verifications of names and civil conditions. The men were examined, and re-examined by the doctor, for all would not be allowed to leave. A card with a number was delivered to every person, and we were all ordered to meet in the yard of the sugar-mill at eight o'clock in the morning on Friday, the 14th of May. Different sentiments prevailed. A few were overjoyed at the news; others showed signs of despairing incredulity.

"God knows where they are going to take us now! What will become of us? You will see they will shut us up in Germany!"

But most of them suspended their judgment. Not daring to hope, they anxiously waited upon events. A still greater misfortune than we had borne lay in store for us, Geneviève had caught a severe cold about a month before, and the day we heard delivery was near she was in bed, shaking with fever. She spent a very bad night, notwithstanding our care. In the morning I ran for the German doctor—as there was no other—despite the patient's protests.

"No, no, I will have no Germans about me. Besides, there is nothing the matter that will prevent me from going."

The fair-haired coxcomb gave a listless ear to my words, looked at me between his eyelids, and asked with his lips:

"Why did not this person come round for medical advice?"

I replied that "this person" was in a high fever, and could not get up. Fortunately another doctor had come to help the former to examine the people before they were allowed to depart. He was a fat, red-faced, jovial fellow, who showed great haste to oblige me, and repeated over and over again as he accompanied me:

"Ah! le kerre! pien ture, pien ture!"

His diagnosis was alarming. A double congestion of the lungs. He prescribed cold water compresses.

"And—and the departure...."

"Oh, it is quite out of the question! The lady could not stand the journey. It is absolutely impossible."

"Then ... we are not going either...."

"That is no business of mine."

And the doctor withdrew with a shrug of his shoulders. Mad with despair we went to the commandant of the camp, Antoinette and I.

"We cannot go. Our sister is ill; we cannot forsake her."

"Why, you must go, you are not ill."

We did not know what saint to pray to; we looked out for help. The mayor of Jouville vainly went to the *Kommandantur* of Marle to plead our cause:

"All emigrants in good health must go." Such was the answer.

Geneviève tossed about her bed, and protested:

"I want to go; I will go. I will not run aground, as we are reaching the port."

But the doctor, once more consulted, repeated emphatically:

"Impossible, impossible."

"Then allow us to stay too."

"Impossible, impossible."

At length, towards evening—the whole camp with the whole village sympathised with us—some one told me:

"An officer from Marle is at the Red Cross. Go and try again."

We ran to see him. I well-nigh fell at his feet, and besought him. He looked somewhat moved.

"Well, let me see what I can do. You are sure the lady is unable to travel?" he asked the doctor.

"Absolutely. She cannot be moved."

"I cannot be moved either," I cried. "Please examine me. You will see there is something the matter with my heart, and if I am driven to go, it will be the death of me."

"Well," the officer said, "let us see."

His eyes gave consent. He turned to the doctor.

"You might examine her, and see if the journey would not endanger her life."

The doctor tossed his head, and smiled an incredulous smile.

"Hum, hum, it can't be denied there is something wrong with her heart," ... and, taking a pen, he signed the slip which I so much desired. What a relief! Geneviève would not be left, seriously ill, among strangers.

"And I, what am I to do?" Antoinette moaned.

"Ah! you must go."

There was nothing else to do. On the way home I tried to encourage her, miserable as she was at going away alone.

The next day I left Geneviève, burning with fever, in Mme. Charvet's care, and went to see the convoy start, heart-broken.

The sun lit up the scene; everybody was in a flutter of excitement. Villagers had been requisitioned, with carts and horses, to convey the children, the infirm, and the luggage. The crowd set out, under the conduct of the soldiers, amid calls and shouts. Many emigrants were crying:

"Where are we going to? Whither shall we be taken?"

Several families were severed one from another, for about fifteen men had been thought too strong to leave the invaded territory. They might turn soldiers, and fight against the Germans!

The charity children, delighted at the prospect, flocked around me.

"You will come later on, won't you, madam?"

Old Mme. Noreau and her grand-daughters faltered some words of sympathy, Antoinette strove hard to restrain her tears, and Pierrot dared not show his joy. I went with them as far as the end of the village, where two gendarmes were busy counting up the herd. I was not allowed to go any farther, and I stood there gazing at the trampling crowd, and until I saw them disappear at a winding of the road.

A halting-place had been arranged four miles from thence, where a train was waiting to convey the emigrants to Hirson. They spent the night in the waiting-rooms, lying on the floor, sitting on benches, all squeezed together with fluttering hearts and anxious looks, disturbed by the squalling of the children and the groans of the old people. In the morning, the poor wretches were carefully searched, and then crowded into the train. Two days after they reached France. With tears and cries of joy they greeted life, at length recovered after so many trials.

CHAPTER XII

After eight months' hopeless waiting, after long weeks spent in a flutter of expectation, we had seen the gate of delivery closed upon us. The others were gone; they were free; and Geneviève and I alone still bore the yoke of invasion, which no one loathed as much as we did. No one had more eagerly wished for freedom, longed to return home, and yearned to meet again those we loved, and alone we stayed behind.

The poor girl thought that she would die of despair rather than of illness, and while she moistened her pillow with tears, I hid my sobs in the attic.

Mme. Charvet took care of Geneviève, and did her best to comfort us both. We did not follow the prescriptions of the German doctor, and never once applied cold compresses. A French matron's experience is at times worth more than the learning of a Teutonic physician. We applied mustard-poultices and cupping-glasses; we gave the patient hot *tisanes* and syrups, which were all the better because they were made in the village.

On the 4th of June, three weeks after the convoy's departure, we arrived at Morny station, in the care of a sergeant. My sister-in-law was still a convalescent, and we trudged along to the Bureau, where our guardian handed over his prisoners. Thus we were restored to liberty; we were no longer emigrants. And with beating hearts we went back home.

On seeing us, my mother-in-law, Yvonne, and Colette well-nigh turned into stone. They thought we had been in Paris for two months at least. We returned to our old habits; five women were again under the same roof, five women in the midst of invasion. One only had succeeded in escaping.

No change for the better in the village. A single detail amused us. The soldiers of the line lived as before in a white house at the corner of the street. For a long time, one of its stout occupants, perched on a ladder, taking great pains and putting out his tongue, had formulated this wish in big black letters:

"God punish England!"

And now, on account of recent events, the painter had added in a fit of rage:

"And the devil run away with Italy!"

The Hussars of the farm were gone, Bouillot at their head, and that day the village had heaved a deep sigh. As a last theft, the Pandours had carried away a cartful of furniture, in order to make themselves comfortable in the trenches which would shelter them.

On the other hand, two convoys were still quartered within our gates, and troops of passage were now and then billeted upon us. We gave hospitality to a young lieutenant, who had succeeded Bubenpech as commandant. He lodged in the two rooms we had abandoned to the Prussians with a heavy heart; he had requisitioned, besides, "the small room" for his servant, and the stable for his horse. Gracieuse and Percinet, shut up in a corner of the coach-house, would gladly have seen the Prussian mare dead, which had usurped their domain. We, too, bore a grudge against the fat Hans, who encumbered our rooms with his person, his pipes, and his clothes.

So, resigned to fate, we established ourselves in the drawing-room, Geneviève and I. One of the windows looks into the street, and when, behind the lace of our curtains, we saw, hour after hour, day after day, the same carts loaded with straw, the same placid-looking Prussians,—they are all alike,—the same stiff and sneering lieutenants, we might have believed our stay in Jouville had been but a dream. The invaders seemed more "at home" than ever. The officers enjoyed themselves according to rule. Of course they had not waited for the spring to lead a jolly life. As early as November 1914 they had had drunken revelries. What merry evenings! What dishes never tasted in Germany! What floods of good wine! What erotic, patriotic, and bacchic songs! "Let us drink and eat, for we shall die to-morrow!"

"But no, we shall not die, we, who shout the loudest, we are safe; we do not go to the front, we stay behind, secure from danger. No other task but to grind down, vex, and punish civilians! Let us profit by the war. Joy's the word! There was a festival yesterday at Laon; it will be at Morny to-day; to-morrow it will be Coucy's turn. Still more revels, still more junketings. It is war, hurrah for the war!"

And all enjoyed themselves: those who cared for nothing as well as those who cared first to save their skin, sybarites as well as sentimentalists, the pompous as well as the dissipated.

But this demands an explanation. We had seen many officers of the reserve, the very men whom the *Gazette des Ardennes* calls "the flower of cultured German manhood"; but we had discovered few varieties among them, and all of them could be comprised in one of the categories we had created for the purpose.

Those who cared-for-nothing deserve careful consideration. They partook of the qualities common to their brothers-in-arms, which I will extol farther on, but their pusillanimity or their indifference belonged alone to them.

Such, for instance, was this lieutenant quartered in Laon, who confided to every one willing to listen to him:

"I don't care a fig for the fate of Germany! If only the war would end soon, and I could get on with my studies and make myself a good position after.... I should be content."

Of the same kind was the young commandant of the village, lamed by a fall from his horse.

"The war!" he said, "what do I care for it? I am unfit for fighting, do you see. I shall neither be killed nor mutilated, and it is all one to me how long the war will last. I have comfortable rooms, and get good dinners without untying my purse-strings. I am well paid, and able to save. When we are at peace again I shall have a jaunt, and then go back to Germany. Men will be rare, and I shall marry whom I choose, the richest girl I can hear of, of course. My future is assured, and so I am quite easy in my mind."

We thought still more disgusting those who first-cared-for-their-skin. We were pleased to observe not a few cowards who strove with feet, hand, and purse to avoid danger and keep behind the line.

Love of life, self-esteem, a dislike for bloodshed, and a natural dread of blows kept them from the front. They thought but of one goal: to cling at any price to safety.

I wrote "at any price" on purpose. Several of them boasted they had paid for not being sent to the front. Where, when, how, to whom, I do not know. By what mysterious bribery, by what surreptitious palm-greasing other people will perhaps establish. The truth of such things is not easy to ascertain. I can only state that two officers and a sergeant, belonging to different regiments, told those in whose houses they lodged, one in Laon, the others in Morny and Jouville, that they had paid from 4000 francs to 6000 francs to get leave to keep out of danger's way. Thus they obtained a few months' respite, after which they had to pay again or endanger their lives.

When we were at Jouville, a stout sergeant, nicknamed Tripe, well-nigh died of an apoplectic stroke on hearing he was ordered to go to the front. "I have paid 4000 francs to be exempted from fighting. I thought the war wouldn't last so long! And now I have no money left!" Mad with rage, he dashed his helmet right across the room, and this martial attribute was picked up with its point all awry. As to private soldiers who told their hosts they had acted in the same way, I will not even try to count them, they are too many.

The other officers owned a certain number of qualities in common. According to the individuals, one of these characteristics eclipsed the others, and the dominant feature helped us to classify the fools.

Of the sentimentalists, Herr Mayor was the best specimen. His eyes cast upon the blue sky, he murmured his regrets in a voice broken by tears: "His wife ... so many griefs ... and so many dead ... how dreadful is war! If only we could make a Holy Alliance of the peoples!" I must say that Herr Mayor kept his sensibility in his pocket, and took it out only at dessert. In the discharge of his duties he forgot this faculty completely.

The pompous officers were more entertaining. Such was a certain cavalry officer who at the end of September put up for a few days at M. Lonet's. His name ended in "ski," he twirled his mustachio after the Polish fashion, and drew himself up most elegantly. Once upon a time he happened to go through the drawing-room, where Geneviève was talking with Mme. Lonet. The surprise sent a thrill through him: "Why! two pretty women! Quick! let us show off!"

And the braggart began to hold forth in praise of Germany.

"Ah! *mesdames*, the emperor is extremely satisfied with the march of our army. Our gallant soldiers laugh at obstacles, and advance as if by miracle."

This speech was made shortly after the battle of the Marne. Unfortunately the hearers, as well as the orator, were unacquainted with the event, which, had they known of it, would have given yet more meaning to the gentleman's discourse.

The same *Rittmeister* could not refrain from delivering high-sounding addresses to all whom he met. In case of need he even fell back on the man who split the wood or the maid of all work. "Have you seen," he would say, "have you seen our splendid Imperial Guard? Have you noticed the gait of our soldiers? Do you know that no troops in the world are to be compared with them?" And for a revictualling cart that rattled by, for a soldier's shirt drying on a hedge, he would pour forth his soul in dithyrambs on Germany's greatness, invincibility, and might. You will think, no doubt, that the first and foremost soldier of the Prussian army, the supreme chief of our enemy, would take his place, not without the radiance of a star, among his *confrères* of pomposity.

Another pompous talker, a sub-lieutenant and former law student, lodged in the spring of 1915 at Mme. Lantois'. He set up for a linguist, and wanted us to believe he knew French better than we. Once I brought him a demand-note to sign. He carped at a word I used. I tried to defend my prose, but he stopped me with a motion of his hand:

"I know the word and how to use it."

I had nothing to do but hold my tongue, so I did, like one thunderstruck. Unfortunately the eloquent rascal took it into his head to turn his stay in France to account. Are we to suppose he thought he would thus acquire a few niceties of speech of which he was ignorant? Nobody knows. But he was often to be seen seated in the big kitchen, devoutly listening to the conversation of the workers, to the stories of the old people of the farm, to whom Mme. Lantois spoke sharply when they lingered too long. The lieutenant knew how to listen, how to learn, how to remember what he heard. For one day we heard him say, thumping his fist on the table:

"Je savions ce que je disions!"

Among our guests were a great many sybarites. Is Barbu's love of creature comforts still remembered? And the many cushions necessary to uphold his person? Can you imagine that some of them, before choosing their room, felt the elasticity of the mattresses, tried the softness of the blankets, inspected the fineness of the sheets? Are the nice afternoon-naps already forgotten?

"We are at war! but that is no reason to give up comfort. Let us have carpets and cushions, wadding and down! We are sybarites!"

The category, to which we come now, the brutes, is the most scandalously celebrated. The present war has been its triumph. I must say we never saw these gentlemen at their best, such as they showed themselves in assaults, in pillage, in massacre, in arson. We did see them as brutes in their treatment of a peaceful, submissive, terrified population,—brutes who thought they had drawn in their claws. Bouillot, for instance, was a beautiful specimen of the kind, but we saw many another. For instance, there was the hero, who had a small boy of Jouville bound fast to a post during an icy cold afternoon. There was that other who knocked down the shepherd-boy of Aulnois, and gave him a good horse-whipping. The poor boy had gone beyond the frontier of the commune with his cattle:

"What am I to do?" he said. "My master's meadow is in Vivaise. I must feed my flock, and at the office they won't give me a pass. They say I don't want one to go those few steps."

I should never finish telling the high deeds of those scoundrels, and I have still to sing the praises of the revellers. They were many in number, and I think more dangerous than the rest. They came to France, allured by the depravity they attributed to us, and it was they who brought to us their vices, particularly those exclusive to their race, on which I had rather not insist. No doubt they thought that they would do a pious work in helping to pervert a country which they hated. Be that as it may, they eagerly exerted themselves to this end, and did their best to transform the country behind the front into a vast brothel. Of course such creatures had not the least respect for the house which sheltered them. An old lady in Morny was deeply shocked at being forced to provide two fast girls of Laon with lodging and board for some days, and many a country house, which had never looked upon other than peaceful scenes, was scared at revels, the noise of which made the very window-panes tremble.

Bubenpech was a remarkably vicious specimen. A bottle of champagne was never emptied in the province without his presence. He was at every feast, he took part in every rejoicing; he rarely came home before two or three o'clock in the morning. He had a pretty taste in wine and nice dinners. Besides, he looked upon himself as Don Juan, and expected every one to yield to him. No thought hindered his caprices. One day he asked a young girl publicly to come and see him in his rooms. Another day we saw him towards dusk kiss two loose girls in the open street. To be at perfect liberty, he sent to prison, under some pretence or another, a man whose daughter he was paying court to. He inscribed, among the women inspected by the police, the name of a young girl who, though not very respectable, had done no harm but reject his advances. With real Gallic humour our good villagers were careful to catalogue the great deeds of our guests, chiefly when heroines from the other side of the Rhine came upon the scene.

One Sunday morning, about ten o'clock, there appeared at our house a little German nurse of the Red Cross, dark-haired, smart, and—a fact hardly to be believed—pretty; but the lady had a peevish air—an air only.

"Lieutenant Bubenpech?"

"Out."

With all possible speed the orderly went to fetch the officer. Bubenpech came back as fast as he could, shut himself up with the little dame, and did not move until four o'clock in the afternoon, forgetful of his lunch. And the orderly, who timidly presented himself for duty, was roughly sent away from the closed door.

"Oh," said Mme. Valaine, shocked, "such impudence! in my house!"

The neighbours made jokes and watched the door. They even laid wagers: they will come out; they won't. At last the couple came out, and disappeared on foot towards Laon.

A moment after a murmur was heard:

"What does it mean?"

To show his disregard of decency, Bubenpech had thrown his window wide open before going out. And now the whole village gathered about our windows and jeered at the shameless disorder of the room and bed.

So, while some officers clearly belonged to such and such a category, they all possessed to a certain degree the qualities peculiar to the other classes. But there were real mongrels among them. For instance, you can imagine for yourself a sentimental-fine-talker and a sybarite-who-cared-for-his-skin or a brutish-reveller. And there was a sameness in all, a family resemblance. Prussian militarism, hypocrisy, and haughtiness were smeared over them all like a thick coat of paint. All showed an extreme satisfaction with their own race and person. In short, you have but to scratch the Prussian to find the barbarian. Should an opportunity offer, or even no opportunity, they can all be unreasonable, harsh, unrelenting.

These gentlemen enjoyed themselves.

In a physical sense, you can easily picture to yourself those revellers. They were not handsome—at least we never came across one we thought handsome, in spite of our efforts to be impartial. Save Bouillot, we never saw a very tall one. They were either long and threadlike, or short and fat. Those who thought they had a look of Apollo you might reproach with thick wrists and ankles, large hips, and heavy feet. Most of them had shapely hands, and very often well-kept nails. Their features were unpleasing from being shockingly irregular or freezingly regular; their hard eyes belied the false kindness of their smile. At a distance, their stiff and starched gait, their mechanical movement; at close quarters, their voice, their smell, their whole being made us bristle with hostility. For a trifle we would have snarled at them like a dog, and every day their presence lay heavier on our hearts.

Their smell! Some people deny its reality. Let them go to the North of France! When you have lodged Prussian officers—very clean people, no doubt—you may air the room eight days running, and it will not lose the smell *sui generis* which impregnates it, and every inhabitant of the village, from the Mayor down to the smallest child, would turn up his nose on entering the room, and say:

"Faugh! it smells of Prussians here!"

Such as they were, the gentlemen amused themselves. Some maintained even that they made conquests. I am touching here on a very delicate subject—the relations between the invaders and the women of the invaded countries. There has been much talk of rape. Compared with the crimes committed in Belgium and in Lorraine, the misdeeds we shall mention are but little things. To be sure, there were rapes, but, thanks be to God, they were few, and they took place at the beginning of the invasion, chiefly after the Germans' retreat on the Marne. In Jouville I heard many a sad story. There was the story of a young woman of Chevregny who went mad after her misfortune, and of several old women too. For, hardly credible as it seems, old women often fell victims to acts of violence, because they lacked agility to run away. At Braye, several soldiers fell upon a woman of eighty, knocked her down, and beat her most unmercifully. At Chamouille, in October 1914, a few women were living in a cellar, frightened to death. "One evening," one of them told me, "we heard a loud cry; there was a falling of stones, and a young woman tumbled down into the cellar through a shell-hole. Thus she escaped from her pursuers, but her companion, an old woman of sixty-eight, fell defenceless into the hands of the filthy fellows."

Ah, we had many proofs of the respect the Germans have for old age!

A woman of Cerny, eighty-seven years old, small and white-haired, with red eyes and a shaking head, told us how she had left her lodging. "I had a small bundle of clothes ready lying on the table. But the soldiers did not allow me to go in and take it; they beat me. As I didn't go—I had money, too, in my bundle—they forced me to go; they all flocked around me, they were twelve, and ... how am I to say it?..." In short, the twelve rascals had driven the poor old woman out of her house by directing towards her that which a famous statue innocently eternises in Brussels. Stripped of her spare clothes and money, filthy, disgusted at what she had seen, the unhappy woman had to go to a neighbour to beg for a bodice and a petticoat, that she might cast away her soiled clothes.

When the Germans settled themselves upon us, these feats of the satyr were no longer common. Here and there evil deeds were still spoken of, and a doctor of the neighbourhood told us in the spring of 1915 that nearly every week there was an act of violence. I must confess that many a woman was the victim of her own imprudence. When you have lived all your life in a quiet village, among kind people, you have some difficulty in believing that you must be on your guard for months together, that you are for ever surrounded with brutes. So more than one villager had reason to regret having gone alone to the forest, or having persisted in living in a lonely house.

But the systematic brutalities, the collective assaults, which marked the beginning, were no longer known. The method had changed. There were acts of violence which were no less terrible for being moral. In many a village whose inhabitants suffered hunger, the children were provided with bread and soup. Yes, but this privilege was reserved for the children whose mothers showed themselves complaisant towards the soldiers. And these women accepted dishonour, because they could not bear to see their little ones pine away and die, while others could not withstand the troubles and vexations that lay in store for good women.

A cry of reprobation and horror arose when we heard that the conduct of all women was not blameless. In the first place there were the women of the lowest class. Even Boule de suif herself would have been tamed after daily relations with the German soldiers. Of course a few black sheep are a disgrace to the flock, and I can fancy women-haters shrugging their shoulders in scorn when they hear of this.

Gently, sir—a truce to jeering. More than one person wearing a beard gave abundant proof of an equal complaisance. Alas, traitors were to be found among us. For instance, there were those who welcomed the Germans with a smile, and revealed to them the resources of the place. There were those, the foulest of all, who denounced French soldiers hidden in the woods or those who fed the fugitives. There were those who, for a little money or food, pointed out the hiding-places of his neighbours, and thus surrendered to the enemy wine, grain, potatoes, even money and jewels. But I am pleased to say that such despicable wretches were rare, and on the whole the population was proud and dignified, and opposed to the invaders' dishonesty a solid brotherhood, which no troubles, no persecutions could lessen or fatigue. And yet we led a grievous life; the Germans seemed to aim at making it as hard as possible, while theirs was as merry as can be.

The winter had been painful, but the summer was still more so. We had less liberty and less food. We were allowed to leave the place we lived in but three times a week, and on stated days. Besides, we had to ask for a pass two days beforehand, and pay seventy-five centimes for it when it was granted, which was not always the case. It was almost impossible to go to the country from Laon, and for weeks together nobody was allowed to leave the town. One day passports had been freely given to the people, tradesmen mostly who went to Marle to buy raw sugar—a yellowish sticky substance with a taste of glue—and a little butter, precious goods that were still to be found there in small quantities. They all came back furious. At different points of the road, level-crossings, outskirts of villages, they had all been arrested.

Men and women had been then entirely stripped of their garments, and searched according to rule. Nurses of the Red Cross and soldiers showed equal zeal in the task, which had a practical object—the gathering of all gold and even silver coins of five francs which pockets and purses might contain. The sum seized, it must be said, was replaced by notes of the Reichsbank.

The victims thought the joke a very bad one, and I am sure Thomas of Marle's bones must have turned in his grave. To think that on this nobleman's own territory soldiers arrested and robbed the passers-by, and he not there to help! And, what is worse, the aggressors were German troopers, and the victims good and loyal French citizens! What does your shade regret, O famous plunderer? To be unable to fight for your countrymen, or to have no share in the robbery?

I need not say that after that no gold pieces ever ventured out on the roads.

A pass also was necessary to go out into the country, and you were expected to have an identity card in your pocket if you but stood on your threshold. All papers had to be renewed every fortnight.

"Fancy," an aged woman said to us, "that I have to pay twenty marks because I forgot my antiquity card!"

One Saturday, a farmer's wife, perched on a ladder out of doors, was eagerly polishing the glass of a bull's-eye window.

Two gendarmes on horseback passed by and gave heed to this commendable zeal:

"Matam! ... carte...."

"Hem, hem! Ah, yes, my identity card; wait a minute, it is lying on the table...."

"Ha! ha! no, not enter ... no card ... fine...."

So she had to pay the fine.

One of our neighbours was taking his cows out of the stable. Suddenly one of them seemed to smell some enlivening odour—was it that of powder?— she bent a frolicsome head on one side, lifted up her sprightly nostrils, raised a swaggering tail, and, as fast as she could tear, went full gallop towards the meadows, the brooklet, the rosy horizon where the setting sun pleased her. The owner took to his heels in his turn, and fled after the giddy-pated creature. The better to run, he tore off his jacket, and succeeded in getting hold of the tether. Then he stopped panting, all in a sweat, and rapped out a tremendous oath.

As if by miracle, a gendarme happened to stand there, his note-book in hand.

"Card, card...."

"Ah! oh, it is in my jacket pocket...."

The jacket was smiling in the distance, a small spot lying on the green.

"Ach!" the Prussian said with a sneer, "not fetch: fine."

Cost fifty francs.

Rascally cow!

I treat the matter as a joke. Sometimes we did joke. We could not have our minds always on the stretch. We already were half-crazy, and we should have gone quite mad if we had not occasionally laughed. We often laughed, with rage, with an empty stomach, with our brain confused after a troubled night. Our race needs to laugh in the midst of tears, and tears are shed in secret, whereas laughter bursts forth in public.

When the Germans laugh, it is always a peal. As to tears, they trickle down their cheeks for a trifle; they bathe in them, they pour them forth everywhere. I had always looked upon this lachrymal faculty so often spoken of as a legend, but we have come to the conclusion that there is nothing more real.

An untoward event, a deception, bad news, or simply home-sickness and melancholy—anything is an excuse for tears. Here is a famous example. Those who have visited the battlefields of Mars-la-Tour and Gravelotte have seen the famous monument—a granite armchair in the midst of a lawn, surrounded with a balustrade. This noble simplicity should speak to the soul of itself. Yet an inscription explains:

"During the battle of Mars-la-Tour, the Emperor Wilhelm the First sat here and wept."

Of course he thought the game was lost. But if his descendants are faithful to tradition, where will they get the torrents of tears they will have to shed within a short time!

However, we are not always crying. We even tried to enjoy the summer, to make up for the sad spring we had spent. As we had to plead a practical object to obtain leave to take walks out of the village, we begged to be allowed "to go and fetch wood."

And, lying on the grass in the open country, we tried to forget the war for a few moments, Geneviève and I, lost in the surrounding calm and beauty; but distant rumours soon belied our short-lived illusions, and dispelled the poor creations of the fancy.

No, it was not peace. Our stomachs, always clamouring for food, never failed to tell us so. During the month of June we hardly ate anything except asparagus and cherries. These things are not highly nutritious. No potatoes, a slice of horrid, sticky, sour German bread. Then came carrots, green peas, and artichokes, and we no longer starved; and when in the second fortnight of August there arrived the food sent by the Spanish-American Board of Relief, we thought we had been transported to a Land of Cockayne. Twenty grammes of bacon daily, a dish of rice on Sunday, a dish of beans on Thursday, eatable bread; what would you ask more? No matter. I wonder, when we are once out of this vale of hunger, how long it will be before we recover our former health.

During the month of July we spent the hot hours of the day out of doors stretched on the grass. Being near a field of corn, we put out a timid hand and from time to time broke off ripe ears; we rubbed them between our fingers, and their plump grains, stripped of the husks, seemed to us delicious food. It was strictly forbidden to pluck corn, "however small the quantity might be." "Our leather bags may be searched," we thought, "but they cannot make a post-mortem examination of us to make sure of a possible theft." For there is no doubt that we were committing highway robbery to the prejudice of the Germans.

When we had yawned the whole long day away, in wearisomeness and hunger, we might have hoped to slumber at night, for sleep is as good as a dinner.

Alas! remember the Germans' revels! These gentry were no longer allowed to find their amusement out of the village in which they were quartered. Every night the officers of Morny will disport themselves in Morny!

Yes, indeed! They spent their evenings in a house which they had transformed into a casino, amid laughter and songs. Only the immediate neighbours were kept awake. But about twelve or one o'clock we never failed to start up in our beds, as the songs and cries came nearer.

"Here are the brutes going home. What whim will they take into their heads to-night?"

We heard them approach to the strains of accordeons and mouth-organs. From upstairs we saw them dressed up like women, with plumed hats on, stopping at every door, trying, it would seem, who could bawl the loudest. Or they tricked themselves out as house-painters, carried buckets and brooms and set high ladders against the walls, and climbed up as if to storm the house. Another time they would pretend to be strolling musicians, and, armed with saucepans and cauldrons, would give a mock serenade that would have put the dead to flight. Or, what was far worse, the noise of their steps would be scarcely audible; they would talk in whispers and stifle their laughter.

And, lying in the dark, we said to ourselves, still half asleep:

"They seem quiet to-night; perhaps we shall be able to go to sleep again."

But all of a sudden: bing, bang, formidable blows with revolvers shook the wooden shutters, and resounded in the room like peals of thunder. The unexpected noise startled us out of our torpor, and we could hardly recover our breath.

The next day, Mme. Lantois, half-sour, half-sweet, asked her lieutenant:

"Well, you had some fun last night?"

"Oh, yes! We knocked hard at the windows of all houses where there are young girls."

Maybe the officer read disapproval in the features of his interlocutor, for he went on:

"We are merry.... You may be sure that the French officers amuse themselves in the same way...."

In the same way? Oh no, Mr. ex-law student of Heidelberg!

One evening, an officer whose rooms were not far from our house refused to take part in a drunken orgy. He was tired; he had a headache; in short, he preferred to go to bed. There were guests in Morny, and before they left to drive home, the whole band made an irruption into the refractory officer's room, tore him from his bed, and, with shouts of laughter, hoisted him into the visitors' carriage and ordered the coachman to drive on.

At the end of the village our man was stripped of his night-shirt, deposited on the road, and his comrades went away at full speed. As naked as when he was born, he had to walk along the high street to get back to his quarters.

The commandant of the village, to whom we gave hospitality, did not care to put a stop to these extravagances. Being but twenty-five, he had little authority over his comrades, and besides, from time to time he liked an orgy himself. He was famous for his worship of Bacchus. He was as long as a day without bread; he had a small boy's head, adorned with large outstretched ears at the top of it. The women of the village, at the sight of his slender calves, had surnamed him "Jackdaw's Leg." More stupid than bad, he felt frightfully dull at Morny, and talked with raptures of his stay in Belgium. "What a good time I had of it!" he used to say. "I was drunk from morning till night!" That he might not get quite out of practice, Jackdaw's Leg tippled as often as he could, and many a night his unsteady legs were at much pains to convey him home without accident. We knew him by his uncertain gait; and when drunk he never failed to prevent us from sleeping the livelong night. He sought laboriously for the dancing keyhole. Then he banged-to the door. At length he succeeded in getting to his room, and his door was hardly shut, when the result of his excess burst forth noisily and—sinister detail—we perceived a characteristic clash of washhand-basin and slop-pail. Then desperate hiccups, groanings, and sighs were audible, and the whole house resounded with his laborious efforts.

Upstairs we heard Colette, furious and disgusted, rail against the tipsy fellow:

"You dirty, loathsome brute ... pig...."

Then nothing was heard but snores. The officer had certainly flung himself upon his bed with his boots on.

And the following morning plump Hans, his servant, was to be seen all a-flutter running to and fro with water, pails, and floor-cloths. Sometimes the painful scene took place in the street; the disreputable traces of it were still to be seen on wall and pathway the next morning, and the lieutenant made for his rooms with deep sighs. Yet he was able to walk by himself to our house. What could we say of that captain who, in Jouville, used to be wheeled home in a barrow by his servants?

At that time an adventure happened by night which I cannot recall without an inward thrill of fear. It was already late in the evening, and we were shut up in our room, Geneviève and I. Our windows were open, and the strong wooden shutters were carefully closed. We had been talking for some time, lying in the dark, and were about to fall asleep, when we heard a carriage rattle by and then stop at the farther end of the house. It was about half-past eleven.

"Kolb, Kolb," cried a loud voice.

Such was the official name of Jackdaw's Leg. A silence followed, then the owner of the voice seemed to grow impatient.

"Kolb ... Kolb ... Kolb...."

No answer came. The uproarious fellow bellowed:

"Kolb ... Kôôôôlb...."

I bounced out of bed, still drowsy.

"This man will wake up the whole street," I murmured. "I believe we had better answer."

"Lieutenant Kolb is at the casino," I cried from behind the shutter.

"What?" asked the voice.

I thought my interlocutor fifteen yards from thence, in front of the gate. My hand leaning against the fastening unconsciously turned it; all of a sudden it was wrenched from my grasp and the shutters flew wide open. As quick as lightning I shut the window, stuck to the wall, and slipped behind the piano. Geneviève had started to her feet and stretched herself at full length along the bed. We saw the man produce an electric lamp from his pocket, and, with his nose flattened against the window-pane, try to catch a glimpse of the inside of the room. The curtains prevented him from seeing clearly anything, but we got a full view of his person.

He was a captain, colossus-like, thick-featured, and red-bearded; he had a helmet and a grey coat on. He sat on the window-sill, and muttered in a clammy, drunken voice:

"Mademoiselle, mademoiselle, open the window.... I want to wish you a good morning ... shake hands with me.... Mademoiselle, open the window."

We held our breaths, we dared not stir a finger.

Then the officer got up, stepped backwards, took a survey of the house, and made for the next window. He shook the shutters, which did not give way, and went to try the others. How eagerly we wished the orderly had shut up everything at his master's! The first window held out, the second too, but the fastening of the third one yielded, and we heard the man jump into the room. As if he knew the ins and outs, he swiftly crossed both rooms and the passage, and stopped at our door.

"Open...."

He gave a knock ... then made an endeavour to open the door.

We were struck with dismay.

With a shove of his shoulders he might have forced the lock. With naked feet and nothing but a nightgown on, how should we have been able to stand up against this booted, armed giant if he had broken in? Noiselessly Geneviève sprang towards me. I softly opened the window overlooking the garden, and we jumped out, careless of the pebbles that bruised our feet, ran along the house with all possible speed, and stopped at my mother-in-law's window.

"Mother, mother, open the window."

Our voices were low, but so anxious that the shutters immediately flew open. We climbed in like cats and hastily closed the window. With strained ears we listened to the intruder's goings and comings, but he soon jumped out of the window, and after renewed calling and knocking we heard his carriage roll away.

We prudently waited some time before venturing out, then we poked our noses into the passage, and, making sure the enemy had really withdrawn, we took once more possession of our own room. But, alas, our emotion had destroyed all chance of sleep.

Day after day, night after night, alarm upon alarm, the summer glided by. Then came the harvest-time. The farmers were much agitated, for the Germans had declared that they would gather in the harvest.

They did so.

Ah, the birds will long remember the summer of 1915!

The harvest lasted three months, and all that time the grain strewed the ground. Every overripe sheaf lost in transport half its wealth.

"They are but lazy-bones, the whole pack of them," M. Lantois muttered between his teeth. "When we gather in the harvest, we get up at three o'clock and work till eight or nine, and we hurry over our meals. But those fellows! they get up at six, leave off work from eleven to one, and have done with it at five!"

If the soldiers did not tire themselves out, the civilians they employed showed no eager haste to do things properly.

The peasants were full of indignation.

"If those idiots had allowed us to gather in the harvest on the condition that we gave them half or even a third of it, they would have had more corn than they have now, and we should have been provided for the whole year!"

However, the Prussians at last understood that more speed was necessary. And since all the able-bodied men were requisitioned, it was the turn of the women. The rural constable announced one evening that women who would work in the fields would receive two francs a day. This aroused a great deal of wonder. In the times we lived in two francs were looked upon as a large sum, and many women hired themselves out willingly. A week after, there was a sudden fall in the tariff. The women heard they would be paid only fourpence a day, and the female workers dwindled to zero. The soldiers, in a rage, tried to enlist the women in their very houses. But they did not succeed. One had a bad headache, another was in bed, a third was nursing her baby, a fourth was sitting up by her sick mother, and so on.

This state of things did not last long. The military authorities issued an order, which enjoined all women from sixteen to fifty to be on the *place* of the village at such an hour, to be enrolled as day-labourers. Mothers of young children alone were exempt. We looked at one another in bewilderment. Why, then, we had to go too! But if we can wield the pen and the needle, and on occasion the broom, we are not trained to handle the sickle, the spade, and the rake. Besides Geneviève was hardly recovered. Colette is as slender as a reed, and if Yvonne and I are far from being viragoes in times of peace, we were still weaker after a year of privation and trouble.

"The little of health and life we have left would be lost in the fields," said Yvonne.

"I won't risk it," said Geneviève. "I had rather go to prison. Let them take me to Chalandry!"

It was at Chalandry that the Germans had installed a prison for women.

Jackdaw's Leg good-humouredly reassured us in his most Teutonic accents:

"The measures in hand concern but the peasants," he said.

It is worth while remarking that the officers did their best to be on tolerable terms with their hosts, and when the inhabitants were ill-treated, the head of the house was sure to be away.

Now, Jackdaw's Leg had been feeling very poorly for some weeks. Was it due to home-sickness and to a longing for sauerkraut and sausages? Or might it not rather come from too many merry parties? In short, the commandant seemed to languish, and ten times a day lay down on his couch. As he had two bedrooms at his disposal, he slept in one bed by night, and—for variety's sake—in the other by day, unmindful of the fact that he thus requisitioned two pairs of sheets a week, that soap was scarcely to be had, and that the poor washerwoman had to whiten the linen with wood ashes. Jackdaw's Leg, being ill, got a month's leave of absence, and disappeared in the background. His place was filled up by the young linguist who had put up at Mme. Lantois'.

He would gladly have seen us dead.

Calling on his brother-in-arms, lingering without a motive, or for a wrong motive, in our garden, in our lobby or on our threshold, peeping through the keyholes—we once detected him in this occupation—he had discovered that our souls were not unworthy of associating with his, mad for music and philology, enamoured of art and culture. Notwithstanding that we had the reputation of hating the Germans, this nice Prussian, who produced in tippling-houses a list of at least one thousand and three names—the list of his conquests in France—this nice Prussian then gave us to understand that he would condescend to enter into relations with us, relations based on philosophy, science, and literature. Why not on politics?

We responded in such a manner to his advances as to convince even a Prussian. And since then the fellow had borne us a dangerous grudge.

Two days after the departure of Jackdaw's Leg we heard a beat of the rural constable's drum ... women from sixteen to fifty ... one o'clock ... market-place.... We hardly listened to it. It was no concern of ours. But at one o'clock Mme. Lantois ran up breathless: "Do you know that the lieutenant just said that *everybody* must go to the market-place? He even told us that if you didn't go, he would send four soldiers to fetch you, and take you off to Chalandry."

Consternation! Alarm! It was twelve o'clock according to German time. Without waiting for luncheon we ran out in all directions to look for substitutes. At one we arrived on the *place*, attended by four old women, still hale and hearty, and well pleased to fill our places, for of course to the scanty pay of the Germans we had agreed to add the usual price of a day's work. The sight of the place suggested a picture of the slave-market. Women, wearing light blouses and coarse linen aprons, had gathered on both sides. To shield themselves from the glare of the sun, the most of them wore a handkerchief tied under the chin; a few of them laughing, tossed their sunburnt hair, and many with weary faces leant against the tools they had brought. There were gloomy-eyed women, who up to that time had never done any work but housekeeping; there were young girls, carefully looked after by their mothers, who did not know what to do with themselves; there were sedate, stern-looking workers, and at last the usual set of soldiers' wenches, laughing at and making fun of the others, noisier than the rest of the company, and thinking that they might do what they liked.

Under the shade of the plane-trees was seated Jacob—such was the Christian name of the lieutenant, and no one gave him another—busy calling the names over. Ours was among the last; we answered without wincing, and then presented our substitutes. Thus did we baffle the trick which Jacob wanted to play us.

This enforced service brought about many troubles between the invaders and the inhabitants, so the Germans had prudently turned the sugar-mill of Aulnois into a prison for male culprits, and converted a house at Chalandry into a jail for women. And if you showed the least disposition to disobedience, you were immediately taken into custody. Did you call a private soldier such names as he had deserved a hundred times? To prison with you. Had you kept back any goods from the perquisitioners? To prison with you. Were you unwilling to comply with the requisitioners' orders? To prison with you. Were you penniless when liable to a fine? To prison with you, to prison, to prison!

Half a dozen men from Morny were for ever ruralising at Aulnois. Of course it is no disgrace to be put into prison by the Germans, but it is a well-known fact that the diet of the Prussian jails is anything but engaging.

A girl of sixteen coming back one evening from the fields threw her pickaxe on her threshold, and cried out in tears:

"I won't work any longer for those barbarians!"

An indiscreet ear overheard the sentence, which was repeated in high quarters.

Now, the word "barbarians" is to a German like a red rag to a bull.

So, two days afterwards, the family of the imprudent little person were awakened out of their sleep at four o'clock in the morning. A sergeant and four men came to fetch the guilty girl and take her to Chalandry. Half an hour was granted her to get ready. Mad with despair and shaken with sobs herself, she left her parents sunk in desolation and in tears. They even did not know how long their child would be imprisoned. Towards evening the father succeeded in seeing the commandant, who told him his daughter would be in prison for three weeks.

"I was not too uncomfortable," the poor thing said afterwards; "one of the 'nurses' was rather nice ... we were sewing the whole day long ... but there were such funny women there...."

I should think so.

Then what an excellent pretext for vexatious measures was this enforced service! A rich landowner of Vivaise, who was ill, sent a servant of his, old but able-bodied, to take his place. One morning the officer asked:

"Why does M. Villars not come himself?"

"He is ill."

"He is not so ill as you are pleased to say. He must come, and we will see what occupation he is fit for."

M. Villars had to yield, and by way of an easy little job he was ordered to clean the soldiers' closet, and gather up dung on the road. Ah, the enslavers knew how to rouse our wrath, and more than one Prussian well-nigh paid with his life for his insolence.

If our men strove hard to be always submissive it is because they knew that a single attempt at revolt might have caused the village to be set on fire and the inhabitants dispersed. Yet once a worker had a quarrel with a Prussian. He was a youth of eighteen, who, when he had seen the convoys go away, had cried for rage and clenched his fists, saying:

"Ah, if I were but allowed to go ... within eight days I should wear red trousers!"

He did not know that red trousers were blue now, but he meant well, and this young fellow one evening gave a sharp answer to one of the soldiers who supervised the work of the fields. The Prussian, not quick at the answer, aimed his revolver at him. The boy stooped down, and the bullet was lost in a bush. At the same time a sudden collective rage seized upon the companions of the young man, who had listened to the quarrel a few steps away. Armed with hay-forks, scythes and spades, they rushed headlong upon the common enemy, who bounded forward and fled across the country. It was a splendid chase: Jacques Bonhomme pursuing Michael. With the whole band at his heels, the Prussian raced across fields and meadows, cleared the hedges, crossed the brooks, got to the village, and went to earth. The pursuers stopped and looked at one another. "What were we going to do?" With a sheepish look and their arms dangling, they went home more than ever depressed beneath a feeling of helplessness.

Our tyrants were not content with worrying us with passports and enforced service. They continued to strip us methodically, poor shorn lambs as we were, to whom the wind was not tempered but whose food was strictly measured. Though the Germans had taken all the fruits of the fields, they were still afraid that something might be left us to eat. So the farmers' wives were forced during the summer to reconstitute their poultry yards. All birds were counted and requisitioned. Besides, the farmers had to deliver to the *Kommandantur* as many eggs as they had hens every fourth day.

"What are we to do if the hens lay no eggs?"

"Do as you will," replied the Germans.

The fruit-trees in the orchards and gardens looked promising. We all rejoiced at it. "If we have nothing else to eat we shall have marmalade." But the first rosy tint had hardly spread over the cheeks of the apples, when the rural constable proclaimed throughout the village: "When good and ripe, fallen apples should be brought to the *Bureau*; a severe penalty will be enforced on the refractory persons."

But the Germans still thought that we might cheat them, and the fruit was unripe when they began to gather it. Children from twelve to sixteen were requisitioned, and under the supervision of two soldiers they knocked down the plums and picked them up. A month later it was the turn of the apples, and then of the pears. The Germans carried off the fruit throughout the country, and we saw hundreds of carts go by loaded with sacks of apples, which were conveyed to Germany.

Among the most troublesome announcements made to the amazed parish—always with a threat against refractory persons—I must recall that which forbade them to cut down grass along roads and paths. This annoyed particularly the owners of rabbits, goats, and kids; the animals were requisitioned, but as long as the Germans were not in need of them the peasant had to take charge of them—had the use of them, if I may say so. And it was no trifle to feed the cattle, as the provender was requisitioned.

In Mme. Lantois' big shed the Germans had heaped up a great deal of hay, and towards evening the farmer's wife used to stand on her threshold, and, after a glance to the right and left, she would run to the shed, gather up an armful of hay, and come back home in a hurry. "My poor beasts," she said, "I can't give them enough to eat. When I hear them move about of nights it nearly breaks my heart; it prevents me from sleeping, it does."

In the autumn the potatoes were dug up and sent to the north. The peasants were furious. One of them, busy digging in his own field behind his house, muttered between his teeth: "Isn't it a shame! The very potatoes I have planted myself! And I shan't have any! Wait a minute!"

He had on a large belt that transformed the upper part of his shirt into a sack. His hand went by turns down to the ground and up to his neck, and he soon had the figure of Punch. While the guard studied the weather, his nose lifted up towards the sky, the man sneaked away, slipped into his house, emptied his belt, came back, and began again. Alas, came the moment when the guard discovered the trick!

This guard was a holy man, fat, stout, demure-looking, a canting preacher, who not only took the apostleship of his nation for granted, but his own too. When the misappropriated potatoes had got back to the Prussian sacks our Mr. Smooth-Tongue looked at the grieved culprit—grieved at having been caught—looked at the hollow-cheeked faces around him, at the sunken, jaded eyes. He paused before speaking, tossed his head three times, and said: "How perverse are the French! Don't you know that stealing is forbidden? And don't you know that the potatoes belong to the Germans? Now then, by taking our potatoes you commit a theft. It is a disgrace. Be sure you never do such a thing again!" Such talk was to be heard from many Germans. It suits them. I delight in hearing them sing this tune, the *Gazette des Ardennes* at their head, and cry up to the skies the good, the beautiful. They go still further, and my joy increases. They laud the love of their neighbour, respect for the property of others, compassion towards the weak; they extol the meekness, the goodness, the infinite sweet temper of Germany. But oh! it is ever to be regretted that so many noble words should be delivered in vain. Such rubbish does not take with us.

"Their *Gazette des Ardennes*!" exclaimed a farmer's wife. "We buy it only to read the list of French prisoners, and because there is no other newspaper. But when my husband reads it, he never leaves off thumping on the table, and rapping out oaths from beginning to end. Since those filthy fellows have settled themselves down here, one has never a fine word in one's mouth!"

"The other day," another woman told us, "my husband had to bring vegetables to Laon. He went to have his pass signed; the sergeant held out his hand to take the paper and said: 'Well, comrade?' My husband gave no answer, but he thought to himself: 'You my comrade! I would rather kick you soundly than call you that.'"

Our sense of impotence was never greater than in the month of August, when the Germans trumpeted abroad with a sneer the defeat of the Russians, and oh, sacrilege! ordered our own bells to be rung to celebrate the glorious deeds of the German army! But in September hope rose in our hearts, and filled them with joy. The offensive began in Champagne. The cannon raged as never before. How they rolled and shook and roared! And to our minds the uproar was suave, the rumbling was blessed.

The French aeroplanes came eight days running to drop bombs on the station at Laon. Six, seven, even ten were to be seen at the same time in the sky; they sparkled like jewels in the deep-blue heavens; they well-nigh drove us mad; we jumped for joy in the garden, cheered them, and would gladly have thrown our hearts out to them. Fortunately no outsiders were the witnesses of our frenzy, or we should have been found guilty. At Laon, two young girls were looking out of an upper window, and at the sight of the dear aeroplanes had screamed with joy, and clapped their hands. Alas, some soldiers saw them from the street, and lodged an information against them! They were immediately arrested, tried, and sentenced to a month's imprisonment. We lived in hope for a whole week. The *Gazette des Ardennes* suppressed the French official reports which they generally gave at full length—at least so they said—and we thought that the offensive, even in the Germans' opinion, bade fair to succeed. Then the cannon was silent once more, and our hearts sank within us.

The fair weather was past. It was cold and rainy, and again, as the year before, we gathered every evening around the lamp—a horrid, evil-smelling horse-oil lamp. Our circle was often out of spirits; our very gestures revealed weariness. Thirteen months of captivity lay heavy on us, and we had received no news whatever of those we loved:

"Oh, they are all dead!" sighed Colette.

Yet we reposed the strictest confidence in our army. We felt sure victory would ultimately be ours. But, oh! how long was victory in coming!

It was cold and damp. We were afraid of the coming winter. Though the summer had brought us many hardships, yet we had made shift to live; but how could we manage in the bad season, when we had neither fuel nor vegetables? They had refused us permission to cut down trees in our own woods, though the invaders had massacred them at will. Besides, the Germans chose this very moment to threaten us with enforced service. We were told that we were no longer allowed to get other persons to supply our places as day labourers.

"The substitutes you find prove that they are still able-bodied. So they must work for their own account, and you for yours."

"Oh!" we moaned, "is there no means of escape from this hell?"

We had made several attempts, had addressed petitions, and written letters that had been either thrown away or answered with a negative. And now they wanted to add penal servitude to imprisonment! They would oblige us to work from morning till night, in the mud, in the rain.

"I prefer going to Chalandry," Geneviève repeated.

But we were excused enforced service, and exempted from prison. A greater misfortune spared us these troubles. One morning I met in the passage two callers who did not ask for Jackdaw's Legs. One of them, very tall, very thin, and very stiff, with Japanese-like features, bent himself down with a low bow. His companion, smaller but just as thin and stiff, copied him hastily.

"Madam," lisped the former in a faint voice, "I should like to see the owner of this house."

I showed both men in, and rushed into my mother-in-law's bedroom. Everybody was in a stir.

"What do they want? This visit foretells no good, of course."

"It is the general's son," Colette said. "I had him pointed out to me a few days ago."

Mme. Valaine walked into the dining-room, where the visitors were waiting. On tip-toe we went into the passage, and holding our breaths anxiously listened from behind the door.

As soon as my mother-in-law entered the room, the officers got up, and bowed themselves at right angles. Then the lisping voice began:

"Madam, I am a staff officer. I have been ordered to inform you of a decision that concerns you nearly...."

"Ah!..."

Behind the door left ajar we strained uneasy ears; the speaker went on with his speech:

"You are not ignorant, madam, of the painful necessities of the war, and I am sorry to have to tell you that we are in need of your house...."

"Oh!"

It was Geneviève who uttered this stifled cry. Mme. Valaine had no voice to answer.

The orator continued:

"... We are in need of your house for a printing office. It corresponds exactly with our wishes."

"But it is my own house; I live in it with my family. I have a right to stay in it...."

"Madam, I am very sorry, but we want it. To-day is Thursday; I think we can wait till Monday next to take possession of the place."

"But it is impossible ... my furniture...."

"Oh, the house must remain furnished. But you may take away such pieces of furniture as the officers do not want."

"But, sir, it is a disgrace!" Geneviève, unable to control her indignation any longer, had pushed the door open, thus unmasking our group, and had entered the lists. Her invasion slightly disturbed the officer.

"It is a disgrace! You pretend that you don't make war upon civilians, and you turn five women out of doors at the beginning of the winter! You offend against the law of nations. But it is your habit. I know you by your handiwork!"

Wholly unmoved, the executioner replied:

"I see you are excited, and I shall not repeat what I have just heard."

"What! Indeed! You may repeat it if you like. I should not be afraid to say so to anybody."

Always calm and stiff and lisping, the Japanese blond went back to what he was saying:

"You will be quieter by and by. I said we want the house to be free on Monday next. As we may stay in France for months, and even for years, it is our duty to settle things as well as can be. It is our right. I am sorry this is disagreeable for you, but it is war." When he had done talking, he bowed himself to the ground, his companion immediately did the like, and both withdrew. In a death-like silence we listened to the retreating steps, to the gate slammed-to, and then burst out into lamentations. A fortnight after we were in Laon.

The dear old house, the garden, the furniture were all violated, lost. As nothing else kept us in Morny, we had asked leave to go to Laon, which by way of compensation had been granted to us. So, we should not be bound to enforced service, and we could make up for the tediousness of the winter by devouring all the books in the town library. And above all, we should not see plundered, and given over to the beasts, the beloved old house, embellished by our love, where the family had lived for several generations, where my husband and my sisters-in-law had been born, where they had spent their childhood.

We should not see the looking-glasses cracked by awkwardness or malice, the hangings splashed with beer, the carpets torn up, the pieces of furniture burnt one after another for firewood, according to the whims of the servants. We should not see the officers walking two by two under our lime-trees, in our long alleys, edged with box—the box, beneath which we hid our Easter eggs!

The rumour of our expulsion spread abroad, and presently we heard the reason of it.

Jacob, the linguist, the pompous talker, not to say the chatterbox, told the Lantois:

"The ladies' troubles are due to an officer's vengeance. Lieutenant Bubenpech had a personal grudge against them; he is the nephew of the brigade-major, and he thought it amusing to give these ladies a little lesson."

Very kind indeed, Herr Bubenpech! But we know what a pretty thing is German vengeance, and it gets home! And after all, life was more easily bearable in Laon than in the country. Friends of ours who lived near the Porte d'Ardon let us have a little apartment in their house. Our windows overlooked the country, and as usual we could watch the bursting of shells, the captive balloons, and the turning beacons. Horse-oil was faithful to our lamps, and we used turf to heat our rooms. I recommend this fuel to those who have a love of dust and smoke. The question of food was hard, but not harder than in Morny. Meat was scarcely to be had. The people dimly remembered the shape of an egg, the colour of butter or oil or grease or milk. Babies I know fed on vegetable-soup alone from six weeks of age. The American Board of Relief distributed provisions similar to those we had enjoyed in Morny—250 grammes of bread a day, a little rice, dry vegetables, from time to time a bit of bacon. Besides, green vegetables were to be had at the greengrocer's. But we were forbidden to buy more than ten kilograms of potatoes a head per month. At Morny the Germans had generously distributed twenty kilograms a head, but half of them were rotten, and then the population had been told that they had received their winter supply.

What we appreciated most in the town was the calmness of the nights. Where superior officers are quartered, subalterns are obliged to save appearances and to conduct their drunken revelries in private. We had no more brutal intrusions to fear; we dreaded no perquisitions, as we had lost everything. And the aspect of so many houses close to one another gave us an impression of security, long since forgotten.

Yet how sad the town looked! Many houses had been emptied according to the Germans' whims. Furniture, bedding, linen, clothes had been carried away. The officers loaded the women who devoted themselves to soothe the boredom of the war with presents, chosen from among this booty. They adorned their apartments with things they had taken from all quarters of the town, and if they did not get from the houses of the absent what they wanted, they applied to those who were still there.

Thus it was that a sergeant and four men once came to the house of the friends who had received us, to fetch away a set of drawing-room furniture. Protestations were of no avail.

"I have my orders. Make out an invoice, take it to the *Kommandantur*, and a note of hand will be delivered to you."

To any complaint which the wronged owner might make an officer answered: "I have but one word of advice to give you: Keep quiet and hold your tongue."

The streets always swarmed with officers and soldiers on foot and on horseback. All shops were open by order of the Germans, but there was nothing to be sold in most of them. No articles of food were to be had, and the stock of shoes, materials, and clothes was nearly exhausted by the needs of the people and by frequent requisitions. In November all silk goods had been requisitioned, even ribbons above ten centimetres' breadth. Many empty shops—which had been plundered after the departure of the owners—had been laid hold of by German civilians, who had lost no time in bringing their little trade to France. Thus you might admire a stationer's and two booksellers' shops, a jeweller's—various kinds of paltry stuff—a boot and shoe warehouse, a hairdressing saloon, and so on. These patriotic establishments were always thronged with customers—in uniform of course.

The *Kommandantur* sold officially in a shop thus installed Belgian lace of great beauty, marvels of point: Brussels, Bruges, Mechlin. After a month it was offered for sale in the town hall alone, and so the sight of these treasures was kept back from French eyes. The officers scrambled for this lace, which, in spite of high prices, sold wonderfully well. For the rest, military men of all ranks spent a great deal of money, and a French jeweller told us that private soldiers often spent upon gold chains and rings all the money they possessed. Was it a way to convert their paper money into something safer? Later on they were forbidden to pay for their purchases in silver or in German notes, and the tradesmen were not allowed to receive anything from the soldiers but municipal banknotes, and were bound to give back only German or French money. These rules were a great hindrance to business.

In the autumn of 1915, the magnanimous, high-souled military authorities decreed that the persons who had concealed wine—well-hidden wine alone had escaped being requisitioned—would avoid close searches and severe punishments by making a statement of the quantity they possessed. Afraid and tired out, many people complied and handed over what they had so long kept out of sight, and thousands of bottles went down the throats of our tormentors.

More serious was the proclamation which granted a delay to the French soldiers still in the invaded territory. The blockade had taken a great many of them by surprise, and had prevented them from reaching the French line; they wore civil clothes and lived under an assumed name. Some of them had surrendered at the beginning of the invasion; others had been discovered and shot. But the new regulation enabled those who were hidden to give themselves up until the 20th of November. From that date every French soldier, caught in invaded territory, would be looked upon as a spy and be immediately shot. As many as eighty surrendered before the stated day, and oh, desolation! the very day after they arrested, in a suburb of the town where he lived disguised as a workman, a French officer, a captain. We read on the bills stuck up in the streets that he had been shot in the citadel.

Another announcement threatened the villagers more than the town's people. It intimated that every criminal attempt made at any point of the railroads would immediately bring terrible reprisals upon the inhabitants of the neighbouring villages. "Whether guilty or not," the unhappy wretches would be "driven from their houses if the military authorities thought proper"; the women would be taken away, and "the men enrolled in the gangs of labourers." Besides, such hostages as the Germans selected might be shot.

On the other hand, the invaders were always in readiness to drain the country of the little money that was left. Many means were at their disposal. Fines were showered down upon the towns and villages. If a French aeroplane dropped bombs on the Laon station, the town was quickly condemned to pay upwards of one hundred thousand francs. In October, to mark, no doubt, the anniversary of the German occupation, the invaded were warned that they would have to pay a second contribution of war. The chief authorities of the communes were told that those under their charge would soon get into the habit of paying tribute, very likely every quarter, to the conquerors. "And when all the money has thus been wrung from all purses, well, you will but have to issue municipal notes, which you will give to us, the Prussians. So, when the war is at an end, when you have all been eaten out of house and home, you will all the same be our debtors!"

They were just as ingenious in fooling the farmers. In that year, 1915, the peasants had tilled the fields themselves. But the Germans are scrupulously honest, as every one knows. "We are going," they said, "to pay you for your trouble and your corn. You will receive twenty francs a hectare!" Splendid amend! Rich indemnity! Morny was entitled to 18,000 frs. "Yes," the Germans went on, "but you remember that old fine of yours, which you never paid entirely. Besides, there is the quarter's contribution to the war, and a thousand francs fine imposed for a passport that was not viséd. In short, when it is all added up, you owe to us 800 frs." The civilians who had to listen to these speeches hung their heads. The account was right: they could not plead false arithmetic. Two and two always make four, especially when the German army maintains it.

This gave heart to the Prussians to go still further: "Let us talk of the future. Next year we shall cultivate the fields ourselves. Of course it is but right that you should remunerate us for so doing. Our tillage is worth fifty-six francs a hectare. Besides, you must pay us our expenses: three hectolitres of seed a hectare ... at the highest possible price. We will be paid beforehand." The sum total was 92,000 frs. for the village of Morny alone. And there were about 1500 inhabitants left in Morny, all in utter poverty after the exactions of which they had been victims. Fortunately the Prussians put the remedy at the sufferers' disposal: "If you have no money left, you possess good pieces of land, which you might pledge. We have just founded a German-Belgian Bank in Brussels, which will lend you some money." These honest offers were made in the month of December, but we do not know how things befell, for the dawn rose again for us. Convoys were organised for a second time.

We blessed the number of the *Gazette des Ardennes* which, at the end of November, brought us the good news. Twenty thousand persons were to be chosen in the invaded territory, first among the poor and the sick and the people whose usual residence was on the other side of the front. We feared lest our demand should be rejected, and we left no stone unturned to prevent refusal. At length we were told that our names had been put down on the list of the emigrants.

It was the end of the year. Colette still hoped to see the French come back before our departure. But, alas! nothing of the kind happened. Christmas, New Year's Day, were kept as they had been kept a year before, sadly by the French, merrily by the Germans. Then the month of January, cold and foggy, glided by, and we were still kept waiting. At length the day of the departure came. The convoy, the mass of emigrants, were strikingly like the herd we had witnessed the year before. Yet I think we saw more sick people. There were many who coughed. When once we were all seated in a carriage, we five, with two little orphan girls, who went to meet their grandmother at Lyons, the train moved off at last, and such an emotion seized upon us that no one uttered a word. The first time our flight had been stopped at Chevrigny, a second time at Jouville. How far should we go now?

We had been told that there would be no quarantine. Was it true? We were travelling through a grey country. The night fell and the dawn rose again: we were in Germany. We made many a long stop in the stations; soldiers distributed coffee and soup in the carriages. We had taken with us, put by from our pittance of a whole week, dry toast, barley coffee, and licorice-wood tea. As to tasting "the soup"—no, thank you. We peered through the windows, but did not see anything worth looking at. Towns and villages were gloomy; in the stations, boys of about thirteen did the work of railway porters.

The night fell again. We reached the Black Forest, which was white with snow. We wound our way up a mountain, and caught sight of a vale far below us. The branches of the fir-trees bent beneath their pure burden, and the cloak spread over the ground was so dazzling that it gave light to the starless night. Houses were to be seen everywhere, grouped together in hamlets and villages, or standing apart in the mountain—good-natured-looking houses nestled in the snow, with gaily-lit-up windows.

Then I cast my eyes about me. My companions were slumbering, and the flickering light brought out the paleness of their uneasy faces. One of the little girls was coughing, and we could hear other people who seemed to echo back the same sad sound. The long train that rolled along was full of wretchedness and misery. And from those snug little houses, from those towns we had just crossed, came the soldiers who had rushed upon our country. From thence the plunderers, the drunkards, the debauchees, the executioners; from thence came those who have carried dismay into a peaceful country, who have converted a happy, industrious population into a fearful, enslaved herd....

May you be cursed ... cursed....

And there, in the big houses, in the towns, live still the accomplices. They are all there. The lamp is bright, the stove lit up. Dinner is over; they are smoking their pipes and reading their papers.

And in the invaded territory thousands and thousands of people have gone to bed at six, because they have no light, no fire, and no dinner. And the others are there. They read the papers. They praise whatever the German army does, they admire the German soldiers, they approve all high-handed measures, and those who are at home, as well as those away from home, lift up their eyes towards the sky, and thank God for not being like the rest of mankind.

Ah no, you are not like the rest of mankind! Could we shout it loud enough? Is there any cry that might pierce your dull conscience? Are there maledictions of sufficient vehemence to penetrate the carapace in which you have wrapped up your understanding?

Ah, I wish I were hundred-tongued, and gifted with more than human genius, the better to proclaim your infamy, the better to cry out upon the sufferings width which you do not cease to load us. I can but repeat what I have seen, what I have heard, what I have borne. I shall never be weary of lifting up a corner of the veil in which you wrap yourselves, you dissemblers, you false-faced, false-hearted men! On your features of brutality and violence you wear a benignant, canting mask, you assume a candid, astonished look, and turn round to the neutrals, to Europe, to all civilised powers, saying:

"We are charged with evil deeds! Look if it is like us?"

You resemble the woman of whom the Bible says: "She wipes her mouth, and says: I have done no harm." You reject with a shrug of your shoulders those of your actions which might make you uneasy. Your accommodating consciences do away with them, and they immediately fall into oblivion. But we are sure to remember what you forget. You have shown yourselves openly, and we know your real faces only too well, their unrelenting harshness, their falseness, their incomprehension, and in your double face we spit out the horror and scorn you rouse in us. And yet we admire you.

Your presence was attended with murder, fire, acts of violence and plunder; you have displayed a powerful, splendid, hideous bestiality, and it is that bestiality which we admire in you.

Do not reject the title of Barbarians. It is the only one that suits you. You might have been fine Barbarians, but for a long time to come you will be only shabby civilised men. I had rather see you stand on a pedestal, and hear you shout, exaggerating your misdeeds, overstraining your cruelty, your vices, your animality:

"Yes, we are Barbarians! and then?"

Thus you might have been great, and since you are strong, since you know how to fight, you would have been like a hero who defends himself as he is, and not like a little girl about to be whipped, who tries to deny her fault, and weeps.

Believe me, you will cut no figure in history as saints. Where your horses have trodden, the grass will not spring up again for long. So make up your minds, unmask yourselves, and cry out:

"We are *the* Barbarians!"

The train had reached the highest point of its journey. All the vale, and the slopes of the mountains, were flecked with a thousand brilliant points. They were the windows of the houses, more smiling than ever. A few moments passed, and then a kind of excitement came over us. Were we approaching the Swiss frontier?

We had still to wait in our carriages for the morning. Long hours together we should have to wait for our turn to be searched, and allow the nurses to examine the soles of our shoes, and the hems of our garments. But what did it matter? We were in raptures! It was over! Our martyrdom was at an end!

We were in Switzerland! We were free!

A fraternal welcome cheered us all along the road. Here was rich Zurich, whose prosperity dazzled our eyes. Then came Berne and fair Geneva, at the end of its blue lake.

Here was at last ... oh, my heart, do not throb so violently! Here she was ... France ... it was France ... unsullied France, where no Germans breathe, living, active France, the France that will crush the enemy. We saw Mont Blanc watch over the frontier; then we came within sight of the valley, of a rocky land, and then of the plain, the plain as vast as the hope which filled our hearts.

And now that we had reached France, now that we rode in a French carriage, we sat close to one another, and with tears in our eyes looked at the landscape.

We felt heavy with an overwhelming joy, and we waited for the morrow, not knowing whether it would bring happiness or mourning.

THE END

9 789357 955201